BLOOMSBURY
DICTIONARY OF
First Names

BLOOMSBURY
DICTIONARY OF
First Names

JULIA CRESSWELL

BLOOMSBURY

First edition published in 1990 by Bloomsbury Publishing Plc,
38 Soho Square, London W1D 3HB

www.bloomsburymagazine.com

This edition first published in 2000
This paperback edition published in 2001

A CIP record for this book is available from the British Library.

ISBN 0 7475 5453 6

10 9 8 7 6 5 4 3 2 1

Typeset by Hewer Text Ltd, Edinburgh
Printed and bound in Great Britain by Clays Ltd, St Ives plc

Contents

This book is dedicated to my mother,
CONSTANCE,
*without whose unfailing help
it would never have been written.*

Introduction

Throughout the time for which we have records, English-language first names have shown two conflicting trends, one a remarkable conservatism, the other a remarkable fickleness of fashion. Names such as *John* and *James*, *Margaret* and *Mary* have remained in steady use for many hundreds of years; other groups of names have come into fashion and then declined rapidly in popularity or even disappeared altogether. The oldest names still in use in this country are perhaps the Welsh names *Caradoc*, a descendant of the name *Caractacos*, used by the British chieftain captured by the Romans in AD 51, and *Buddug*, a descendant of the name *Boadicea*, the woman who led the revolt against the Romans in c. AD 60. Many other Welsh names are of great antiquity. Some are forms of Latin names which show signs of having been adopted during the Roman occupation of Britain, others are native names which may well date from before this time. There are names found in the earliest surviving Welsh literature and recorded in early saints' lives which are still in use. The other branch of the Celtic language, Irish and Scots Gaelic, also provides many early names recorded in saints' lives. Again, these Dark Ages names may well be even older, but we lack written evidence to prove this.

These ancient Celtic names have continued in use amongst the minority of Celtic speakers in Great Britain, and have increased in popularity in modern times, many of them having been revived in the nineteenth century with the rise of Celtic nationalism. However, for the English-speaking majority the main sources of names have been the traditions of the various Germanic tribes of northern Europe, and the names introduced by the Church: either the Hebrew names of the Old Testament, or the Greek and Roman names of the New Testament and saints. Truly 'English' names are those made up of elements brought over to England by the invading Anglo-Saxons, a motley collection of peoples from various Germanic tribes, speaking various dialects of what is correctly called Old English, although the terms Anglo-Saxon and Old English have been used more or less interchangeably in this book. These peoples used the Germanic tradition of name-formation, where most names were made up of two elements, each of which has a recognizable meaning, but which do not necessarily make much sense when combined. Thus *Alfred* ('elf-counsel') and *Alfwine* ('elf-friend') make some sort of recognizable sense, but *Edward* ('fortunate' and 'guard') is a lot more difficult to rationalize. The sense of the name was obviously not the most important aspect of it. What was important was the source of the name, for often the names given to children were coined from name elements used by other members of the family and used to identify them as members of that family. Alfred the Great was as exceptional in his name as in so much else, being the first bearer of his name in a family which traditionally used *athel* ('noble') or *ed* ('fortunate, prosperous, happy') to start names. His father was *Athelwulf*, his three elder brothers *Athelbald*, *Athelbert* and *Athelred* (the second elements of these names meaning 'wolf', 'bold', 'bright', 'counsel'), his son was *Edward* and his grandsons *Athelstan* ('noble stone'), *Edmund* ('fortunate protection') and *Edred* ('fortunate counsel'). The few names we find that do not fit this pattern tend to be nicknames, often descriptive, or shortened forms of these double names. This system is found in all those names descended from the northern tribes; not just the obvious names we have inherited or adopted from Germany and Scandinavia, but even in some Italian names which descend from names used by the invading Germanic tribes who took over the north of Italy in the Dark Ages, and especially in names brought to England by the Normans. It may seem odd that so many of the names introduced by the French-speaking Normans were Germanic, but not only were they descended from Viking raiders, but the French aristocracy was itself descended from the Franks, another of the Germanic tribes that invaded the crumbling Roman Empire in the Dark Ages.

This pattern of forming names is very marked among the Germanic peoples, but is common throughout Europe, being inherited from our Indo-European ancestors, so it fitted in well with the already-established Celtic system, where names could come from nicknames, particularly those associated with complexion or colouring, or were also made up of two elements. The two-part system can be seen in the large number of Welsh names containing the element *gwen*, which means 'white, fair, good' and so by association with purity, 'blessed'. The two halves of a name are not always as clear in Welsh as in English, for the form changes with the sex of the name so that *gwen* becomes *gwyn* in the masculine. In addition, Welsh is one of the languages that has a peculiar system known as lenition, where the initial sound of a word can change to show grammatical function, so that in a name like *Bronwen* ('breast + white'), *gwen* becomes *wen*. The same system is found in Gaelic, which explains some of the differences between the original and anglicized forms of the name. Moreover, the Irish and Scottish spelling system is based on the ancient pronunciation of a language that has changed radically, causing immense difficulties in seeing the relationship between the letters and sounds for the uninitiated, and even sometimes for the initiated.

As well as bringing over their own forms of Germanic names which often replaced the Anglo-Saxon forms, the Normans also brought with them the habit of using truly Christian names – those taken from the Bible and the saints. Before 1066 such names are very rare in England, the few examples found being mainly adopted at ordination by those taking holy orders. Hebrew names fall into several main categories. There are those that express a particular characteristic or occupation of a person (or that the givers of a name hoped that a child would have); those that come from the natural world, some of which may reflect ancient tribal symbols or totems, but many of which show the worldwide desire of parents for their children to emulate certain admired qualities in the natural world; and, very noticeably in those adopted into English, those names containing one of the many elements referring to God, expressing a hoped-for relationship with Him. Many of these names reappear in the New Testament, sometimes in a form altered to fit the Greek in which its books were written. Thus the Old Testament name *Simeon* appears in the New both in this form and as the Greek form *Simon*, while *Joshua* becomes *Jesus*. Other names in the New Testament reflect its times, when the eastern Mediterranean was heavily influenced by Greek culture overlaid with the influence of the Roman Empire. Thus the names of many early Christians are Greek or Roman. Greek men and women normally had only one name, although nicknames could be added and further identification made by describing someone as the son or daughter of their father. Most Greek names were made up from everyday or 'vocabulary' words, but a good proportion, like the earlier Hebrew names, describe the bearer as having a relationship to a god or goddess. With the coming of Christianity such names remained in use, despite their pagan meanings.

Roman names were rather different. All Roman males had three names, a personal name drawn from a very limited stock that among the aristocracy boiled down to a mere 15 or so; a clan name; and the name of the family within each clan, although other names could be added on to these three. Women were usually known by the feminine form of the clan name, but this could vary and we do have records of women's personal names. In modern times any of these three classes of names can be used as a first name: *Marcus* is a Roman personal name, *Claud* and *Anthony* derive from clan names and *Adrian* is from a family name.

Thus by the early Middle Ages the main sources of British first names were established. Since then new names have been added, and old ones have disappeared, but the changes have on the whole been ones of fashion and emphasis rather than radical. There have always been parents who have wanted to give their children names that are different, and who have gone to unusual sources or made up names. As a result, one can never be categorical about when a name was first or last used, or why it has been used, but can only deal with general trends. For example, the next main change in names comes with the Renaissance when there is a growth in the use of non-biblical names from the classical past, but this does not mean that such names were never found in the Middle Ages. *Diana*, *Lavinia*, *Leda*, *Antigone* and *Cassandra* have all been recorded from the late twelfth or early thirteenth centuries. However, such names are found more frequently as a knowledge of Greek spreads. At first it was mainly a literary phenomenon, with authors using names taken from classical literature in their own works, or making up names such as *Pamela* and *Stella*, based on Greek and Latin, for their heroines. As would be expected, this is found again in the late seventeenth and eighteenth centuries, when everything classical was the rage. Literary heroines were given names like *Clarissa* and real-life heroes had names like *Horatio* Nelson or *Lucius Quintus Cincinnatus* Lamar. There was also a tendency to use the Latinate form of girls' names, so that *Louisa* became more common than *Louise*. The introduction of classical names has continued since then, although less markedly, and many that were at one time exotic are now so thoroughly naturalized that they hardly seem anything but English. A name like *Penelope*, first used in the mid-sixteenth century with conscious reference to Homer, is now so at home that it has lost most of its associations with faithful wifehood, and has become as English as its short form, *Penny*.

Even more important than the Renaissance in changing the pattern of naming are the effects of the Reformation. For the majority, naming patterns remained much the same, with the perennial *William*, *John* and *Thomas* still the most common names for boys, and *Elizabeth*, *Mary* and *Anne* for girls, but there was a decline in the use of names more obviously associated with the saints of the Roman Catholic Church, and a distinct increase in the use of names taken from the Bible. This trend became even more marked with the rise of the Puritans, who sometimes wished to mark their rejection of past ways by cutting their children off from the associations of well-established names. Thus they would seek out the more obscure biblical names such as *Malachy* and *Shobael*, and also use vocabulary words as first names. Some of these, such as *Hope* and *Patience*, have survived, but the more astonishing, such as *Tribulation*, *Ashes* or *More Trial*, had only a brief fashion, although writers on names have tended to over-emphasize this trend, as it is so striking.

American names

The Pilgrim Fathers took these new trends with them when they moved across the Atlantic. Politics and fashions led to a rapid decline in Puritan names in Britain, but they remained in use for longer on the new continent, and so entered the mainstream of American names, many of the biblical names remaining in use to this day and once more becoming fashionable. It is important not to exaggerate this trend. Studies of American names in the seventeenth century have shown that while biblical names were in use, and names such as *Jered*, *Lemuel* and *Zeruiah* can be found, the majority had well-established names, and certainly no more than 15 per cent bore vocabulary names such as *Mourning*, *Free-Grace* and *Wrestling*. Moreover, we can also find pagan names such as *Atlanta* and *Lucrecia* (although one must be careful with names such as *Phoebe*, which are in fact found in the New Testament), as well as non-religious vocabulary names such as *Lady*.

However, there is no doubt that naming in the United States started out with a desire to break away from some of the old traditions, and that ever since there has been a freer attitude to choosing a child's name than in many countries, although other countries without a long burden of tradition, such as Australia, show a similar independence. There have been a number of contributory factors. One is the large number of different ethnic groups that have made up the population. Thus the people from the old French territories followed French patterns of naming, using both French forms of names and from the early nineteenth century following the French fashion for classical names. These naming habits have remained in use to this day, although they are now less marked. Later on, Scandinavian, German and Jewish immigrants brought their name-forms and preferences with them, and more recently Spanish names have had their influence. All this has made the pool of names that can be drawn on much greater, and the variety available to parents must have helped to form a much less rigid attitude to what constitutes a 'normal' name. In 1959 Thomas Pyles formulated another theory about American naming habits, in an article which he gave the tongue-in-cheek title of 'Bible Belt Onomastics or Some Curiosities of Anti-Pedobaptist Nomenclature'. Here he pointed out that a quarter of American Christians belong to sects that practise adult baptism (Pyles's 'anti-pedobaptism'), and that therefore the conservative influence of a clergyman does not affect the choice of a child's name. 'Where name-giving is no part of the sacrament of baptism, and where consequently a clergyman with some sense of traditional onomastic decorum has no say, individual taste and fancy may run riot – and usually do.' The family he cites where the women were called *Hoyette*, *Norvetta*, *Yerdith*, *Arthetta*, *Marlynne* and *Wilbarine* has become well known in name studies. It is interesting to note that a number of the names he lists as remarkable – *Leroy*, *Prince*, *Amber*, *Orlando*, *Kimberly*, *Kelley*, *Fawn*, *Melody*, *Madonna* and many others, have now become much more widely known. The fertility of invention among American parents and the freedom that their history gives them to choose, means that the United States in the twentieth century was the major influence in changing patterns of naming in the English-speaking world. Because of this, careful attention has been given in this book to the more recently coined American names. These generally spread to other English-speaking countries, and even if they should not, will be met through American television and film.

Surnames as first names

The use of surnames as first names goes back to at least the sixteenth century. Initially the most usual reasons for giving a child such a name was to preserve a mother's maiden name, or in honour of a godparent (usually, it is to be feared, in the hope that the godparent would reward the child for this compliment). This pattern of naming continued to be used quietly but increasingly. From the eighteenth century onwards another use of surnames as first names becomes more common, that of naming a child for a famous person admired by the parents. The author, for example, has an ancestor (whose own father had done well through being christened after a wealthy godfather) who chose to mark his views about English conduct during the American War of Independence by christening his son *Washington Lafayette*. In the nineteenth century this tendency became more general, and aristocratic surnames, with which the bearer had no connections but which sounded grand, became fashionable. Another peculiarity of the nineteenth century was a fashion for giving a child the same first name as his surname, so we find such oddities as a judge called *Sir Cresswell Cresswell*.

Surnames as first names have been particularly popular in the southern United States, where it has been calculated that in the mid-nineteenth century 10 per cent of names were of this type. Heroes from the Civil War were popular as names, which explains the spread of Lee as a first name. Surnames have always been used as first names for both sexes – *Douglas*, for instance, is quoted as a woman's name in the seventeenth century, and *Beverly* and *Shirley*, which we now think of primarily as first names, started as surnames – but this trend is again more marked in the southern United States, which probably explains why so many modern names based on surnames can be used for either sex in the USA.

Another markedly American fashion is to look to the famous and worthy of the past for first names. Some of these such as *Cyrus*, *Darius* and *Myron* cannot be classed as surnames, but *Milton* is a typical American name of this class.

The use of surnames as first names became very marked in the twentieth century. In America and Australia, Irish surnames have been particularly popular, presumably a fashion which started with emigrant communities, and many of these are now widely used in the United Kingdom as well. The fashion is now so firmly established that almost any surname can be used as a first name without raising eyebrows. Consequently it has been impossible to include any but the most popular here, and readers wanting more information on such names should turn to a good dictionary of surnames.

Names in the nineteenth and twentieth centuries

As well as the growth in surnames and the steady increase in Latinate forms, which have already been discussed, certain other trends can be found in the nineteenth and early twentieth centuries. One of these was the interest shown in old names, which led to a revival of many of the Anglo-Saxon names such as *Alfred* and *Edred* that had disappeared with the Norman Conquest. This antiquarianism is a good example of the way in which fashions in names reflect the cultural fashions of the times: medieval names went hand in hand with Victorian Gothic architecture and a general revival of interest in the Middle Ages. Another example of names reflecting current taste is the way in which, more recently, names that seem to have a Victorian feel – *Victoria* itself, *Emily*, *Charlotte*, *Flora* – became fashionable at the same time as Victorian architecture and furnishing became popular once more.

In the Victorian and Edwardian periods we find four main sources of new names. The custom of naming a child after the place where he or she was born, or with which a parent was particularly associated, has a long history, but became much more popular at this time. Moreover, once the name came to public attention, it could then be adopted by parents who had no association with the place. The most obvious example of this is *Florence*. Florence Nightingale was named after the town in which she was born, just as her elder sister was called *Parthenope* from the old name for *her* birthplace, Naples. Florence's fame turned a one-off name into a highly popular one which entered the main stock of British names. For further information on this subject see under *Kim*. This naming habit has been strongly revived in recent years, with the change that the name is often where the child was conceived rather than born. Sometimes the place name is simply where the parents spent their honeymoon or had a particularly happy holiday, or even just somewhere they like the sound of. A recent prominent name in this class is *Brooklyn* Beckham, the son of 'Posh Spice'.

Another fashion of this time was for jewel names, with names like *Pearl*, *Beryl* and *Ruby* having a particularly turn-of-the-century feel to them. Again this fashion has not died out, but the jewels chosen have changed, with a distinct leaning towards the semi-precious such as *Amber*, *Jade* and *Topaz*, which may well reflect a rise in the use of such stones in jewellery. Flower and plant names were another fashion of this time, with many girls being christened *Violet*, *Rose* and *Ivy*. Once more this fashion did not die out, but changed over the years with new plants such as *Bryony*, *Heather*, *Holly* and *Saffron* coming into use. Some of the old flower names such as *Poppy* and *Daisy* are once again popular with parents, and new ones are always being coined. In one 12-month period the author has found in the newspaper birth announcements *Japonica*, *Briar*, *Moss*, *Tamarisk*, *Clematis* (sister of *Poppy* and *Fleur*) and two *Fuchsias*.

Another new source of names has been books, and more recently other media. Obviously the book of books, the Bible, has been a major source of names for centuries, and for this reason biblical quotations in this book have been taken from the Authorized Version, as the translation that has had most influence on the history of names. Writers and stories had long influenced parents, but the nineteenth century saw the rise of the novel as an important influence on names, introducing exotic names such as *Mavis*. Moreover, names were taken more freely from older authors, with Shakespeare and Spenser being particularly favoured. Books have continued to be influential. *Gone with the Wind*, among the most influential, is credited with a rise in popularity of a number of names including *Ashley*, *Melanie* and *Tara* as well as the more obvious *Scarlett*. *Gone with the Wind* introduces the influence of the cinema and later television and pop music. Frequently visual adaptations of books have had a greater influence in making a name popular than the written original, while the influence that film and pop stars (as well as idols from sport) have had on parents' choice in recent years is too obvious to need elaboration.

Modern trends

It would be a brave person who confidently predicted what was going to happen next with names. However, certain recent and current trends can be determined, and tentative suggestions made about the future. The mixture of conservatism and innovation we have seen throughout the history of names continues. On the conservative side boys' names like *James*, *Thomas*, *William*, *Edward* and *Charles* which have been around for hundreds of years are still the most common, while the majority of girls have 'old-fashioned' sounding names like *Alice* and *Emily*, or perennials like *Catherine*. On the innovatory side a whole new crop of surnames – *Darren*, *Paige*, *Courtney*, *Ryan*, *Hayley*, *Kelly* – have become established as first names. From abroad we have taken the foreign forms of names which already existed in English – *Karen*, *Marie*, *Anton* – or feminines of names which were hitherto only masculine – *Michelle* and *Michaela*, *Danielle* – or adopted new names – *Natalie*, *Kyle* – to a greater extent than before. The return of some of the old saints' names may also be due to foreign influence, as names like *Damian* and *Dominic* remained in use in Catholic countries when they died out in predominantly Protestant ones. Ireland may have contributed here, for it has certainly been a source of a number of newly popular names in the rest of the English-speaking world. In fact all the Celtic languages have spread outside their old boundaries when names are being chosen. The Scottish *Kirsty* has been particularly popular recently, and Welsh *Bethan* is firmly established as an 'English' name. For boys, Welsh *Gareth* has been very popular, and the Irish *Shaun* is also widely used.

What about the future? A few tentative suggestions can be made about where names are going. As the generation of women who were given Victorian names come to have their own children, there is an indication that some are choosing to revive slightly more recent names from the beginning of the twentieth century, such as the currently fashionable flower names listed above. There also seems to be a minor revival of names based on abstract nouns, with *Clemency* and the like occurring surprisingly frequently in the birth announcements. Fashions in names include fashions in sounds, with new names at different times sharing similar sounds. For example, a look under the letters K and T in this book will show how many new names starting with these sounds have been introduced in recent years.

There has undoubtedly been vast growth in the variety of names in recent years. In particular, parents have been making new forms of old names (variants); joining together bits of different names (blends) to give names like

Floella, *Alondra*, *Delbert*; or simply inventing names. This has made life much more difficult for the writer on names. It is impossible to record all such blends and variants, and no such attempt has been made in this book. In addition, double names such as *Mary Lou* have been ignored. With the greater freedom in forming names, it is also much more difficult for a writer to be didactic about a name. If you find a name like *Kerryn*, do you class it as a variant of *Karin* or *Kerry* or as a name in its own right? Is *Tonya* really a short form of *Antonia*, or a variation of *Tanya*? Nowadays it is impossible to draw any strict lines between names.

The question remains: why are there so many new names nowadays, and why do fashions in names seem to change more rapidly? The answer must surely lie, to a large extent, in the changes that occurred over the twentieth century in the way we address each other. The rise in informality over the century has meant that the surname has become less and less important, while the first name has become more significant. The stock of surnames has always been greater than that of first names, and they, combined with the first name, have served to mark the person as an individual. The less surnames are used, the more important it becomes to make a child stand out by its first name.

What is in this book, and how it got there

Since I started writing on names, I have often been asked where I get the information. The simple answer is that all writers on first names depend to a large extent on the work of others. There are hundreds of books on names, ranging from awesomely academic studies of Anglo-Saxon naming habits to booklets handed out in maternity wards. I have consulted and made use of a good number of these, as well as reading many articles, particularly in the two major journals devoted to names, *Nomina* in England and *Names* in America. In 1863 Charlotte M. Yonge published her *History of Christian Names*, which is really the first, and still one of the most readable, of the modern books on names. Although some of what she wrote has now been superseded, most modern books rely heavily on her either directly or indirectly. Another influential work is E.G. Withycombe's *Dictionary of English Christian Names*, first published in 1945 and still going strong. This is particularly useful for anyone wanting the history of names in the Middle Ages and the forms they took then. The most prolific of recent writers on first names has been Leslie Dunkling. Of his numerous books, the most useful is his *Dictionary of First Names*, written with William Gosling, which probably lists more variants than any other work. Much of the information on Irish names in this book will be found in my *Gem Dictionary of Irish First Names*, while much of the information on Welsh names comes from T.R. Davies' *A Book of Welsh Names*, updated by more recent works. Dictionaries and a concordance to the Bible give information on where to find out more about biblical names (if you are looking for the source of a particularly obscure name, it is always worth checking a concordance). Standard classical and literary reference works are another useful source of information. Many of the comments on twentieth-century fashions are based on an analysis of entries in the births, deaths and marriage announcements in newspapers, supplemented by other readings in the press, and by more informal sources such as conversations with midwives about naming trends in the local hospitals. Since the first edition of this book was written there has been a new Oxford *Dictionary of First Names*, which is particularly strong on European names, and for the USA, I have made extensive use of Cleveland Kent Evans' authoritative *Unusual and Most Popular Baby Names*. There is now a new and very important source of information on names – the Internet. There is a vast amount of information available on the net, and anyone interested in the subject should spend some time looking at what is there. Its quality is very variable, ranging from downright misleading to the highly reliable, such as the UK government figures on the most popular names (separate lists for England and Wales, and for Scotland). Anyone who doubts that the range of names listed in this book is really in use should look at the web site of the Wandsworth Register Office (http://www.wandsworth.gov.uk./reg/ngame.htm), which has put out a list of all the names registered there since 1991, and they will see quite how diverse a range of names is used.

In this book I have tried to show the relationship between different branches of the same name. These have been grouped under one main 'root' form of the name, with each version of the name printed in bold so that it can be picked out for quick reference. These variants have also been listed alphabetically in the book, with where to find them, except where they would appear immediately before or after the root form. Names in small capitals mean that there is an entry under that name, where the reader can find more information. Where an entry covers both male and female names, the headword is usually in the masculine form, unless the feminine is much more common. This is not sexism, but because it is much more common to have a feminine name coined from a masculine than vice versa. Moreover, naming conservatism has been much stronger for boys than girls. Parents have had the feeling that it is better to give a boy a 'safe' name, but that they can look for something more glamorous and exotic for girls, so it has been easier to find a single main form of the masculine than of the feminine.

Finally, I would like to thank some of the people who have helped with this book. Fred McDonald, Elizabeth Pearce, Ferelith Hordon and Jean Buchanan supplied me with valuable information. My husband, Philip, has also made many useful suggestions and comments on the work, and given me all the help a spouse can give, as well as giving me the benefit of his expertise in computers. My mother, Constance Fishwick, not only read the whole manuscript as it was originally being written, making many corrections to content, grammar and spelling, but also gave up much of her time to look after my son, Alexander, for the first seven months of his life.

Aa

Aaron

In the Bible, Aaron is the brother of MOSES and is traditionally regarded as the founder of the Jewish priesthood. The meaning of the name is not known, although meanings as diverse as 'mountain of strength' and 'brightness' have been suggested; indeed, we do not even know if it is a Hebrew or Egyptian name. The plant Aaron's Rod is so-called from the story that when Moses and Aaron's right to the leadership of the exiled Children of Israel was challenged, Aaron's rod, or staff, budded and blossomed when laid upon the altar, as a sign that he was chosen by God. The name has become much more popular in recent years – since the late 1970s in the USA, but only in the later 1990s in the UK – which no doubt owes at least something to the fame of Elvis Aaron Presley. This popularity is reflected in a change in pronunciation of the double 'a', which was pronounced in the past with the same sound as 'care', but which is now usually pronounced with the sound found in 'cat'. This in turn has led to new spellings of the name such as **Aron** and **Arron** (but **Aran** can also be a separate Welsh boy's name, from a Welsh place name). **Ron** and **Ronnie** are used as pet forms.

Abby see ABIGAIL

Abel

Abel is the name of the second son of ADAM and EVE, who was killed in a fit of jealousy by his brother **Cain**. As in the case of so many early biblical names, it is difficult to work out the meaning. It has been suggested that the name comes from a word meaning 'son' or perhaps from another word meaning 'breath'. It is an uncommon name, although used rather more now than in the past.

Abigail

Abigail is a Hebrew name which means 'father rejoiced'. The biblical Abigail was a wife of King David. It was a popular name in England until the seventeenth century, when it became a term for a lady's maid, probably because the original Abigail often describes herself as the king's 'handmaiden'. This use, not unnaturally, led to the name falling out of favour. However, it was revived in the nineteenth century, and has remained in steady use, growing in popularity in the later 1990s. It can be found spelt **Abigayle**, and **Abby** (**Abbey**, **Abbi**, **Abbie**) is a short form (shared with GABRIEL), which is also used as an independent name. **Gail (Gale, Gayle)**, its other short form, is well established as an independent name and was well used in the USA in the 1950s.

Abraham

Another Hebrew name, Abraham means 'father of a multitude'. In the Bible, Abraham was originally called **Abram** ('high father'), but as the patriarch of the nation, his name was changed to fit his role. Abraham Lincoln's nickname 'Honest **Abe**' shows one short form of the name; **Aby** is also used, and **Bram** Stoker, the creator of Count Dracula, illustrates another short form. In recent years there has been an increased interest in the name in the USA, although it is still uncommon. Black Muslims have also used the Arabic form of the name, **Ibrahim**.

Achilles see HECTOR

Ada, Adah

These two names actually come from different roots, although in practice they are probably used interchangeably. **Ada** is a short form of the names in the ADELA group and came into use as an independent name in the last century, although it is also recorded as a name used in Asia Minor in the fourth century BC, having been the name of the sister of Mausolus, who built the first mausoleum. **Adah** is a Hebrew name, given to a number of women in the Old Testament, meaning 'an ornament', although it has been interpreted as meaning 'brightness' in contrast to one Adah's co-wife ZILLAH ('shadow'). The computer language Ada is named in honour of Byron's daughter Ada, Countess of Lovelace (1815–52), who was a gifted mathematician in her own right and a patron of Charles Babbage, encouraging him to develop his prototype computer. Ada and Babbage tried to apply their mathematical skills to predicting the outcome of horse races, and Ada died heavily in debt.

Adam

The name of the first man created, Adam comes from the Hebrew word for 'red', referring either to the colour of his skin or to the earth from which he was made. It has been a very popular name for the last 25 years throughout the English-speaking world. Historically, it has particularly strong associations with the Celtic areas of Britain. In Scotland its early popularity led to the development of many variants and pet forms, such as **Adie**, **Edie**, **Edom** and **Yiddie**. There is also a rare Scots feminine form **Adamina**. The Welsh form of Adam is **Adda**, and the Irish have a subsidiary form of the name, **Adamnan** which means 'little Adam'. This was the name of an Irish saint and bishop of the seventh-eighth centuries who was renowned for his work for peace and for his writings, and who also made the earliest recorded 'sighting' of the Loch Ness Monster.

Adela

The early Frankish nobility were very keen to stress their daughters' pedigree (and thus marriageability) and were particularly fond of giving them names compounded with Adel- ('noble'). This is the source of Adela, the name of one of William the Conqueror's daughters, as well of **Adelicia** or **Adeliza** ('noble cheer'), the name of the mother of William the Conqueror and of another of his daughters; **Adelina** ('noble manner'); **Adelaide** ('noble kind'), now also spelt

Adalaide and Adelaida, and Adelinde ('noble snake'), a name that developed into our 'Sweet Adeline' and also shortened forms Alina and Aline. Addie and Addy are used as short forms for all these names. Adèle is the French spelling of Adela, which became popular in the nineteenth century, and Aleida is a German name from the same root, spelt Alida in Hungarian. Adela is also spelt Adella, which is the source of the now independent name Della. There are faint signs of a revival of interest in this group of names. (See also ADA, ALICE, HEIDI.)

Aden see AIDAN

Adina
Adina is an obscure biblical name, the name of a chief of the tribe of Reuben in Chronicles, but is now understood as a feminine name. It is rarely used, but is saved from total obscurity by being the name of a character in Donizetti's opera *L'Elisir d'Amore* and the title of a work by Henry James.

Adlai
Adlai is another rare biblical man's name from the same root as ADAH, meaning 'my ornament'; it was made known to the general public by the politician and wit Adlai Stevenson (1900–65).

Adolf
Meaning 'noble wolf', Adolf has never been popular in Britain, and has little chance of improving its prospects since it became so closely associated with Hitler. However, its Latinate form Adolphus, with its short forms Dolph or Dolphus, was popular in the eighteenth century, when it was given in honour of the Swedish King Gustavus Adolphus, and it is still occasionally encountered.

Adrian, Adrienne
The Adriatic Sea probably got its name from the Latin word *ater* meaning 'black', possibly from the black sand of its beaches. The sea in turn gave its name to the town of Adria, and it was from this town that the family name of the Roman Emperor Hadrian (Latin *Adrianus*) came, which gave us the name Adrian. The only English pope, Nicholas Breakspeare, took the name of Adrian or Hadrian IV, perhaps from St Adrian of Canterbury (d. 710), a man who twice refused to become Archbishop of Canterbury, preferring to remain in a local monastery. The French form of the name is Adrien, and from this comes the most common feminine form Adrienne. Adrianne, Adriane and Adrian(n)a are also used, and can be shortened to forms such as Riana. In the United States, Adrian and Adrien can also be found used as girls' names, the spread of the use perhaps influenced by the character of Adrian Balboa, the hero's wife in the *Rocky* series of films made from 1976 onwards.

Aegidia, Aegidius see GILES

Aelwyn see ALVIN

Aeneas, Aengus see ANGUS

Aeron, Aeronwen

The meaning of the Welsh name element Aeron is disputed. The word *aeron* in Welsh means 'fruit, berry'; but it has also been suggested that the name comes from the ancient Celtic goddess of battle, *Agrona*, or, particularly when used for boys, from the river name which, despite being the least romantic option, is probably the most accurate. Aeron is used for both sexes, but there are specifically feminine variants in **Aerona** and **Aeronwy**. Another feminine, **Aeronwen**, is formed from Aeron plus the suffix *gwen*, which means both 'white' and 'blessed'.

Affery, Afra see APHRA

Afric, Africa

These are forms of a woman's name used in Ireland and the Isle of Man for the Celtic name **Aifric**, meaning 'pleasant', and in Scotland for the Celtic name **Oighrig**, of disputed meaning, possibly 'new speckled one'. It is an old name, going back to at least the eleventh century, and has no connection with the name of the continent, although Africa has been used by Black American parents to mark pride in their origins. It is also found as **Affrica**, while the form **Aphria** may sometimes lead to confusion with APHRA. It has also been confused with the short forms of the name EUPHEMIA which, particularly in the form Effie, was used in Scotland to anglicize Oighrig.

Agatha

Agatha comes from the Greek word meaning 'good'. St Agatha was a third-century martyr, about whom little is known for sure. She is the patron saint of bell-founders, owing to misinterpretation of pictures of her martyrdom. One of the tortures that she was supposed to have suffered was to have her breasts cut off, and she is often painted bearing them on a dish. The bell-like shape of these objects led to her association with campanology. **Agate** is the old form of the name.

Agnes

Derived from the Greek word for 'pure', Agnes was early on associated with the Latin word *agnus*, meaning 'a lamb', and the lamb is her symbol in art. St Agnes was an early Christian martyr and her popularity is attested by the various forms her name has taken. The old English forms of the name were **Annis**, **Annes** or **Annot**, reflecting the medieval pronunciation, and they may be one source of the name **Nance** or **Nancy**. In Scotland, as well as the common shortening **Aggie** or **Aggy**, **Nessa** and **Nessie** are used as pet forms, whence the use of Nessie for the Loch Ness Monster. There is also the peculiar development in Scotland in which the name **Senga** is formed by spelling Agnes backwards (although it has also been suggested that this could come from the Gaelic word *seang* meaning 'slender'). In Wales, the name became **Nest** or **Nesta** and one eleventh-century holder of that name became a byword for her beauty. **Agneta** is both a Latin and Scandinavian form of the name and gives a pet form **Netta**, while the Spanish form gives us **Inez** or **Ines**.

Aibhilin see EILEEN

Aidan

Aidan was originally a pet form of the Irish name **Aodh** (pronounced'ee'), the name of the old Celtic god of the sun and fire, and so means 'little fire'. St Aidan was a seventh-century missionary from Ireland who played an important part in the conversion of the pagan north of England. As a result, his name has long been used in the north, and has in recent years spread to the rest of the UK. The name can also be found as **Aiden** or **Aden**, and is **Aodán** or **Aodhan** in Irish. Aidan is sometimes found given to girls in Ireland, although **Enat** (Irish spelling **Aodhnait**), **Ena**, **Aida** and **Edana** are alternative feminines.

Aifric see AFRIC

Ailbe, Ailbhe see ELVIS

Aileen see EILEEN

Ailie see ALICE

Ailis, Ailish see EILIS

Aily see EILEEN

Ailsa

Some authorities have argued that this Scottish girl's name is a form of ELSA, or of Ealasaid, the Gaelic form of ELIZABETH, or of **Ailsie**, sometimes spelt Ailsa, used in Scotland as a pet form of ALICE. These have no doubt been an influence, but most people identify the name with the island, Ailsa Craig, in the Firth of Clyde. The island's name comes from Old Norse, Ailsa originally meaning 'Alfsigr's Island' (from a masculine Norse name), but it seems to have been popularly understood as 'Ailsa's rock', and so Ailsa came to be thought of as a first name. Ailsa started being used for girls some 100 years ago. Further south, Ailsa Craig became familiar to vegetable growers as the name of popular varieties of tomato and onion. Since Craig is more familiar to southerners as a surname than as a form of the word 'crag', and as many plants are named after people, this may have helped to establish Ailsa's currency as a name.

Ailsie see ALICE, AILSA

Aimé, Aimée see AMY, ESMÉ

Aine

In Irish mythology, Aine is a goddess whose name means 'brightness, splendour', and who was particularly associated with Knockainey (Aine's Hill) in County Limerick. In later legend she became a fairy woman, queen of the fairies, and the kings of Munster claimed to be descended from her. So too did the Fitzgerald family, to whom we owe the name GERALDINE, and Aine became a traditional name in their family.

Ainsley, Ainslie

This is one of the twentieth-century names that has been used equally well for both sexes, although its popularity is well past its peak, and like most of these names it comes from a surname. The surname in turn comes from a place name. Depending on which place with this name the family bearing the surname comes from, it can mean 'lonely clearing' or 'hermitage in a clearing'.

Aisha

Aisha is an Arabic name meaning 'alive and well'. It was the name of the favourite wife of the prophet Mohammed. After he died in her arms, she played an important part in the political and religious events which followed his death. In the form **Ayesha** it was used by Rider Haggard for the name of She-Who-Must-Be-Obeyed in his novel *She* (1887). It is also, by tradition, the name of the wife of the Pharaoh who was drowned in the Red Sea when the Children of Israel escaped from Egypt. **Ayeisha** is also used, while in the United States, where the name has been popular with Black parents, the form **Iesha** or **Ieasha** has developed. The occasionally found **Asia** probably owes as much, if not more, to Aisha as to the name of the continent, as it reflects an alternative pronunciation of the name.

Aisling see ASHLING

Al see ALBERT, ALEXANDER

Alaina, Alayna see ALAN

Alan

A Celtic name of unknown meaning, Alan is found in early Welsh records. It seems to have died out in Britain, until it was reintroduced at the time of the Norman Conquest by Duke William's Breton followers, who used it in honour of a local saint. It is also found in forms such as **Allan, Allen, Alyn, Alleyn** which probably show the influence of surname spellings. Attempts have been made to distinguish the form **Alun** from other spellings, linking it with a Welsh river name, but in practice only a minority of parents seem likely to be aware of this distinction.

Feminine forms of the name, which have become much more common since the 1950s, include **Alana, Alan(n)ah** and **Alanna**, and the short form **Lan(n)a**, made famous by the film star Lana Turner. Forms such as Alannah may be influenced by the spelling of names such as Hannah, although some authorities claim that this group of female names come not from Alan, but from the affectionate Irish interjection *alannah*, which comes from the Irish Gaelic *a lenbh* ('o child'). In recent years **Alaina** and **Alayna**, perhaps a blend of Alana and ELAINE, have begun to be used in the USA.

Alaric

Alaric was a traditional name for the kings of the Ostrogoths, the most famous of which, Alaric I, sacked Rome in 410. The name means 'noble rule'. For some reason, perhaps as a part of the admiration of things 'Gothic', perhaps in honour of the blessed Alaric, a prince who became a monk in Switzerland in the tenth century, it was revived in the nineteenth century, and is still occasionally used.

Alasdair, Alastair, Alastrina, Alastriona see ALEXANDER

Alban

St Alban, who gave his name to the town which grew up around his supposed place of death, was the first British martyr. He is said to have been a Roman soldier who swapped clothes with a Christian priest who was being hunted for his faith, and was executed in his place. Alban seems to have lived in the third century, but dates suggested for his death range between 209 at the earliest to as late as 304. The name, which comes from Latin, and can be interpreted either as meaning 'white' or '[man] from the town of Alba' ('white town'), was revived in the nineteenth century, but is now rare. It is also found in the form **Albin**. Feminine names from the same root are **Albinia** and **Albina**, the name of a third-century martyr, which can be shortened to **Bina**, while BLANCHE is an alternative name with the same meaning, 'white'.

Alberic see AUBREY

Albert

Albert means 'nobly bright'. The Anglo-Saxon form of the name was **Ethelbert**, which more or less died out after the Norman Conquest until revived as a rare name in the nineteenth century. Albert was introduced from Germany by Queen Victoria's husband, and by the end of the nineteenth century was extremely popular in the UK; it was also quite popular in the 1930s in the USA. Short forms are **Al** (particularly in America), **Bert** and **Bertie**. **Alberta** was coined for a god-daughter of Queen Victoria, and other feminine forms such as **Albertine** – familiar as the name of a popular rose – and **Albertina** are also used.

Albin, Albina, Albinia see ALBAN

Alby see ELVIS

Aldous

A man's name derived from a Germanic root meaning 'old', Aldous is an uncommon name given fame by the novelist Aldous Huxley (1894–1964). **Aldis** is an occasional variant.

Aldred see ELDRED

Alea see ALIA

Alec, Aleck, Alessandra see ALEXANDER

Aled

Aled is a Welsh name taken from the name of a river and lake in Denbighshire. It was used by the fifteenth- to sixteenth-century poet Tudor Aled (d. c. 1526). The Welsh singer Aled Jones has recently made the name widely known outside Wales.

Aleesha see ALICE

Aleida see ADELA

Alethea

A woman's name which comes from the Greek word meaning 'truth', Alethea first came into fashion in the seventeenth century, perhaps as a part of the Puritan movement for naming children after abstract virtues such as PATIENCE and CHARITY. It has a variety of spellings such as **Alithea**, **Alithia**, **Alethia** and **Aletheia**. ALTHEA comes from a different root, although the two names are often confused.

Alewyn see ALVIN

Alexander, Alexandra

Alexander is a very ancient and widely used name, which has been particularly popular in the UK for the last 25 years, and popular in the USA since the 1990s. The Greeks believed it came from words meaning 'defender of men', and it is generally so interpreted; but there is some evidence that it may be an even earlier name coming from the ancient Hittite. According to Greek legend, the first holder of the name was the Trojan PARIS, abductor of HELEN; he was nicknamed Alexander by some shepherds whose flocks he defended from robbers. Much later it was adopted by the Macedonian royal family, who followed the Greek custom of alternating pairs of names between generations. Thus PHILIP II of Macedon was the son of an Alexander, and his son was Alexander III, better known as Alexander the Great (356–323 BC), whose conquests of Asia as far as India spread his name in forms such as **Iskander** through much of that continent (see also OLYMPIA, ROXANA). The fame of Alexander the Great also meant that the name was found throughout Europe, spread by the medieval fictional account of his life in *The Romance of Alexander*, which, like a modern bestseller, was translated into a wide range of different languages. The name is found in England from at least the twelfth century, but has special associations with Scotland. St Margaret of Scotland (c. 1038–93) was the daughter of an exiled Anglo-Saxon prince and a Hungarian princess. She married King Malcolm III of Scotland and one of her sons was christened Alexander, a name that had not been used in the Scottish royal family before, but which was popular in Hungary. Alexander I of Scotland reigned for 17 years, and in the following century two more Alexanders succeeded each other; their combined reigns, lasting from 1214 to 1286, firmly established the name in Scotland. Thus it is not surprising that Scotland provides a multitude of pet forms of the name, including **Alec** and **Aleck**, **Alick**, **Eck**, **Ecky**, **Sander**, **Sandy**, **Elshander**, **Elshender**, **Elick**, **Allie** and **Ally**. In Gaelic the name became **Alasdair** (also spelt **Alastair**, **Alistair**, **Alister**), which had been adopted by the Lowland Scots by the seventeenth century, and became popular outside Scotland in the twentieth century. Other pet forms are **Al**, **Alex**, **Lex**, and in the north of England and Scottish Lowlands **Sawnie** was an old pet form.

English speakers have also adopted forms from other countries. Thus the Russian Aleksandr has pet forms **Sasha** or **Sacha** and **Shura**. These are male names in Russia, but because English speakers think of names ending in -a as feminine, they are now often given to girls. The Hungarian **Sandor** is occasionally found. From Russia we also get the related name **Alexis**, or **Alexei** ('helper'), the name of a popular Greek saint. Again these are masculine in origin, but now used as feminines. Alexei is currently one of the most-used girls' names in the USA.

Alexandra, made popular by the Danish princess who married King Edward VII, and back in fashion on both sides of the Atlantic, is the most widely used female form of the name, but **Alexandria, Alexandrina, Alexandrine,** and **Alex(i)a** are also used. They can be shortened to **Alex** and **Lexie. Alix** and **Alyx** look as if they should also be forms of the name, but historically they are medieval spellings of ALICE. From the Italian **Alessandra** we get the names **Sandra, Sondra** and **Zandra,** while in France they use **Xandra** and **Xandrine** as pet forms. There are rare Irish feminine forms of Alasdair: **Alastrina** and **Alastriona.**

Alfred
An Anglo-Saxon name meaning 'elf-counsel', Alfred was made famous through the work of Alfred the Great (849–901), who was not only an inspiring leader of men and a successful general, forcing the invading Danes out of southern England, but also a great patron of learning. Short forms are **Alf, Alfie,** and **Fred.** The name, which had become obsolete, was revived in the nineteenth century, and its very popularity then and in the early part of the twentieth century has led to a decline in its use, although there is a mild revival in use on both sides of the Atlantic. **Alured** is coinage of the nineteenth century, formed from a mis-understanding of the Latin form of the name, the 'u' being a misreading of the 'v' used for the Old English 'f'. **Avery** is a surname, now also used as a first name, which arose because the Norman French who came to rule England in the eleventh century had great difficulty pronouncing English words with groups of consonants in them, and so mangled Alfred to Avery. There is currently a mild fashion for Avery or **Averie** as a name for both sexes in the USA. **Alfreda** is a feminine version of the name which can be shortened to **Freda.**

Alfwine see ALVIN

Algernon
Algernon means 'with whiskers' and started life as a nickname; for instance, William de Percy, who took part in the Norman Conquest and founded the PERCY family, was called Algernon on account of his moustache. It has often been described as an aristocratic name, and certainly has aristocratic associations; but recent research has shown that in the Middle Ages at least, it was used through all strata of society. **Algy** or **Algie** is the short form.

Alia
Alia is an Arabic feminine name, introduced to America by Black Muslims. It means 'sublimity, loftyness', and is also spelt **Alya, Aliya(h)** and **Alea.** The common Muslim man's name **Ali** comes from the same root.

Alice
This name comes ultimately from the old German name Adelaide (see under ADELA) via the French shortening Adaliz, which came over to England as **Aliz, Alys, Alyx** or **Alix** (see also under ALEXANDER). The Latin form of the name gives us **Alicia,** which has recently developed the forms **Alis(i)a, Aliss(i)a** and **Alyss(i)a,** which in turn have developed such forms as **Aleesha** and **Alisha. Elysia** (also found in forms such as **Eleasha, Elissa, Elisha** and **Ellicia**) can be thought of as either a development of Alicia, a blend of Elise and Alicia or a development of Elizabeth. Pet forms of these names are **Ali, Allie** and **Ally.**

ALISON, an old pet form of Alice, is now regarded as a name in its own right. In Scotland, Alice has pet forms **Ailie, Ellie, Ailsie** (sometimes written AILSA), and this, alongside ELIZABETH, is one of the sources of **Elsie. Elke** or **Elkie** is a German pet form of the name. Alice can also be found in such spellings as **Alyse** or **Alyce.** (See also **Eilis.**)

Alick see ALEXANDER

Alida see ADELA

Alienor see ELEANOR

Alina, Aline see ADELA

Alisa, Alisha see ALICE

Alison
Alison, found more often in the USA spelt **Alisson,** is a pet form of ALICE which has become an independent name. Both Alice and Alison have been popular in the UK for most of the twentieth century, while Alisson was well used in the USA in the 1990s. Forms such as **Al(l)yson** and **Alysson** are also found.

Alistair, Alister see ALEXANDER

Alithea, Alithia see ALETHEA

Alix, Aliz see ALICE

Aliya, Aliyah see ALIA

Allan, Allen, Alleyn see ALAN

Allegra
This name means 'lively' in Italian. The poet Byron chose it for his daughter (1817–22), and his choice has been followed by later English-speaking parents particularly in recent years.

Ally see ALEXANDER, ALICE

Allyson see ALISON

Alma
Those wanting to use this girl's name can choose from three different sources. The Latin word *alma*, as in the term Alma Mater for one's school or university, means 'loving, nurturing', and is one source of the name. Then, in the sixteenth century, Edmund Spenser created a character called Alma for book II of his *Faerie Queene*, deriving the name from the Italian for 'soul'. The name remained rare until after 1854, when the British and their allies defeated the Russians in the Crimean War at the battle of Alma, named after a Crimean river. This third source gave the name a popularity which lasted well into the twentieth century, but it is now out of fashion.

Almeric

This Germanic man's name formed from elements meaning 'work' and 'rule' was introduced at the time of the Norman Conquest. It is also found in the form **Almery**. In Italy the name became Almerigo, then Amerigo, as in Amerigo Vespucci (1451–1512), after whom the continent of America is named.

Aloisa, Aloys, Aloyse see HELOISE, LEWIS, LOIS

Alondra

This is a girl's name that became fashionable in the later 1990s in the USA, apparently as a new creation. It could be analysed as a blend of two such names as Alison and Sondra, but may simply have been used because parents liked the sound of it.

Aloysius see LEWIS

Althea

Althea is a Greek name meaning 'wholesome'. In the form **Althæa** it occurs in Greek mythology, as the mother of the hero Meleager, who was told at his birth that he would live as long as a certain log of wood on the fire remained unburned. She kept the wood safe, thus protecting him, until the day he got into a fight and killed her two brothers. In fury she threw the wood on the fire, and her son immediately died. The form Althea was introduced by the Cavalier poet Richard Lovelace as one of his poetic names for Lucy Sacheverell (see LUCASTA).

Alun see ALAN

Alured see ALFRED

Alvin, Aylwin

Two Old English names, **Athelwine** ('noble friend') and **Alfwine** ('elf friend'), lie behind this name, both taking on the forms **Alwin** or **Alwyn** after the Norman Conquest. The name was used quietly until given a boost by the publication of Theodore Watts-Dunton's romantic novel of Gypsy life, *Aylwin*, in 1898. **Alvin** is the form of the name most popular in the United States and may show a Dutch influence. Other forms of the name are **Alvyn** and **Alewyn**. A feminine form, **Alvina**, is found in a Flemish legend in which a king's daughter of that name was rejected by her parents for marrying unsuitably. It is said that her crying can still be heard in the howling of strong winds.

The history of the name is complicated by the existence of a group of similar Welsh names – **Aelwyn, Alwen, Alwyn, Eilwyn** and various other forms – which could be from the same Old English source, or from a jumble of Welsh sources, the second element meaning 'white, fair', the first any one of 'great', 'child' or 'brow'. A related name is **Alvar**, which can be analysed as a form of the Old English name *Alfhere*, formed from 'elf' and 'warrior', or as a form of the Spanish *Alvaro*, another Germanic name, introduced to Spain by the Visigoths, formed from elements meaning 'all' and 'war'. This is the name of a number of characters in the great Spanish epic the *Cantar de Mio Cid* ('Song of My Cid'), but to any British person above a certain age it is best known from the veteran broadcaster Alvar Liddell.

Alwen, Alwin, Alwyn see ALVIN

Alyce see ALICE

Alyn see ALAN

Alys, Alyssa see ALICE

Alysson see ALISON

Alyx see ALICE

Amabel see AMY, MABEL

Amadea, Amadeus see THEODORE

Amalia see AMELIA

Amanda
Amanda means 'worthy of love', and it is one of a large group of names connected with love, for which see further under AMY. The name probably goes back to the seventeenth century when descriptive names based on Latin roots were popular. It was much used for literary heroines in the eighteenth century, and it has been particularly popular as a given name in the second half of the twentieth century, often in its short form, **Mandy**. It peaked in popularity in the 1960s in the UK, but not until the 1980s and 1990s in the USA.

Amandine see AMY

Amaryllis
Amaryllis is a name used by pastoral poets of the classical world for a fair country girl. The name probably derives from a Greek root with the sense 'sparkling of the eyes' or 'darting quick glances'. It was taken up in their pastoral poetry by Spenser and then Milton, who immortalized the name when he wrote of the shepherd's opportunity 'To sport with Amaryllis in the shade' (*Lycidas*). It is only in modern times that Amaryllis has come to be a plant name. The similar-sounding **Amarantha**, another of Lovelace's poetic names (see ALTHEA), is however an ancient Greek flower name, the word meaning 'unfading flower'.

Amata see AMY

Amber
Amber, the name of the fossilized resin used as a jewel, was used occasionally for girls in the nineteenth century, but became fashionable in the 1960s; it has again been popular, particularly in the United States, in the 1980s and 1990s.

Ambrose
Ambrose, from the same Greek root as the food of the gods, ambrosia, means 'belonging to the immortals' and was the name of one of the great doctors of the early Christian Church, the fourth-century St Ambrose, bishop of Milan.

The name is found in British history in the fifth century in the person of Ambrosius Aurelianus, traditionally the uncle of King Arthur. From this Ambrosius the Welsh name **Emrys**, now more common than Ambrose, developed. There is a very rare feminine, **Ambrosine**.

Amelia

Although Amelia looks as if it should be from the Latin family name of Aemelia, the latter has become EMILY, and Amelia, sometimes found as **Amalia** or **Amalie**, actually comes from a Germanic word for 'work'. However, Emily and its related forms are also found as pet forms of Amelia, and may well have influenced the name's development. **Emmeline** (French **Ameline**) is another form of Amelia and the source of the rare name **Emblem**. **Amelina**, **Ameline** and **Amelita** are all developments of the name. **Millie** or **Milly** are used as short forms for these names as well as for MILLICENT. Long out of fashion, there has been a greater show of interest in the name on both sides of the Atlantic since the late 1980s.

Amethyst see JEWELL

Amice, Amicia, Amie see AMY

Aminta see ARAMINTA

Amos

Amos is the name of an Old Testament prophet who foretold the destruction of Judah and Israel if the people did not reform. The name probably means 'bearer of a burden', although others have interpreted it as 'borne by God'. Although popular in the sixteenth century among Puritans, and well used for the next 300 years, it is not much used today.

Amy

Amy means 'loved' (from the French name **Aimée**) and is one of a group of names given to children as an expression of their parents' love. Amy becomes **Amicia** in Latin, which in turn became **Amice** in the early Middle Ages which is still found, if rarely. As well as AMANDA ('worthy to be loved') there is a French name of the same meaning, **Amandine**. **Amata** means 'beloved' and **Amabel** (Amabilla in the Middle Ages), which became MABEL, means 'loveable'. **Amorée** is a recent addition to the list, while Amy can also be found in spelling such as **Amie** or **Amye**. In the past there were male equivalents of many of these names, but the only one to have survived is **Amyas** ('loved'), kept alive by its use by Charles Kingsley for the hero of his *Westward Ho!* (1885).

Amynta, Amyntas, Amyntor see ARAMINTA

Ana, Anabel, Anabella, Anabelle see ANN

Anaïs

This is a French feminine name, derived from the Greek meaning 'fruitful'. It is found as a character in Colette's *Claudine* books, and has a certain notoriety from the French author Anaïs Nin, but more recently became widely known as the name of a perfume.

Anastasia

St Anastasia was a Christian martyr who died about 304, whose feast day is on Christmas Day. Although there are wild and wonderful legends, almost nothing is known about her for sure. The name was found from the early twelfth century onwards in England, often in the forms **Anstace** or **Anstice**. We now tend to think of it as a Russian name, thanks to the fame of the Russian princess who is rumoured to have survived the massacre of the last Tsar and his family. Anastasia comes from the Greek word for 'The Resurrection'. Short forms include **Stacey** or **Stacy** (see also EUSTACE) and **Tansy**, although this can also be thought of as a use of the name of the yellow wild flower (*Tanacetum vulgare*).

Anchoret see ANGHARAD

Andrew, Andrea

Andrew comes from the Greek meaning 'manly'. The Apostle Andrew became the patron saint of Scotland, so it is not surprising that there it has developed its own forms **Andra** or **Andro** and **Dand, Dandie** or **Dandy**. Other pet forms are **Andie, Andy** and **Drew**; the latter is often used as an independent name and can also be derived from a Germanic-French name **Drew** or **Drogo** meaning 'trusty'. The French form, **André**, has now spread to English-speaking countries as well, while the form **DeAndre** is a well-used Black American name.

Andrea, the most common of the feminine versions of the name, is from the Italian (where it is a masculine name), which also gives **Andreana**. **Andrée** is the French form. There are also a number of feminine versions which probably started life in Scotland, as they show typical Scots forms, but which are now by no means restricted to Scotland. Included in this group are **Andrina, Andrene, Andrewena, Andrine, Andreena** and their diminutives **Dreena** and **Rena**. All these can be shortened to Andie or Andy.

Aneurin, Aneirin

This is usually said to come from the Latin name *Honorius* (see HONORIA), which would mean it was adopted before the end of the Roman occupation of Britain; but it has also been suggested that it should be derived from Welsh roots giving a meaning of 'little one of pure gold'. It is certainly a very old name, for it was borne by one of the earliest known Welsh poets, who lived in the sixth century. Its short forms are **Nye** and **Neirin**. It is perhaps best known from the Labour politician Nye Bevan (1897–1960), who as minister for health was largely responsible for the introduction of the National Health Service after World War II.

Angela

Angela means 'angel', a word that comes from the Greek word for 'a messenger', and has pet forms **Ange, Angie** and **Angy**. Variants include **Angelica, Angelina, Angeline, Angelique, Angelia**. **Angel** is occasionally found for girls; but while it is very common in Spanish-speaking countries, or with those of Spanish descent, as a man's name, it is not much used elsewhere, although we do have the literary character Angel Clare in Thomas Hardy's *Tess of the D'Urbervilles* (1891). Another masculine form is the Italian **Angelo**, which has a pet form **Lito**, and **DeAngelo** is also used in the USA.

Angharad

Angharad, also spelt **Anghared**, is a Welsh name meaning 'much loved', which has been in use since at least the ninth century. It is the name of the fair lady in the medieval Welsh romance *Peredur*. It was out of favour for a while because the element 'an', which in this name is an intensifier indicating 'very, much', could be understood as a negative, giving a meaning 'unloved'; but in the twentieth century it was well used in Wales and occasionally outside the country. It is one of the few Welsh names adopted by the English in the Middle Ages, anglicized to the now rare **Anchoret** or **Ankaret**.

Angie see ANGELA

Angus

The Scottish form of a Gaelic name, Angus means 'one choice'. It is an important name in Scottish history, as it was the name of one of the first Irish settlers who founded the Scots nation. The Irish form is **Aonghus** or **Aengus**, which has given the Scots surname **Innes**, reflecting the Irish pronunciation of the name. This is occasionally found as a first name. **Aeneas** or **Eneas**, the name of the Trojan founding father of the Roman people, whose name means 'praiseworthy', was used in the past when Gaelic names were frowned on, as the equivalent of Angus, and is still used in some Scots families. (For a similar use of a Trojan hero see HECTOR; see also under JULIA.)

Angy see ANGELA

Anika, Anita, Anja see ANN

Ankaret see ANGHARAD

Ann, Hannah, Nancy

This disparate-looking group of names all derive from the Hebrew name **Hannah** ('God has favoured me'). Tradition, rather than the New Testament, makes it the name of the mother of the Virgin Mary, and this tradition led to its spread throughout Europe, where it took many forms. **Anna** is the Greek form of the name, and at the moment is considerably more popular with both American and British parents than the more traditional **Ann** or **Anne**. **Ana** is also found. The pet form **Annie** is used as an independent name, and leads other pet forms, such as **Nan**, **Nan(n)a** and **Nanny**. These in turn are one source of the name **Nancy** and its short form **Nance** (see also AGNES); **Nansi** is the Welsh spelling. Hannah, particularly popular at the moment, was the name of the mother of SAMUEL in the Old Testament.

Many foreign forms of the name have been adopted by English-speaking parents. From France we get **Annette** (which in Scotland became **Annot**) and the diminutives **Nanette**, **Ninette** and **Ninon**. **Anita** (shortened to **Nita**) and **Anya** come from Spain, and **Anneka**, **Anika** and **Annika** are Scandinavian pet forms. The actress **Anouk** Aimée has made the Russian form better known, and Russia also gives us **Anushka** and **Nina**. Respellings of Anna, such as **Anja** and **Annah**, are not uncommon, and Anne and Anna are often combined in forms such as Anna Mae or **Anneli** (a shortening of the German and Scandinavian **Anneliese** formed from Anne and Liese, a pet form of ELIZABETH, which is sometimes spelt **Annalise** to reflect its pronunciation).

An(n)abella (**Anabel, Anabelle**) presents a problem, as it is found in Scotland well before Anne, so it is difficult to derive it from the obvious combination Anna-Belle ('fair Anna'). It may well be a form of Amabel, the source of MABEL. Its short forms are one of the sources of **Bella** and **Belle**.

Annes, Annis, Annot see AGNES

Anorah, Annorah, Annora see ELEANOR, HONORIA

Anouk see ANN

Anselm
Anselm was the name of a twelfth-century archbishop of Canterbury, canonized for his theological writings. It is a Germanic name, meaning 'divine helmet', despite the fact that St Anselm himself was born in Italy.

Anthea
Derived from a Greek word meaning 'flowery', Anthea was an ancient title of Hera, the Greek queen of the gods, and has been in use as a literary name since the fourth century AD. In this country it was taken up and given currency by the poets of the seventeenth century, in particular Herrick, but has only been popular as a given name since the mid-twentieth century.

Antony, Antonia
These names come from the Roman family name of the Antonii, best known through Julius Caesar's follower Mark Antony (in Latin, Marcus Antonius). The meaning of the name is not clear, but the Romans derived it from a word meaning 'inestimable' or else as signifying descent from Antius, one of the sons of the hero-god Hercules. **Anthony** with an 'h' (never found in Latin) came into use in the sixteenth century in an attempt to derive the name from the Greek *anthos* (a flower), as in ANTHEA. **Tony**, and in the past **Nanty**, are pet forms. The name became popular throughout Europe through the fame of two saints, St Antony the Hermit, a third-century saint regarded as the founder of monasticism, and St Antony of Padua, a thirteenth-century saint famous for his preaching, and still one of the best-loved saints of the Roman Catholic Church. The French form of the name **Antoine**, and **Anton**, found in both Germany and Russia, have recently become more popular, particularly in the USA, where the Spanish form **Antonio**, and its shortening **Tonio** are also well used.

Antonia is the Latin feminine of Antony and is similarly abbreviated to **Tony**, or more commonly **Toni(e)**. **Tonia** and **Tonya** are also used. The French form **Antoinette**, famous from the beheaded Marie Antoinette, is shortened to **Net**, **Nettie** or **Netty** (see also JANE), and in the United States phonetic respellings of both Antoinette and Antoine using a 'w' or 'u' after the 't' are to be found.

Anushka, Anya see ANN

Aodán, Aodh, Aodhan, Aodhnait see AIDAN

Aoife

Aoife, one of the most popular choices among Irish parents for girls in recent years, is an ancient Irish name meaning 'radiant, beautiful', and was originally the name of a goddess. It is anglicized as Eva (see EVE), which both reflects the name's pronunciation and explains why Eva has always been such a popular name in Ireland.

Aonghus see ANGUS

Aphra

This name comes from a misunderstanding of a biblical passage when, in the book of Micah (1:10) the translators have 'in the house of Aphrah roll thyself in the dust', where the word 'Aphrah' actually means 'dust'. It is possible that the name is also confused with **Afra**, an obscure early martyr, and with forms of the Irish AFRIC. It was a not uncommon name in the seventeenth century, but its use today is almost entirely due to the fame of Mrs Aphra Behn (1640–89), spy, playwright and author of the first anti-slavery novel in English, who is reputed to be the first Englishwoman to have earned her living by her writing. She was nicknamed by her contemporary admirers 'The Incomparable **Astrea**'. Records of her life show her name spelt Afra, Aphra and **Ayfara**. In *Little Dorrit* (1857) Dickens has a character called **Affery** Flintwinch, which illustrates the pet form of the name.

Aphrodite see JULIA

April

April is the name of the month used as a first name. Perhaps April, May and June are all used as girls' names not only because they are short, making them more suitable than, say, October, but because the months' associations with spring and early summer are so attractive. They are chosen surprisingly rarely because the child is actually born in that particular month. April was particularly popular in the USA in the 1980s. In Wales the equivalent name is **Ebrilla**, with **Ebrillwen** as a variant. The French form of the name, **Avril**, is also used, although it is not noticeably common in France. Avril probably owes something to the name Averil, from the Old English name **Everild** or **Everilda** ('boar-battle'), the name of a rather obscure Yorkshire saint. Everild became **Averilla** and thence **Averil**. The older forms are still found today, although rarely, Averil being much more common.

Arabella

This is a Scottish name, probably a form of the name Annabel (see ANN), although as the name is found in early documents as **Orable** it has been argued that it comes from a Latin word meaning 'easily moved by prayer', or even that it comes from a word meaning 'Arab'; but these are much less likely sources. **Arbel** was a common early form, and **Arabel** seems to be a bit older than the Latinate Arabella. Its pet forms **Bel, Bell, Belle** and **Bella** are one of the sources of this name.

Araminta

This is an elaboration of the name **Aminta** or **Amynta**, itself derived from the Macedonian Greek masculine name **Amyntas** ('defender'), used by that country's royal family from at least the fourth century BC. The masculine name was used by Spenser in his autobiographical poem 'Colin Clout' (1595) and by the Earl of Rochester (1647–80) in 'Phyllis', and in the form **Amyntor** by Beaumont and Fletcher, but the masculine name does not seem to have caught on with parents. The feminine forms have an equally literary pedigree, being poetic names of the seventeenth century; both are used by Vanbrugh, and Sir Charles Sedley addresses poems to Aminta. Aminta had already been used in the previous century by the Italian poet Tasso. Virginia Woolf's **Minta** Doyle in *To the Lighthouse* (1927) shows one short form of the names, the other being **Minty**.

Aran see AARON

Archibald
Archibald is a Germanic name formed from elements meaning 'truly bold'. It has particular associations with Scotland, where the Campbells used it to anglicize the native name **Gillespie** (Gaelic **Gilleasbuig**), meaning 'servant of the bishop'. Short forms of the name are **Arch, Archie, Archy, Baldie** and in Scotland **Erch** and **Erchie**. It has become quite fashionable in the UK in recent years, particularly when shortened to Archie.

Ardal
Ardal (**Ardgal** or **Ardghal** in Irish) probably comes from words meaning 'high valour', but may belong with other Celtic masculine names such as ARTHUR, that come from the element *art* meaning 'bear'.

Arel see ARIEL

Aretha
Made famous by the singer Aretha Franklin, this unusual name comes from the Greek word for 'virtue'. It is also spelt **Areta**. From the same root comes the rarely used **Arethusa**, the nymph who, in classical mythology, was chased from Greece to Sicily by an amorous river god until she turned herself into a spring to escape his attentions.

Arfon
A Welsh place name in Gwynedd meaning 'opposite Anglesey', Arfon is used as a boy's first name. **Arfona** and **Arfonia** are the female equivalents.

Ariadne
In Greek mythology, Ariadne is a Cretan princess who falls in love with Theseus and helps him to escape from the Minotaur, only to be abandoned by him. The name means 'the very holy one' and was probably originally used as a title for a goddess. Recently interest has been shown in the French form **Ariane**, perhaps because it has become well known as the name of the European space rocket. The Italian **Arianna** is also found.

Ariel
As a girl's name, this became well used in the United States after it was the name given to the heroine of the Disney cartoon *The Little Mermaid* (1989). In origin it probably owes something to Shakespeare's island spirit Ariel in *The Tempest*. It is also found in the form **Arielle** and **Arial**. As a masculine name, it is a

Hebrew name, from a biblical place name, said to mean 'lion of God'. It is a popular name in Israel and can be found used in the USA. It has pet forms **Arel** and **Arik**.

Arlene
Also spelt **Arleen** and **Arline**, this seems to be a fairly modern coinage, possibly derived from Charlene (see CAROL). Similarly **Arlette**, a French name made well known here through the Van der Valk novels of Nicholas Freeling, is thought to be formed from a pet from of Charlotte.

Armand, Arminel, Arminelle, Armine see HERMAN

Arnold
Arnold is a Germanic name, formed from elements meaning 'eagle' and 'rule'. Its popularity in the Middle Ages is shown by its frequency as a surname, but it later died out, only to be revived, with so many other old names, in the nineteenth century. Short forms are **Arn** and **Arnie**. The success of the Austrian-born actor Arnold Schwarzenegger does not seem to have increased the popularity of the name, perhaps because he came to fame playing rather unearthly roles.

Aron, Arron see AARON

Art, Artan see ARTHUR

Artemis, Artemisia see DIANA

Arthur
The meaning of this name is much disputed, the two main theories being that it comes from a Celtic root meaning 'bear', or that it is a form of some Roman name, such as the clan name Artorius. The name is inextricably linked with that of King Arthur of legend and possibly history, but despite its link, over-use of the name in the nineteenth century led to a decline in its popularity in the twentieth. **Art** and **Arty** are its short forms, but Art can also be a traditional Irish name (also meaning 'bear') with pet forms **Artan** and **Artin**.

Arwel
Arwel is a Welsh masculine name meaning 'prominent'.

Arwyn, Arwen
These are Welsh names meaning 'fair, fine', the former masculine, the latter, along with the variant **Arwenna**, feminine.

Asa
Asa is a Hebrew name meaning 'physician', and was the name of one of the Old Testament kings. It is particularly associated with Yorkshire, and is perhaps best known today from the historian Asa Briggs.

Ashanti
Also spelt **Asante**, this is one of the new names chosen by Black parents to mark their pride in their ancestry. The Ashanti are a West African tribe, mainly based

in Ghana, who, in the eighteenth and nineteenth centuries ruled a great empire which also had a fine artistic tradition. The name is used for both sexes, but is mainly female. The name **Shante** may be a short form of this.

Asher

According to the Bible (Genesis 30. 13), when one of Jacob's twelve sons, who gave their names to the tribes of Israel, was born, his wife, Leah, said 'Happy am I, for the daughters will call me blessed; and she called his name Asher', the name meaning 'fortunate, blessed'. The name was originally restricted to Jewish use, but has recently begun to be more widely used, and has even been recorded as a female name, perhaps under the influence of ASHLEY.

Ashley

This is a surname originally given to someone who lived in an ash wood (or a clearing in one); it is now used as a first name for both sexes. It is also spelt **Ashleigh** and **Ashly**. It has been particularly popular in Australia and the United States. Its spread may owe something to its use by Margaret Mitchell for one of her male characters in *Gone with the Wind* (1936), for this book and film has influenced the popularity of several names; but see further under EARTHA. The name was at first predominantly masculine, but was being used increasingly for girls in the USA from the 1940s, becoming even more popular through the 1980s, until it became the most popular name for American girls in 1991; it was still in the top three five years later. In the UK the spread between girls and boys has been more even: it ranked 33rd for girls in 1985, but was not in the top 50 for boys, yet in 1997 it did not make the top 50 for girls but was 46th for boys.

Two related names have recently begun to make an impact in the USA. **Ashlyn**, used for girls, may be a development of Ashley, or else an American version of ASHLING. **Ashton**, another surname, from a place name meaning 'settlement where ash trees grow', is now used as a first name for both sexes.

Ashling

Ashling is the phonetic spelling of the Irish feminine name **Aisling**, also found as **Isleen**. It is a modern name which comes from the Irish word meaning 'dream, vision' and has been particularly popular in the last 30 years.

Ashton see ASHLEY

Asia see AISHA

Astrea see APHRA

Astrid

Astrid is a Scandinavian name formed from elements meaning 'god' and 'beauty'. It has been used in Scandinavian royal families since at least the tenth century, but only since the twentieth century in the UK. Its spread may owe something to the popularity of Queen Astrid of the Belgians (d. 1935).

Atalanta

Atalanta is an ancient Greek name that has slowly been coming into use over the last 10 to 15 years. In Greek mythology Atalanta was a maiden-huntress who was determined not to marry. To this end, knowing how fast she could run, she said she would only marry the man who could beat her in a footrace. She was finally outrun by Hippomenes, who had obtained three golden apples from Aphrodite, goddess of love. Every time Atalanta was about to overtake him, he rolled one of these apples in front of her and pulled ahead as she stopped to pick them up; in the end, he just beat her. Atalanta's name and story became widely known through Swinburne's much-anthologised poetic drama *Atalanta in Calydon*, published in 1865. **Lanty** has been used as a pet form of Atalanta. The similar sounding **Atlanta** comes either from the Atlantic Ocean or from the city in Georgia. The Atlantic got its name because it was the ocean near where Atlas stood. He, in Greek myth, was a giant who held up the sky on his shoulders. Since his picture appeared in many early books of maps, these came to be known as 'an atlas' after him.

Atheldreda, Athelthryth see AUDREY

Athelstan

Also spelt **Athelstane**, this is an Old English name meaning 'noble stone'. It suffered the same obscurity after the Norman Conquest as most other Old English names, but was revived in the nineteenth century, and as a result is still occasionally found.

Athelwine see ALVIN

Athene

Athene was the great patron-goddess of the city of Athens, a warrior goddess, but also the bringer of many skills and crafts, and goddess of wisdom. The meaning of her name is not known, but it is thought to go back at least to Mycenean times. Both Athene and the alternative form **Athena** are occasionally used, rather more often than her Roman equivalent **Minerva**.

Athol

The earls and later dukes of Athol played a prominent role in Scottish history, and the name may have come into use from the title, in much the same way that CLIFFORD and HOWARD did in England. It is also a surname and place name in Perthshire (which gave the dukes their title). The place gets its name from the Gaelic *ath Fodla*, meaning 'new Ireland', a name given it by the Gaels who immigrated to the area from Northern Ireland. As a masculine first name it is also found as **Atholl**, **Athole** and **Athold**.

Atlanta see ATALANTA

Aubrey

Aubrey is the Norman French form of the Germanic name **Alberic** ('elf-ruler'). Alberic was the name of the Scandinavian king of the elves, who plays such an important part in Wagner's *Ring Cycle*. **Auberon** seems to have been a pet form of this name, and had already been used as the name of the king of the fairies before Shakespeare used the name in the form **Oberon** in *A Midsummer Night's Dream*. Throughout most of its history, this name has been a boy's name, but in recent years, perhaps influenced by AUDREY, the name has begun to be used for girls, particularly in the USA. For girls it can also appear as **Aubree**, **Aubri(e)** and **Aubry**.

Audrey

This is a contraction of the Old English name of St **Etheldreda**, or **Ethelthryth** ('noble strength'). The full form of the name is also spelt **Atheldreda, Etheldred,** and **Athelthryth**, and is also one of the sources of the name ETHEL. St Etheldreda was a seventh-century East Anglian princess who founded an abbey at Ely on the site where the cathedral now stands. The name St Audrey was itself contracted to the word 'tawdry' (the 't' being run on from the end of the word 'saint'), first used to describe the sort of cheap but glittering goods sold at the famous St Audrey's Fair. Audrey is not a frequent choice of British parents at the moment, but is more likely to be found in the USA, where variants such as **Audreen** and **Audrianna** can be found. All forms can be shortened to **Audie**.

Augustus, Augusta

Augustus is a Latin word meaning 'majesty', given as a title by the Roman Senate to the first Roman Emperor in 27 BC and adopted by him as a name (see also OCTAVIA). Augusta is the feminine form of the same word. **Gus** and **Gussie** are used as pet forms of these names and of **Augustine**, pronounced with the stress on the second syllable in Britain, but on the third in the United States. Augustine was the name of an early saint and one of the great doctors of the Christian Church, and was derived from Augustus. Augustine was also the name of the man sent in 596 to England by Pope GREGORY the Great to convert the heathen Saxons to Christianity. In medieval England this name was contracted to **Austin** or **Austen** and used both as a surname and as a first name. Austin is currently one of the most popular choices for boys in the USA.

Aure see DAWN

Aurelius, Aurelia

These are the masculine and feminine forms of a Roman family name meaning 'golden'. **Aurelian**, the name of one of the Roman emperors, is an alternative masculine form. From Aurelia come **Auriel** and **Auriol; Oriel** and **Oriole** are spelling variants of this name. ORLA is the Irish equivalent of this name.

Aurnia see ORLA

Aurora, Aurore see DAWN

Austen, Austin see AUGUSTUS

Autumn

This vocabulary word, with its associations of glowing leaves and the richness of the harvest, is the most popular of the seasons used as a girl's name. Although it was used in the 1980s and earlier, it only made its mark in the 1990s. **Summer** is the next most popular of the seasons, followed by **Spring**, but the month names – APRIL, MAY, JUNE – also cover these seasons. Winter has too many negative associations ever to become popular. All the season names are most frequently found in the USA.

Ava

This name is found in the early Middle Ages, where it is probably a pet form of names, such as Avaline, beginning 'av-', but then disappears until the twentieth century, where it was strongly associated with the film actress Ava Gardner. It may be a form of Eva (see EVE), from the Latin *avis* ('a bird'), or a pet form of a name containing 'ava'; but it is just as likely to be a Hollywood invention like Lauren (see LAURA).

Aveline see EILEEN

Averie see ALFRED

Averil, Averilla see APRIL

Avery see ALFRED

Avice, Avis
This is an old Germanic feminine name of unknown meaning, although the form Avis has led to its association with the Latin for 'bird'. Some French writers associate it with the German name **Hedewig** or **Hedwige**, meaning 'combat', the source of the pet forms found in Ibsen's **Hedda** Gabler and the film star **Hedy** Lamarr. **Hedwig** has enjoyed new prominence as the name of Harry Potter's pet snowy owl in the popular *Harry Potter* series of novels by J. K. Rowling.

Avril see APRIL

Ayeisha, Ayesha see AISHA

Aylmer see ELMER

Aylwin see ALVIN

Aymé see ESMÉ

Bb

Babette see BARBARA, ELIZABETH

Babs see BARBARA

Bailey
This surname, originally given to someone who had the job of bailiff, has become fashionable as a girl's name in the USA. The second syllable can have all the variant spellings found in the name LEE, giving forms such as **Bailee** and **Baileigh**, while spellings with Bay-, such as **Baylee**, are also found. The name has also been recorded as a masculine name.

Baldwin, Baldric
The name-element 'bald' has nothing to do with hair growth, but represents the Germanic form of the English 'bold'. Thus Baldric means 'bold-rule' and Baldwin 'bold-friend'. Baldwin is a popular name with the Belgian royal family, although it is usually used in the French form of the name Baudoin.

Balthazar see JASPER

Bambi see FAWN

Barbara
Barbara comes from the Greek word for 'foreign, strange': the same root gives us the word 'barbarian'. It may have started as a name given to a foreign slave. St Barbara, virgin and martyr, was a very popular saint from the ninth century onwards. Her symbol is the brass tower in which her father shut her before executing her for her faith. Since he was punished by being struck down by a thunderbolt, Barbara is invoked against lightning and, by an association of ideas, is also the patron saint of gunners and miners. Her story has elements found in many folk tales, and there is no evidence that she ever existed. Short forms are **Babs, Barbie** (as in the doll) and, in the US, **Bobbi**. The French pet form **Babette** (also used for ELIZABETH) is sometimes found, and **Barbra** Streisand has popularized a variant spelling. Barbara was popular in the United States through most of the twentieth century, but it is less well used now, and has been in decline in the UK since the 1950s.

Barnabas

In the Bible, Barnabas is defined as meaning 'son of consolation', although a more correct interpretation would be 'son of exhortation'. The biblical St Barnabas, 'a good man, full of the Holy Ghost and of faith' (Acts 11. 24), was closely associated with St Paul in spreading Christianity through Asia Minor. **Barnaby** is an old short form of the name which has been revived as an independent name in recent years. **Barney**, a short form shared with BERNARD, is now probably best known to millions of children as the name of a lurid purple singing and dancing dinosaur.

Barney see BARNABAS, BERNARD

Barry

Barry is a Celtic name with several origins. There are three main sources, which have become so confused as to be indistinguishable. There is an Irish name Barry (**Bearach** in Gaelic), which comes from the word for 'spear'. In Wales the name can be a form of the surname 'ap Harry' (son of Harry); but it can also be derived from the place name of Barry Island, in which case it comes from the Welsh word *bar* meaning 'a dune or mound'. In addition, Barry can be used in Ireland as a pet form of Finbar ('fair head') (see FINLAY), in which case it is sometimes spelt **Barra**.

Bartholomew

Bartholomew is a Hebrew name meaning 'son of Talmai', Talmai itself meaning 'abounding in furrows'. It is thought that the apostle Bartholomew is probably the same as NATHANIEL, Bartholomew being the equivalent of a surname. **Bart** is a common short form; **Bartlemy** and **Bartly** are less common old shortenings, and **Tolomey** is also found. In Ireland, Bartholomew is used to anglicize the Gaelic name **Parthalon** or **Partholon**.

Basil

Basil comes from the Greek word for 'kingly', and is thus the Greek equivalent of the Latin REX. It was the name of several saints in the Orthodox Church, and is very popular in Slavic countries, usually in a form beginning with a 'v', as in the Russian **Vasilie**. Short forms are **Baz** or **Bas**, and there are rare feminine forms **Basilia** and **Basilie**.

Bastian see SEBASTIAN

Bathsheba

This biblical name means 'opulent' or 'voluptuous' – apt for a woman whose naked body, seen while she was bathing, led King David to bring about the death of her husband **Uriah** the Hittite, so that he could marry her. It is nowadays better known as a literary name from Bathsheba Everdene in Thomas Hardy's *Far From the Madding Crowd* (1874) than as a real-life name, but it was popular with the Puritans, presumably more as a warning than as a model for the bearer. The short form **Sheba** is occasionally found used independently.

Baudoin see BALDWIN

Baylee see BAILEY

Baz see BASIL

Bearach see BARRY

Beatrice

This name has variant forms **Beatrix, Beatris** and, in Wales, **Bet(t)rice** or **Bet(t)rys**; and short forms **Bea, Bee, Beatty, Trix, Trixie** and **Triss**. The earliest, Late Latin form of the name appears to have been *Viatrix* ('voyager'), but seems to have been changed under the influence of the Latin *beatus* ('blessed'). The choice of the name by the Duke and Duchess of York for their first child, in 1988, seems to have led to some increase in its popularity in the UK. In the USA the name, which is not a particularly common choice, is most likely to be given in its Spanish form, **Beatriz**. **Beata** is from the same Latin root and means 'blessed'.

Beau

This boy's name is almost entirely restricted to American use. It comes from the French word for 'handsome'. Although it was used as a nickname for the Regency dandy Beau Brummell (1778–1840), it was not noted as a given name until the twentieth century. Two books brought it to the general public: P.C. Wren's novel *Beau Geste* (1924) (where it was again a nickname) and, more importantly, Margaret Mitchell's novel *Gone With the Wind* (1936), which featured the character Beau Wilkes and was the inspiration behind the growth in popularity of a number of names, including ASHLEY, MELANIE and SCARLETT. Beau is also found spelt **Bo** and **Boe**, and can also be a short form of **Beauregard** ('handsome look'), a name sometimes given in honour of the US confederate general Pierre Gustave Toutant Beauregard (1818–93), particularly in his native New Orleans.

Becka, Becky see REBECCA

Bedelia see BRIDGET

Belinda

Strictly speaking Belinda is an old Germanic name, with an unknown first element and the '-linda' part meaning 'serpent', a symbol of wisdom. However, most users today probably think of it as a combination of the French 'belle' (as in the name **Bella**, also used as a short form of this name) and of the Spanish 'linda'; both mean 'beautiful'. Alexander Pope seems to have had the connotations of beauty in mind when he gave this name to the heroine of *The Rape of the Lock* (1712–14). The name is one of the sources of LINDA.

Bell, Bella, Belle see ANN, ARABELLA, BELINDA, ISABEL

Ben see BENJAMIN

Benedict

Benedict comes from the Latin meaning 'blessed' and owes its use as a name to St Benedict (490–c. 542), founder of the Benedictine order. **Benedick** is an old variant form of the name, as is the surname **Bennet(t)** once used as a first name.

Benedicta and **Benedetta** are uncommon female forms of the name, while **Benita** comes from the same root.

Benjamin

Benjamin is an Old Testament name meaning 'son of the right hand', indicating qualities of strength and good fortune. In the Bible, Benjamin is the youngest of the twelve sons of JACOB, and the pet of his father and brothers, so the name has sometimes been used to signify a favourite child. Short forms are **Ben**, **Benjie**, **Bennie** or **Benny**. Both Benjamin and Ben have been particularly popular with parents on both sides of the Atlantic in recent years.

Berenice see VERONICA

Bernard

This is a Germanic name meaning 'strong or brave as a bear'. **Barney**, shared with BARTHOLOMEW, is a short form used particularly in the United States. The feminine form **Bernadette** (sometimes **Bernardette**) was given popularity by St Bernadette of Lourdes. **Bernardine** and **Bernardetta** (shortened to **Detta**) are feminine variants, and **Bernie** is used as a short form for both sexes.

Bernice, Bernie see VERONICA

Berry see BERTRAM

Bert, Bertie see ALBERT, BERTRAM, GILBERT, HERBERT, ROBERT

Bertha

This is an old Germanic name meaning 'bright'. It is found in various forms throughout Europe, and has been used in England since Anglo-Saxon times. Bertha Bigfoot, the mother of the emperor Charlemagne (c. 742–814), was an early holder of the name. She appears in medieval fiction as the heroine of highly romantic stories, but in her real life she was much admired as a fine ruler and a power behind her son's throne. A less attractive use of the name is Big Bertha, the name given to each of a set of four guns made by the Krupp armaments firm and used by the Germans to bombard Paris in 1918. They were named after Bertha Krupp, the heiress to the firm, and their range of 76 miles was the greatest of any gun yet made. (See further HERBERT.)

Bertram, Bertrand

Strictly speaking Bertram means 'bright raven' and Bertrand 'bright shield', but these two Germanic names early on came to be regarded as variants of the same name, with Bertrand the French form of Bertram. The commonest short forms are **Bert** and **Bertie**, but **Berry** (as in the case of the Dornford Yates character) is sometimes used, although this can also be derived from the surname, which comes from either the type of fruit or the French place name. There have been recent signs of a revival of interest in these names among parents in the UK.

Beryl

This is one of the gem names popular in the late nineteenth and early twentieth centuries. It came into use rather later in the American Middle West, where it has also been regularly recorded as a man's name.

Bess, Bessie, Bessy, Bet, Beth, Bethan, Bethany, Bethia, Betsy, Bettina, Betty, Bettyne see ELIZABETH

Betrice, Bettrice, Betrys, Bettrys see BEATRICE

Beulah see HEPHZIBAH

Beverly, Beverley
This comes from a place and surname meaning 'beaver stream'. While it can be used as a name for either sex, it is now rare as a male name, although the novelist Beverley Nichols keeps alive an awareness of its masculine use. **Bev** is the short form. The name was popular in the USA from the 1920s to the 1950s, and in the 1960s in the UK, but is little chosen now.

Bevis
An old French name, Bevis was famous in the Middle Ages as the name of the hero of the inordinately long but very popular romance *Sir Bevis of Hamtoun* (i.e. Southampton). In 1882 Richard Jefferies published a very successful book, *Bevis, the Story of a Boy*, which helped to revive the name.

Bianca, Bibi see BLANCHE

Biddie, Biddy, Bidelia see BRIDGET

Bill, Billie, Billy see WILLIAM

Bina see ALBAN

Birgita see BRIDGET

Blain
Blain is a Scottish surname that has recently found some favour with parents in the USA as a boy's first name. The surname was originally an affectionate nickname probably given to someone with blond hair, as it is a pet form of the Gaelic word *bla* ('yellow').

Blair
Like BLAIN, Blair is a Scottish surname and place name used as a first name. The place name means 'marshy plain'. It is now being used for girls as well as boys, in which case it can appear as **Blayre**.

Blaise
Blaise has been derived from the Greek *basileios*, meaning 'royal', but is more likely to come from a Latin nickname *blaseus*, meaning 'stuttering, deformed'. In Arthurian legend it is the name of Merlin's secretary, who is supposed to have written down his master's sayings. The name is more popular in France than in English-speaking countries, no doubt due in part to the fame of Blaise Pascal (1623–62). **Blaze** and **Blase** are variants.

Blake
Blake is a surname meaning 'black, dark-complexioned', but is also used as a

first name. It is usually a masculine name, but feminine uses have been recorded.

Blanche

Occasionally spelt **Blanch**, this is an old name meaning 'white'. A fourteenth-century holder was Blanche, Duchess of Lancaster, the wife of John of Gaunt and heroine of Chaucer's elegy *The Book of the Duchess*. **Bianca,** which can be shortened to **Bibi,** and **Blanca,** the Italian and Spanish forms of the name, are also found.

Blase, Blaze see BLAISE

Blayre see BLAIR

Blodwen

This is a Welsh feminine name made up of elements meaning 'flower' and 'white' and therefore belongs with the flower group of names (see FLORA). Another Welsh flower name is **Blodeuwedd** ('flower-form'), the name of a woman magically created out of flowers in the medieval Welsh story of *Math son of Mathonwy*. She was unfaithful to her husband for whom she had been made, and as a punishment was turned into an owl. The legend has become familiar to modern children through its retelling in Alan Garner's *The Owl Service*. **Blodyn** or **Blodeyn,** which simply means 'flower, blossom', is another member of this group.

Blossom see FLORA

Blythe see BONNIE

Bo see BEAU

Boadicea see VICTORIA

Bob see ROBERT

Bobbi see BARBARA

Bobbie, Bobby see ROBERT

Boe see BEAU

Bonny, Bonnie

This is the Scottish word for 'fair,' used as a first name. It is a comparatively recent introduction, which has been particularly popular in the USA. It is yet another name that may have been popularized by Margaret Mitchell's *Gone with the Wind*. The rarer **Blythe** ('happy') is a companion name to Bonnie, the two words frequently being linked in old verses.

Boris

Boris is a Slavic name meaning 'fight, battle'. In early Russia it was frequently used as a royal name. Its associations are still predominantly Russian, but it is occasionally found in English-speaking countries.

Braden, Bradon see BRANDON

Bradley
Bradley is a boy's name that has been popular in Australia and the United States for some years, but only became noticeably popular in the UK in the late 1990s. It derives from a surname taken from a place name meaning 'broad clearing'. **Brad** is used as a short form and also as an independent name, sometimes in the form **Bradd**. A related surname, **Bradford**, from a place meaning 'broad ford', is also found.

Brady
This surname has been moderately fashionable as a boy's name in the USA in the 1990s. The surname can have a number of origins, the most common of which is an Irish surname of uncertain meaning, perhaps originally a nickname given to someone with a broad chest.

Bram see ABRAHAM

Brandi see BRANDY

Brandon, Brendon
Brendon with an 'e' is the name of more than one Irish saint, the most famous of which is St **Brendan** the Navigator, who sailed his coracle in the Atlantic and whose legend has been interpreted as an account of a pre-Columbian discovery of America. The meaning of the name is disputed, perhaps coming from the word for 'prince', but often interpreted as the unflattering 'stinking hair'. The Irish form of the name is **Breandán**. Brandon, a name used by Charles Kingsley in *The Water Babies* (1863), is often a variant of Brendan, although it can have other sources, including a surname, in its turn derived from either the Old English meaning '(person from the) broom-covered hill', or from the French for 'sword'. While Brendon has been used steadily in the UK, Ireland and the USA, Brandon (or **Branden**) has been popular in the USA since the late 1970s, and entered the UK most popular lists only in the late 1990s. The choice of **Braden** (**Bradon**), another Irish surname meaning 'salmon', sometimes found as a boy's first name, may owe something to the similarity of its sound to Brandon.

Brandy
Sometimes spelt **Brandi**, this is a feminine name more likely to be found in the United States than in the UK, although it is being used increasingly in England. Although it appears to be the drink used as a first name – not unknown, since **Chardonnay** has been recorded more than once as a first name – it is more likely to be a feminine echo of the name Brandon (see BRENDAN), which is also very popular in the United States.

Branwen see BRONWEN

Bree see BRIDGET

Breeanna
This name, which has enjoyed considerable popularity in the United States, can be analysed as a variant of Brianna, a feminine form of BRIAN, or as a blend of

Bree (see BRIDGET) and Anna, but probably owes its popularity as much as anything to the fashion for names combining 'br-', a long vowel and an 'n', as a number of these have been popular recently in the USA. These include **Brenna** and **Brennan**, Irish names meaning 'tear', 'sorrow', as well as other names listed here under Br-. Breanna is also found as **Breeanne**.

Brenda
Brenda is a name made popular by Sir Walter Scott, who used it in *The Pirate* (1821) for one of his heroines. It is a name from the Shetland Islands, and is probably a feminine form of the old Norse name **Brand** ('a sword'). In Ireland it is used as the feminine of BRENDAN. It was popular in the 1950s and into the 1960s, but is little used in the UK today, although it is still found in the USA.

Brendan see BRANDON

Brenna, Brennan see BREEANNA

Brent
Originally a surname, Brent comes either from an Old English word meaning 'burnt', or from a West Country place name meaning 'hill, high place'. It has been in regular use as a boy's name, particularly in the USA, for a number of years. The similar-sounding **Brenton**, probably primarily an elaboration of Brent, is another surname from a place, this time meaning 'Bryni's homestead', Bryni being an Old Norse name.

Bret, Brett
This name comes from the surname meaning 'Briton' or 'Breton'. Its best-known holder is probably the American poet and short story writer Bret Harte (1836–1902), whose work, now little read but at one time very popular, helped give literary form to the legends of the Far West. It has been fashionable for some time in the USA, usually as a boy's name, but occasionally as a girl's.

Brian
A Celtic name, Brian probably comes from the word for 'a hill'. In Ireland it is famous as the name of Brian Boru, High King of Ireland (1002–14), who defeated the Viking invaders. The name was also used by Celtic-speaking Bretons who probably introduced the name into England in the Middle Ages. The common alternative **Bryan** reflects the spelling of the surname. The popularity of the name has varied from country to country. In the UK it was popular from the 1920s to the 1960s, but is now out of fashion, but in the USA it has been steadily popular since the 1960s, and the surname that derives from Brian, **Bryant**, can sometimes be found as a first name. In the United States, feminine versions of the name are also popular, in the form **Brianne** (**Briann**, **Bryanne**), or most commonly, **Brianna** (**Briana**). (See also BRYN, BREANNE.)

Brice see BRYCE

Bridget
The Irish form of this name, meaning 'the High One', is **Brighid**, which seems to have been the title of an ancient Celtic goddess whose name may also be

connected with the ancient British tribe of the Brigantes. The popularity of the name is due to St Bridget (c. 450–c. 523), the greatest of the Irish female saints, though little is known of her for sure, for her legend seems to have attracted stories of the original pagan goddess. **Brigid** is an alternative form of the name, while the form **Bride** (Irish **Brid**) with its pet forms **Bridie**, **Biddie** or **Biddy** reflect the Gaelic pronunciation of the name. **Brigitte**, occasionally **Brigette**, comes from the continental form, and **Bidelia** or **Bedelia** is an Irish gentrification of the name, which has fallen out of favour as it was felt to be over-genteel. **Birgit** or **Birgita**, the Swedish form, gives us **Britt** as a short form. The name **Bree**, with its elaboration **Breeda**, can either be interpreted as an independent name from the same root, or else as a pet form of Bridget, and may be a source of Breeanna.

Brittany

One of the most popular girls' names in the USA in the late 1980s and early 1990s, Brittany is now being used in the UK as well. It comes in a wide variety of spellings, and is sometimes reduced to two syllables, in forms such as **Britny**. Although place names are increasingly popular as first names, and the choice of a French place is by no means unique, being found in names such as **Normandy** or **Normandie**, and to some extent **Rochelle**, no one has come up with a convincing explanation of why this district of France should be used, but the sounds that make up the name can be found in other popular names, so the attraction may be the same as in the use of blends.

Brock

Brock or **Broc**, from a surname, had a mild popularity as a masculine name in the 1990s, mainly in the USA. As a surname, it can either be a form of the surname Brook or Brooks, or may derive from an old word for 'a badger'. In Ireland, Broc has been used as a rare first name since the Middle Ages.

Broderick see RODERICK

Bronwen

This is a Welsh feminine name meaning 'fair or white breast'. The similar-sounding **Branwen**, origin of **Brangwain** or **Brengwain**, the name of ISOLDA's maid in the TRISTAN legends, means 'fair raven', indicating a dark beauty, and is the name of the heroine of one of the medieval Welsh *Mabinogion* stories. Her name may be of divine origin as the names of her father Llyr and her brother Bran are both those of Celtic gods.

Brooke, Brook

Brook or Brooke is a surname, meaning 'brook' which has recently come into use for both sexes, although thanks to the fame of the actress Brooke Shields it is now usually female. **Brooklyn**, the name of a borough of New York City, may look as if it too comes from 'brook', but is in fact a form of the Dutch *Breukelen* meaning 'broken land'. Although recently chosen as the name of the son of David Beckham and 'Posh Spice', it is more likely to be found in the USA as a girl's name, sometimes in the form **Brooklynn** or **Brooklynne**, as if a blend of Brooke and Lynn.

Bruce

The fame of the heroic King Robert the Bruce (1274–1329) is probably the cause of this surname being adopted as a Scottish first name, which has since spread throughout the English-speaking world. Despite its Scottish associations, the surname comes from a Norman place name, although experts cannot agree which particular place with which particular meaning is the exact source.

Brunella see PRUNELLA

Bruno

Bruno simply means 'brown', and is a German name which has become more common in English-speaking countries in recent years, probably via German immigrants to the United States, although the popularity of names beginning Br- may also have been influential. The rare feminine equivalents, **Brunella** and **Brunetta**, show the influence of Romance languages.

Bryan, Bryanne, Bryant see BRIAN

Bryce

Bryce is currently the more popular form in the USA of the name traditionally spelt **Brice**. St Brice was a fifth-century Frenchman, who succeeded the great St Martin as bishop of Tours. **Bryson**, the surname that comes from Brice, can also be found occasionally as a first name.

Bryn

This is a masculine name from the Welsh for 'a hill', and thus shares the same root as BRIAN. The elaboration **Brynmor** means 'big hill'. They are both place names which have become first names.

Bryony

Bryony is a plant name introduced in the twentieth century. Unlike most of the plant names which are those of striking flowers, this is an insignificant hedge climber. It may owe its use in part to its role as a feminine form of BRIAN.

Buddic, Buddug see VICTORIA

Bunnie, Bunny see VERONICA

Bunty

Bunty is usually a nickname rather than a given name. Its popularity is said to date from 1911 when there was a successful comedy performed in London called *Bunty Pulls the Strings*. The name comes from the same source as the nursery song 'Bye, baby bunting', 'bunting' being a dialect word for a pet or hand-reared lamb, which came to be used as an endearment.

Burt

An alternative spelling for Bert, originally short forms of ALBERT, BERTRAM, CUTHBERT, EGBERT, GILBERT, HERBERT, HUBERT, LAMBERT, OSBERT, ROBERT, WILBERT.

Byron
Byron is the name of the Romantic poet George Gordon, Lord Byron (1788–1824), used as a first name. The first Lord Byron was John Byron (1600–52), who was created Baron Byron as a reward for his support of Charles I in the Civil War. However, the meaning of the name is far from aristocratic as it means 'at the cattle sheds', and would have been a name given to a cowman.

Cc

Caddy see CAROL

Cadel, Cadfael, Cadwallader

The Welsh name-element *cad* means 'battle' and is used in a multitude of Welsh masculine names, some of them the names of warriors in our earliest records. **Cadel** or **Cadell**, combining 'battle' with an affectionate ending, is both a name in its own right and a pet form of these names. **Cadfael**, a name familiar as the hero of Ellis Peters' medieval whodunnits, means 'battle-metal', a suitable name for an old and experienced soldier. **Cadwallader** (also spelt **Cadwalder** and **Cadwaladr**) means 'battle prince' and is a name found as early as 681. The most famous holder of this name was a Welsh ruler who led his people against the troops of Henry II and who died in 1172.

Cædmon see HILDA

Caelia see CECILIA

Cahir, Cahal see CATHAL

Cai, Caio see CAIUS

Caiseal see CASHEL

Caitlin

Caitlin is an Irish form of CATHERINE. The Anglo-Norman conquerors of Ireland brought the name with them in the form *Cateline*, and this became Caitlin in Irish, which was later anglicized to **Kathleen**. In Ireland the first syllable is pronounced as in 'cat', but in the USA, where the name was among the most popular girls' names of the 1990s, it is pronounced as if a blend of 'Kate' and 'Lynn'. This is reflected in the spelling variants which can include **Katelyn(n)** and **Kaitlyn(n)**.

Caius

Caius or **Gaius** is a Roman first name which comes from the Latin *gaudere* ('to rejoice'). The name seems to have passed into use among native Britons during the Roman occupation, for it is the source of Sir **Kay** or **Kai**, King Arthur's foster-brother and steward in the legends. His is one of the earliest names associated with King Arthur and it is still used in Wales in the forms **Cai, Caio** and **Caw**.

Caleb

In the Bible, Caleb is one of only two men, among the many who leave Egypt with Moses, who lives to see the Promised Land (Numbers 26. 65). The name comes from the Hebrew word for 'dog', and is usually interpreted as indicating a dog-like faithfulness and devotion to God. It was popular with the English Puritans, but thereafter became associated with rusticity, and became rare. However, the Puritans took it with them to America. It has been used there ever since, if uncommonly, and has recently enjoyed a revival, which is beginning to be felt in the UK as well. **Cale** is a shortened form, and the recent name **Kalin** or **Calen** appears to be a development of this.

Caleigh, Caley see KAYLEIGH

Callie

Callie, more common as a girl's name in the USA than in the UK, has a number of sources. It can be a pet form of CAROLINE, but also a short form of two names based on the Greek word *kalos* ('fair, beautiful'). **Calliope** ('beautiful voice') was the name of the Muse of Heroic Epic in Greek myth. **Calista** (sometimes **Callista**) is the Latinate form of a Greek name meaning 'most beautiful'. In Greek, the name was **Callisto**, and was in legend the name of a maiden loved by Zeus and turned into a bear by Hera, Zeus's jealous wife. However, since Callisto is used in Italian as a man's name, and the -a is more obviously feminine, the Latin form is more usual. Callie has also been recorded as a short form of **Caledonia**, the ancient name for Scotland, and of **Calvina**, the feminine form of CALVIN. Some variant forms blend imperceptibly into variants of KAYLEIGH.

Callum, Calum see MALCOLM

Calvin

Currently moderately popular in the USA, Calvin came into use as a first name in honour of John Calvin (1509–64), the French Protestant theologian who gave his name to Calvinism and who was famous for his strict morality, his learning and his support of austerity. The French surname means 'bald'.

Cameron

A Scottish clan name used as a male first name, Cameron comes from the Gaelic *cam sron* ('crooked nose'), perhaps a nickname given to an early clansman. It is currently a popular first name on both sides of the Atlantic, and is being used increasingly for girls.

Camilla

Camilla is a figure from Roman legend, whose name, it has been suggested, means 'one who assists at sacrifices to the gods'. In VIRGIL's *Aeneid*, she figures as a warrior queen who fights with Aeneas, and is described as so fast a runner that she could run over a field of wheat without bending a blade, or over the sea without getting her feet wet. The French form of the name, **Camille**, can be used for either sex. Camilla has been quite fashionable in the UK in recent years, but

Camille, as a girl's name, is the more popular form in the USA. This latter is shortened to **Cammie** or **Kami**, sometimes given as an independent name, but because of its association with underwear, it is rarely used in the UK, where the name is more likely to be shortened to **Milla** or **Milly**.

Candace, Candice
This name, which was formerly pronounced 'can-day-see' but is now usually 'can-dis', is an ancient title of the queen of Ethiopia. The name was introduced into the body of European first names through its mention in the Acts of the Apostles. **Candy** is a pet form of the name, shared with CANDIDA.

Candida
Candida comes from the Latin for 'white', the same word that gives us 'candid' (originally 'unblemished') and 'candidate' (from the white robes worn by Roman politicians when standing for office). Although it is found as a woman's name in Roman inscriptions, it was not used thereafter, until it was 're-invented' by George Bernard Shaw for the heroine of his play *Candida* in 1897. He in his turn modelled the name on the naive hero of Voltaire's allegorical novel *Candide* (1759). The similar-sounding **Candia** is not, as it would appear, a variant of Candida or of the pet form **Candy** which it shares with CANDACE, but (according to E.G. Withycombe) a name first given to one Candia Palmer who was born while her father was travelling to Candia, the old name for Heraklion in Crete, and which then passed into use among certain families.

Cara
Cara is the Italian for 'dear' used as a girl's name, and therefore the equivalent of the French Chère (See CHERYL). The affectionate diminutives **Carina** and **Carita** are also used. These names are recent introductions. They have all had a certain popularity in the USA, particularly Cara, which is more likely to be spelt **Kara** there, while Carina is often **Karina**, with forms such as **Karena** shading into variants of Karen. (See also under CATHERINE for some of these forms.)

Caradoc, Caradog
This comes from the Welsh word *cariad* ('love') and is therefore the masculine equivalent of the feminine names found under CERI. It is one of the oldest recorded British names, for it is the same as **Caractacos** (Latin **Caratacus**), the name of the captured British chief taken in chains to Rome in AD 51, whose noble bearing won him his liberty. Caradoc is also the name of a character in the Arthurian legends, chiefly famous for being the only man at the court who came through various magical tests to prove he had a faithful wife.

Cari see CERI, CERIDWEN

Carina, Carita see CARA

Carl see CHARLES

Carla, Carleen, Carlene, Carlina, Carlota, Carlotta, Carly, Carlyn see CAROL

Carlton

Carlton is a place and surname meaning 'settlement of the free men or peasants'. **Carleton** is an alternative spelling. The name **Charlton**, as in the actor Charlton Heston, comes from a variant form of this surname.

Carmel

Carmel is the Hebrew word for 'a garden' and the name of a mountain in Israel, famous in the Bible for its fruitfulness. A monastery, dedicated to the Virgin Mary, was established there by Crusaders, and the name originally given in honour of Our Lady of Mount Carmel. **Carmella** is a diminutive form, and **Carmen**, famous from the Bizet opera (1874), is the Spanish form of the name.

Carol, Caroline

The feminine forms of the name CHARLES are very varied, depending on whether they are based on the German form Carl, the Latin *Carolus* or on Charles itself (see under the entry for CHARLES for the history and origin of the name). **Carla** or **Karla**, with their variants **Carly, Carlyn, Carleen** or **Carlene**, are comparatively recent introductions which reflect the original form of the name. **Carlina** has also been described as a modern coinage, but has been in use in the author's family since at least 1803. **Carlotta** or **Carlota** are the Italian and Spanish versions of the name, with the pet form **Lola** being shared by Carlota and DOLORES, and a diminutive **Carlita**. From the Latin form of the name come the best-established forms, **Carol** (sometimes chosen because a child is born near Christmas) and **Caroline**, with their variants **Carole, Carola, Carolyn, Carolina** (one of the sources of LINA), **Karol, Karoline. Caryl** (see also CERI) is used as a variant. These names give us the pet forms **Carrie** (and nowadays **Kari**), CALLIE, **Caddy** and **Caddie**. From Charles come **Charlotte** (enormously popular in the UK since the 1970s) with its variant **Sharlotte** (in use since the end of the nineteenth century, and not a recent form as one might expect) and the Irish forms **Charlot** or **Searlait**. Charlotte gives us the pet forms **Charlie** (pronounced with either a 'ch' or a 'sh' sound), **Sharley, Chatty** and **Lottie. Charlene**, and its variants **Charleen** and **Sharlene**, are modern feminine forms of Charles (see also ARLENE).

Caron see CATHERINE

Carrie see CAROL

Carson

Carson is a Scottish surname, perhaps meaning someone who lives in a marsh, which has had a certain popularity as a boy's name in the USA. It does not seem to be much used as a girl's name, despite the fact that its most famous bearer, Carson McCullers (1917–67), author of *The Heart is a Lonely Hunter* and *Reflections in a Golden Eye*, was female.

Carwen, Carwyn see CERI

Cary

Although the actor Cary Grant (Archibald Leach in real life) was not the first man to use the surname Cary as a first name, it was he who popularized it, and it has been used steadily, if quietly, ever since. The surname is usually an

English West Country one, from a river whose name may mean 'pleasant stream', but it can also be from the Irish *O Ciardha* ('son of the dark one').

Caryn see CATHERINE

Carys see CERI

Casey
This is well used in the United States for both boys and girls, but is not yet very common in the UK. Although the name can be a pet form of CASIMIR, it is more obviously linked to the Irish surname *Cathasch*, meaning 'descendant of the vigilant one'. The most famous Casey of all, the American folk hero celebrated in song, Casey Jones (1863–1900), was in fact a railway engineer christened John Luther Jones; he was given the nickname 'Casey' because he was born near Cayce in Kentucky. As a masculine name, Casey is sometimes spelt **Casy** or with a 'K', while as a girl's name it can be found in all sorts of elaborate spellings.

Cashel
This is an Irish man's name meaning 'fortified house, castle', which comes from the city's name, the ancient capital of the province of Munster. The Irish spelling is **Caiseal**, and there is a pet form **Cashlin**.

Casimir
Traditionally Casimir or **Kasimir** has been interpreted as meaning 'proclamation of peace', but recent scholars have suggested it actually means the opposite and comes from words meaning 'to spoil peace'. It is a Polish name, used here in the nineteenth century among supporters of Polish independence, and introduced to the United States by Polish immigrants. CASEY (now used for both sexes, but formerly masculine) can be a diminutive of Casimir, but is more likely to be the Irish surname meaning 'descendant of the vigilant one'.

Caspar, Casper see JASPER

Caspian
This is a name used by C.S. Lewis for the hero of his children's novel *Prince Caspian* (1951), part of the Narnia series, which has occasionally been used for a real boy.

Cassie
Cassie is a short form, now more common than its original (particularly in the USA) of **Cassandra**, a character from Greek legend. She was a Trojan princess and priestess of Apollo, who agreed to let him sleep with her in return for the gift of prophesy. However, she reneged on her side of the bargain, and as a punishment the god condemned her to prophesy the truth, but to be believed by no one. Thus she is often used as a symbol of one who foretells unpleasant events, but is ignored, and as such her name was chosen for the name of the famous column in the *Daily Mirror* whose criticisms so annoyed Churchill during World War II. Despite the unpleasant aspects of her story, this is one of the earliest classical names found in England, having come into use in the thirteenth century owing to the popularity of the romanticized story of Troy in

the Middle Ages. British use may owe something to Jane Austen having a sister called Cassandra, to whom many of her delightful letters were written. **Cass** or **Cassy** are also used. Another source of Cassie in the United States is the Irish surname **Cassidy** (Gaelic *O Caside* means 'descendant of the curly-haired one'), which is not an uncommon girl's first name.

Castor see COSMO

Cathal
This is an Irish name meaning 'battle-mighty': **Cathair**, from the same root, means 'warrior'. Both versions have the anglicized forms **Cahal** and **Cahir**. For the related name **Cathan** see KEENAN.

Catherine
Although a name of unknown meaning, Catherine was early on associated with the Greek word for 'pure' (an appropriate sense for the name of so many virgin saints) and this is frequently given as its meaning. It is a name spelt in a variety of ways. This is partly due to the fact that the original Greek form of the name was *Aikaterine*, giving the spellings with 'e' in the middle, while the Greek word for 'pure' was *katharos*, which led to these being 'corrected' to the 'a' spelling. The commonest forms are **Catherine, Catharine, Katherine, Katharine** and, more recently, **Kathryn**. A wide variety of forms from other languages has also been adopted by English speakers. **Caterina** and **Catherina** show the Italian form, while the similar **Katerina** technically comes from the Swedish. **Karen, Karina** (although this may owe something to Carina – see under CARA), **Karin** and ultimately their variants **Caryn** and **Caron**, are further Scandinavian forms of the name. **Katja** or **Katia** is a little-used Russian form. There is an important group of names from the Celtic areas of Great Britain: **Kathleen** is the Irish form of the name, with CAITLIN showing its Gaelic form; **Catriona**, given wide currency by R.L. Stevenson's 1893 novel of that title, is the Scottish Gaelic form, with **Catrina, Katrina** and **Katrin(e)** as variants; Wales gives us **Catrin, Cadi** and **Cati**. Short forms of these names include **Cathie, Cathy, Kate, Katie, Katy, Kathie, Kathy, Kay** (which can be used for any name beginning with 'K'), **Kit, Kittie, Kitty** and, less frequently, **Trina**. KERRY is said by some to be an Irish or Irish-American pet form.

Cecil
Although Cecil is sometimes thought of as a masculine form of CECILIA, it has a different origin. The Latin name **Sextus**, originally a name given to a sixth son, developed the form *Sextilius*. This was brought by the Romans to Britain, where it developed into the Old Welsh name **Seisyllt**. This in its turn became the family name Cecil, and the surname of this noble family came to be used as a first name.

Cecilia
The use of this ancient Roman family name (probably derived from a word meaning 'blind') is due to the popularity of St Cecilia, the patron saint of music, whose 'life' is now thought to be largely, if not wholly, mythical. The name was current in England from the early Middle Ages, when it generally took the form Cecily. The first syllable of this can be pronounced either 'ses' or, as was more usual in the past, 'sis'. This second pronunciation gave rise to the variants **Cicely** and **Sisley**, and the short forms **Sis, Cis, Sissy, Sissie, Cissy** or **Cissie**.

Cecile is the French form of the name, used for both sexes in France, but in the English-speaking world feminine. **Celia** is often used as a short form of Cecilia, but is in fact a separate name. It comes from another Roman family name, that of the *Caelii*, which was interpreted as from the word *coelum* ('heaven'), which gave rise to the old spelling **Coelia** as well as to the Latin **Caelia**. This derivation is incorrect, and as the family was supposed to have been founded by an Etruscan, it seems probable, that the name comes from one of the few Etruscan words we can understand: *celi* meaning 'September'. Either Cecilia or Celia was the origin of the Irish name **Sile**, anglicized to **Sheila**, also found in a variety of spellings such as **Shiela** and **Sheelagh**.

Cedric

Cedric is a name invented by Sir Walter Scott in his novel *Ivanhoe* (1819) for the father of his hero. Cedric represents all that is good about the old Saxon landowners, in contrast with the rapacious Norman invaders. It used to be said that the name came from a misreading of **Cerdic**, a very early Saxon name meaning 'amiable', but others have pointed out that there is a Welsh name **Cedrych**, meaning 'pattern of bounty'. Since Scott's other 'Saxon' names are suspiciously Celtic, it seems more likely that Scott got his cultures mixed, and is using a form of this Welsh name. Long out of fashion, there has been a mild revival of use of the name in the United States, where it is occasionally found as **Sedrick**, and can be shortened to **Rick**.

Ceirios see CHARITY

Celeste

Celeste and its diminutive form **Celestine** come from the Latin word for 'heavenly', and therefore has links with Celia (see CECILIA). Forms such as **Celesta** and **Celestina** can also be found.

Celia see CECILIA

Celina, Céline see SELINA

Cenydd see KENNETH

Ceri

This is one of a large group of Welsh girls' names that comes from the word *caru* ('love') and it is therefore the Welsh equivalent of the English AMY. Ceri (which can also be used for boys) and **Carys** are probably the most used, but other forms include **Ceril**, **Cerys**, **Cerian**, **Cari** and **Caryl**, which is also used as a form of CAROL. Carys should not be confused with CHARIS which, although pronounced in the same way – both with a hard 'k' sound – comes from the Greek. Ceri, particularly in the form **Keri** which is sometimes found, may have contributed to the development and popularity of KERRY. From the same root comes the name **Carwen**, the second element meaning 'white, blessed', with its masculine form **Carwyn**. For other masculines see CARADOC.

Ceridwen

This is thought to be the name of the Celtic goddess of poetic inspiration. Her name is made up of elements meaning 'poetry' and 'white, fair, blessed'.

Traditionally she is the mother of TALIESIN, one of the great early bards of the Welsh. Like all Welsh names beginning Ce- the 'c' is hard. It can be shortened to CERI or **Cari**.

Cerys see CERI

Chad

This was the name of an Anglo-Saxon saint and bishop whose history is told by the Venerable Bede. He was bishop of Lichfield, and the cathedral there is dedicated to him. This kept the name of this rather obscure saint current, at least locally, while in the twentieth century it was widely known thanks to the fame of the Rev. Chad Varah, who founded the Samaritans. The meaning of the name is obscure. Although he was a Saxon, it may be Celtic in origin, from the same *cad* ('battle') element that is found in names such as CADEL. Chad is also the name of a little cartoon figure shown as a bald head, two eyes and a nose peering over a brick wall associated with the phrase 'Wot, no . . . ?' which was created in World War II by the cartoonist Chat as a comment on shortages, and which worked its way into popular culture. The name has been well used in the United States since the 1980s, and has seen a mild revival in the UK. In the USA, **Chadwick** – a surname from various place names mostly meaning 'Chad's farm' – is also used as a first name.

Chae see CHARLES

Chance see CHAUNEY

Chandler

This is a surname used as a first name. The surname comes from the French word *chandelier* ('candle maker'). Already moderately well used as a boy's name in the USA since the late 1980s, we can expect an increase in popularity from the use of the name for a character in the very successful television series *Friends*.

Chanel

The name of the famous French perfume has been in use as a first name, particularly among Black Americans, since at least the 1980s. This particular brand name was probably chosen because the sounds fit in with other popular names, the 'cha-' sound linking to names such as CHANTAL, and the '-el' ending being a popular feminine ending. There are a number of variant spellings such as **Chan(n)el(le)** and **Shanel(le)**. The perfume took its name from the fashion designer Coco Chanel (1883–1971). For another influential perfume name see Ciara (under KIERAN).

Chantal

St Jeanne de Chantal was a seventeenth-century French saint associated with St Frances de Sales. As well as being the grandmother of Madame de Sevigné (1626–96), she combined a romantic life-story with great worldly wisdom and true piety. She is a most attractive figure, and it is not surprising that French parents should want to name a child after her. The name was first officially accepted in France as a Christian name in 1913, and spread rapidly thereafter. It arrived more recently in the UK, but has already developed variants including

Chantelle and even spellings with Sh- such as **Shantal**. The name ultimately comes from the southern French word *cantal* ('a stone').

Chardonnay see BRANDY

Charice see CHARIS

Charis
Charis (the 'ch' is pronounced as if a 'k') is the Greek word for 'grace'. It is tempting to link the increase of its use to the appearance of a character of that name in Georgette Heyer's novel *Frederica* (1965); but it may also be linked with the use of the Welsh name Carys (see CERI), which is pronounced in the same way. **Charissa** is a Latinate form of the name, created by Edmund Spenser for *The Faerie Queene* (1590–96), but it could also be interpreted as a variant of Carissa (see CARA). **Charisse** is a French form of the name (pronounced with an initial 'sh' sound), which has found some popularity in the United States, often in the form **Cherise**, but variants such as **Charice, Cherice, Sharice** and **Sherise** are also found. Use of this form may owe something to the film star Cyd Charisse (1921–). However, there is a number of names that seem to be developments of the sounds involved in this name, for example Cherry (see below) and Cheryl, and it is impossible to work out if they are names with traceable histories, blends or fashionable innovations. This includes **Cheryth**, or **Cherith**, and **Cherish** (possibly the vocabulary word), as well as some of the names under CHERYL.

Charity
Formed from the same root as CHARIS, Charity is with FAITH and HOPE one of the three great Christian virtues, and all are used for girls' names. **Cherry** started life as a pet form of Charity, rather than being derived from the fruit, but it is now an independent name. The Welsh name **Ceirios** comes directly from the plant name 'cherry'. After many years out of fashion, Charity is beginning to be fashionable again. For related names, see above and at CHERYL.

Charles
The Old German word for 'a man' was *carl*, a popular name among the Frankish ruling class that dominated western Europe in the Dark Ages. The name was Latinized as *Carolus*, which in turn became Charles in French. These three forms have developed into a vast number of names for both sexes, found throughout Europe. The German and Scandinavian forms **Carl** or **Karl**, now popular in English-speaking countries – probably via their use by Scandinavian immigrants in the United States – reflect the original form of the name. From *Carolus* comes the eastern European form **Carol** or **Karel** occasionally found, but usually only for those of eastern European descent. The Irish also use the surname **Carroll** (**Cearbhall**), meaning 'champion warrior', as a first name. Charles has spawned a large number of diminutives such as **Charlie** (currently more popular as a given name in the UK than the full form) or **Charley, Chas** from the old abbreviated written form of the name, **Chae** or **Chay** in Scotland, **Chuck** mainly in the United States, while **Chilla** is said to be a form used in Australia. For the feminine forms see under CAROL.

Charlton see CARLTON

Charmaine

This is a name of debated origin, particularly used in the mid-twentieth century thanks to a popular song. It now has the variant **Sharmaine**. Its origin is often linked to the much older name **Charmian**, the Greek for 'joy' and used by Shakespeare for Cleopatra's maid in *Antony and Cleopatra* (this is strictly speaking pronounced with a hard 'k' sound, but the pronunciation with a soft 'ch-' is often found), perhaps with what was felt to be a French twist; but it may simply have been invented at the time.

Chas see CHARLES

Chase

This surname, from the Old French word *chaceur* ('hunter'), grew steadily in popularity as a boy's name throughout the 1990s in the USA.

Chastity

This Christian virtue has a long, if infrequent, history as a girl's name. In 1969 Cher and Sonny Bono chose it as the name for their daughter, and this has led to an increase in its use. It has also been suggested that the rise of the curious name **Chasity** – 255th for girls in the USA in 1991 – comes from a misunderstanding of Chastity Bono's name.

Chatty see CAROL

Chauncey

Chauncey or **Chauncy** is a masculine name used in the United States since at least the early nineteenth century. A surname deriving from a village near the French town of Amiens, it was used as a first name in honour of Charles Chauncey (1592–1672), the second president of Harvard College (later Harvard University). The short form **Chance** is currently more popular as a given name than the full form.

Chavon see JANE

Chay see CHARLES

Chelsea

The use of this place name as a girl's name presumably owes something to the fame of Chelsea as a glamour spot in London (although there is also a Chelsea, New York); the football club seems an unlikely inspiration for a girl's name, except for the real fanatic. In use from at least the 1950s, the name first reached a wider public in the late 1970s when the actress Chelsea Brown was prominent in the American television comedy show *Rowan and Martin's Laugh-In*. It has been popular in Australia, and was in the top two dozen most popular names in the USA by 1990, but took a few more years to become popular in Great Britain. Chelsea Clinton, the US president's daughter, was given her name from a favourite song of her parents, Joni Mitchell's *Chelsea Morning* (1969).

Cher, Cheralyn, Chère see CHERYL

Cherida, Cherie see CHERYL

Cherise see CHARIS

Cherokee see DAKOTA

Cherry see CHARITY

Cheryl
A modern formation, Cheryl has had currency since the 1920s. It is probably based on the name Cherry (see CHARITY) or on the French word **Cherie** ('darling'), used as a first name. Cheryl rapidly developed a number of variants, including **Cheralyn** (the most popular) and **Cheryn**. Both Cheryl and Cheralyn are found in a number of different spellings including **Sheryl, Sher(r)el(l)** and **Sheralyn**. **Cher** is a short form popularized by the singer of that name (whose given name is Cherilyn), which sometimes appears as **Chère**, the French for 'dear'. Cherie is also found in the form **Sherry** or **Sherri**. **Cherida** is a rare variant, blending the Spanish and French for 'dear'.

Chester
This is the town name, derived from the Latin *castra* (a camp), used as a first name.

Cheyenne
This is the name of a Native American nation, now an increasingly popular first name, particularly in the USA. The meaning of the name is not known. It is sometimes spelt **Sheyenne**, while spellings such as **Shianne** or **Shyann(e)** reflect the pronunciation.

Chiara see CLARE

Chilla see CHARLES

China see INDIA

Chivonne see JANE

Chloë
This name comes from the Greek for 'a green shoot' and was one of the names for the fertility goddess Demeter (see DEMETRIUS) in her summer aspect (see also MELANIE). Its use is usually ascribed to the name appearing as a minor character in the New Testament, but since early uses are mainly literary it is more likely to be inspired by the Greek pastoral romance *Daphnis and Chloë*, probably from the second or third century AD. The name was not very common outside literature until about 30 years ago, when new interest was shown in it. By 1997 it had become the most popular parental choice for a girl's name in the UK, but was less well used in the USA. **Chloris**, occasionally **Cloris**, is an unusual name related to Chloë since it comes from the same root, which means 'green'.

Christine

This is the most popular of the feminine names meaning 'Christian'; **Christian** itself was used originally for boys (and is currently increasingly popular), but is now used for both sexes, along with its pet form Christy. **Christy** or **Christie**, along with **Chris** and **Chrissie**, are also used as pet forms of Christine, with **Kirsty** or **Kirstie** in Scotland. **Cristyn** is the Welsh version of the name. **Christina**, with its pet form **Tina**, are popular variants, and the Scandinavian forms **Kirsten** and **Kersten** have recently come into use. **Christabel** is mainly literary, although it is found in the suffragette Christabel Pankhurst (1880–1958). Other variants include **Christiana**, **Christiane**, **Kristina**, **Krystyna**, **Kirsteen** and **Kirstine**, **Kirsta** and **Kristin**. (See also CRYSTAL.)

Christmas see NOEL

Christopher

Christopher comes from the Greek for 'Christ carrier', and was the name of the giant in legend who carried the Christ Child over a river and thus became the patron saint of travellers. **Kester** is an old pet form now generally replaced by **Chris** or **Kit**, with **Christy** being more common in Ireland. A Scottish form of the name was **Crystal** or **Chrystal**, which is also used in Ireland, and found as an occasional masculine name along with the pet form **Christy**. Christopher has been a very popular name for boys since the 1990s on both sides of the Atlantic.

Chuck see CHARLES

Chynna see INDIA

Cian see KEENAN

Ciara, Ciaran see KIERAN

Cicely see CECILIA

Cilla see PRISCILLA

Cillian see KILLIAN

Cinaed see KENNETH

Cindy see CYNTHIA, LUCY

Cis, Cissie, Cissy see CECILIA

Clare

Clare and its French spelling **Claire** come from the Latin word *clarus*, literally meaning 'bright, clear' but also used in the sense 'famous'. The name owes its popularity to St Clare of Assisi (c. 1194–1253), companion of St Francis and foundress of the Poor Clares. Her Italian name would have had the form **Chiara** or **Clara**. **Clarice** is an Italian diminutive of Clara, and featured as a literary name from the fifteenth century onwards in various romances. Other literary forms of the name are **Claribel** (masculine in Spenser), **Clarinda**, also found in

Spenser, and **Clarissa**, best known as the heroine of Samuel Richardson's novel *Clarissa or The History of a Young Lady* (1747–49). **Clarry** or **Clarrie**, once almost obsolete but now familiar to listeners to *The Archers*, is used as a pet form of these names, particularly of Clarice. **Clarence** is the masculine form of the name. This derives from the surname Clare, transferred to the Irish county, from which the dukes of Clarence took their title.

Clark

Clark comes from the surname, and means 'cleric'. It has become well known from the actor Clark Gable and from Clark Kent, *alter ego* of Superman. **Clarke** is also found.

Claudia

Claudia is another name which comes from that of a Roman family. The Claudii interpreted their name as coming from the Latin word *claudus* meaning 'lame', from the nickname of an ancestor; but this may be mere folk etymology. **Claudette** and **Claudine**, as in the novels of Colette, are further forms of the name. Claudia has a place in British folk history, for the Claudia found in the New Testament (II Timothy 4. 21) is traditionally held to be the daughter of a British prince, sister of LINUS and wife of Pudens, mentioned in the same verse. The name Pudens has been found on Roman inscriptions at Colchester, and the first-century Roman poet Martial refers to a friend Pudens who has a wife 'Claudia, the foreigner from Britain'. The Welsh name **Gladys** (**Gwladys**, **Gwladus**) is traditionally said to come from Claudia, but in fact probably comes from a word meaning 'ruler'. The masculine form of the name, **Claud**, once popular, is now rare; even rarer is the full Roman masculine form **Claudius**. The French form of the name **Claude** (pronounced 'clohd') can be used for either sex, but in this country is usually feminine.

Claus see NICHOLAS

Clay, Clayton

These are surnames, originally given to someone who lived in an area of clay soil, used as first names. They have been in use since at least the nineteenth century, and are currently mildly fashionable in the USA, particularly Clayton.

Clementine

This name means 'mild, merciful' and is probably best known from the song 'My Darling Clementine'. **Clementina** is a variant. There has been something of a revival of these names in recent years, including the use of the abstract noun **Clemency**, a name used by the Puritans, along with its counterpart MERCY. **Clement**, the masculine form of the name, popular with popes, has been less well used. The short forms of this group of names can be illustrated from the political world, the prime minister Clement Attlee (1883–1967) being known as **Clem** and Sir Winston Churchill addressing his wife Clementine as **Clemmie**.

Cleo

Cleo is the short form of the Graeco-Egyptian name **Cleopatra**, meaning 'glory of her father', which is more frequently used than the full form. The fame of the first-century AD queen of Egypt has been too strong for the name to be more than quietly used, although there has been a certain usage among Black Americans, particularly those wanting to emphasize their African roots. **Clio**, with the 'i' usually pronounced as in 'mine', is not a variant, but the name of the Greek muse of history.

Clifford

This, with its more common short form **Cliff**, is a surname used as a first name, originally given to someone living near a cliff and ford. The name was probably adopted because it was the surname of a prominent aristocratic family.

Clinton

Like CLIFFORD, this is an aristocratic surname used as a first name. Henry de Clinton, founder of the family of the dukes of Newcastle in the twelfth century, held land at Glympton in Oxfordshire and the name is probably a corruption of this place name, meaning 'settlement on the River Glyme'. The actor **Clint** Eastwood has given fame to the short form of the name.

Clio see CLEO

Clive

Clive is another surname used as a first name, in this case probably in honour of Robert Clive (1725–74), whose exploits in India did so much to lead to the East India Company's domination of the sub-continent, leading ultimately to the formation of the British Empire. The surname is an Old English one meaning 'dweller by the cliff'.

Clodagh

This is the name of a river in Tipperary. It was first used as a girl's name by the family of the marquesses of Waterford. Its use outside Ireland may have spread through the success of the singer Clodagh Rogers.

Cloris see CHLOË

Clovis, Clova, Clover see LEWIS

Clyde

This is the Scottish river and surname, used as a masculine first name. The river's name has a long history, being a pre-Roman Celtic name which probably comes from a word meaning 'to wash'. It has been suggested that it was originally the name of a pagan goddess.

Cody

This is an Irish surname used as a first name. It has been a popular name for boys in the USA since the 1990s, but is less frequently found for girls, when it is usually **Codi**. Spellings such as **Codie** and **Codee** and those beginning with a 'k' can also be found. As a surname there are two possible sources. One is a Gaelic name meaning 'descendant of Cuidightheach' (originally a nickname meaning 'helpful person'), the other the Gaelic *Mac Oda* ('son of Oda'), where the meaning of Oda is not known.

Coinneach see KENNETH

Cole, Colton
The choice of this as a boy's first name is probably inspired by the fame of the music and sophisticated lyrics of Cole Porter (1891–1964). As a first name, Cole can have a number of origins. It is an old pet form of NICHOLAS (see also COLIN). It can be a use of the surname Cole, which can either be from Nicholas again, or from the Old English *Cola* or related Old Norse name *Koli*, both meaning '(char)coal', and probably given to someone with particularly dark colouring. It can also be a shortened form of two other surnames used as first names: **Colby** from an English place name meaning 'Koli's settlement', and – the most popular choice of the three names – **Colton**, another place name with the same meaning as Colby. **Coel**, a Welsh name with the same pronunciation, comes from a word meaning 'trust'. Coel the Adulterous, a Scottish king of the sixth century, was the original of the Old King Cole of nursery rhyme fame.

Colin
Colin, now sometimes **Collin**, started life in France as a pet form of NICHOLAS, although in Scotland and Ireland it has also been associated with a Gaelic word meaning 'pup, cub' and hence 'young man'. The relationship between Colin and Nicholas can be more clearly seen in the feminine **Colette** (sometimes **Collette**) from Nicole, Nicolette. **Colinette** and **Colina** have also been recorded as feminine forms.

Colleen
This the Irish word for 'a girl' used as a first name. It is rarely found in Ireland itself, but has been popular in the United States and Australia.

Colm, Colmcille, Columba see MALCOLM

Conal, Conan, Conchobar see CONN

Conn, Conor, Conan
The Irish name Conn or **Con** means 'high', and is used either as a name in its own right or, with **Connie**, as a short form of a number of names. Thus we have Conor or **Connor**, the anglicized form of the Gaelic **Conchobar**, probably meaning 'lover of hounds', but often interpreted as 'high desire', the name of the king of Ulster in the great Irish epic of *The Tain*: **Conal** ('high and mighty') and **Conan** (sometimes **Conant**), as in the *Conan the Barbarian* stories, also meaning 'high'. Conan is found as the name of the early dukes of Brittany, and it is possible that it is a Breton name which has since passed into Irish use. Connor has recently become a very popular choice for boys throughout the UK.

Connie see CONN, CONSTANCE

Conrad
This is the English form of the German name **Konrad**, meaning 'bold counsel'. There is an old pet form **Conradin**, the name of the last of the Hohenstaufen Holy Roman Emperors; it is also used by 'Saki' (H.H. Munro, 1870–1916) for a character in his short stories. The more usual short form now is **Curt** or **Kurt**.

Constance

With its masculine form **Constant**, as in the composer Constant Lambert (1905–51), Constance is a name which celebrates the Christian virtue of steadfastness. **Constancy** has also been recorded as a girl's name. There is a further Christian connection in the related **Constantine**, for it was the name of the Roman emperor who formally brought the empire into the fold of the Church. They all share the short forms **Con** and **Connie**. The Welsh form of Constantine is **Cystennin**. Constance was a very popular name in the nineteenth century and into the early twentieth, but then went out of fashion. However, there has been a slight revival of interest in the name in Great Britain in recent years.

Cora see CORINNA

Coral

Coral is one of the gem names introduced in the late nineteenth century. The French form is **Coralie** and dates from some 100 years earlier.

Corbin

This surname has been mildly fashionable as a boy's name in the USA in the 1990s, no doubt helped by the success of the actor Corbin Bernsen. It comes from the French word for 'raven' and is also found as **Corben** or **Corbyn**.

Cordelia

This is one of the less frequently used Shakespearean names, but one which appears to be being used increasingly. The name may be the same as the continental **Cordula**, one of the virgins martyred with St Ursula. The name is thought to be connected with the Latin word *cor, cordis* ('heart').

Corey

This surname, of uncertain meaning, is used as a first name for both sexes, but more commonly for boys. As a girl's name it is often **Cori**, which some users may interpret as a pet form of a name such as Cora or CORINNA. The spelling **Cory** is not uncommon.

Corinna

Corinna was the name of an early Greek poetess, probably of the sixth century BC. Her name possibly comes from the Greek *kore* ('a maiden'), one of the titles of the goddess of the underworld, **Persephone**. A less respectable Corinna is the object of the poet's pursuit in Ovid's *Amores*, and it is from this source that the seventeenth- and eighteenth-century poets adopted the name for their inamorata, as in Robert Herrick's 'Corinna's going a-Maying'. **Corinne** is the French form of the name, made popular by Madame de Staël's 1807 novel of that name. **Cora** is probably an invention of James Fenimore Cooper for a woman in *The Last of the Mohicans* (1826), whence the name's popularity in the United States; but it is thought to be based on the same root. **Corisande** appears to be an elaboration of this. There is a masculine form also found in Classical poetry, where it is a typical name for a shepherd, **Corin**, which is now used for women. It is rarely found for men, but is kept in the public eye by the actor Corin Redgrave.

Cormac

This is a Gaelic name, borne by a legendary Irish king. Its meaning is doubtful and interpretations vary widely, but include 'charioteer' and 'son of the raven'.

Cornelius

Cornelius, with its short forms **Corney** or **Corny** and **Cornel**, comes from the Roman clan name of the Cornelii, which probably means 'war horn'. The feminine form, **Cornelia**, is strongly associated with the famous Cornelia, mother of the Gracchi, the second-century Roman tribunes. She represented all matronly accomplishments, and devoted herself to the raising of her children. When a visitor showed off her jewels and asked to see her hostess's, Cornelia is said to have produced her sons with the words 'These are my jewels'. The Romans erected a statue in her honour.

Cory see COREY

Cosmo

Saints Cosmas and DAMIAN are said to have been twin brothers who practised medicine for free among the poor, and were martyred for their faith. Beyond the fact that they probably existed and belong to the early period of Christianity, little is known of them for sure, for their legend has become heavily adulterated by memories of the pagan heavenly twins **Castor** and **Pollux**, the sons of Zeus. Cosmas (whose name means 'order') and his brother became the patron saints of Milan, and from there the name spread throughout Italy in the form **Cosimo**. In the eighteenth century, Cosmo came to Britain via the dukes of Gordon, who had links with the dukes of Tuscany, and the name became traditional in their family. **Cosima**, the feminine form, is also used occasionally. Its use is probably inspired by the fame of the romantic Cosima, who was daughter of Franz Liszt (1811–86) and wife of Richard Wagner (1813–83).

Courtney, Courtnay

Courtney is another aristocratic surname used as a first name. The family came from a Norman village called Courtenay, which would have been named from a Gallo-Roman landlord called *Curtenus* or *Curtius*, but from early on the name was thought of and used as a nickname *court nez* ('short nose'). It was originally a masculine name, but more recently has been used for both sexes, and has become particularly popular in both the UK and USA as a girl's name.

Craig

Craig means 'cliff' and is still used in Scotland in that sense (see under AILSA). It has a long history as a surname given to someone who lived near a cliff, but only came into use as a first name in the twentieth century. It was particularly popular in the 1970s and 1980s in the UK, and is still reasonably popular in the USA.

Cressida

Considering her history, it is surprising that this attractive-sounding name has come into use. Giovanni Boccaccio (1313–75), in his *Il Filostrato*, told the story of the love of Troilus for Cressida, showing her as a heartless and faithless woman. Chaucer (c. 1340–1400) in *Troilus and Criseyde* gives a rather more sympathetic version of her, showing her as easily led and timid rather than vicious; but by the time that Shakespeare deals with the story, she has become a downright wanton, while her uncle's name, Pandarus, became that of the common pander. However, her story must have its attractions as her name became increasingly popular through the twentieth century, while the virtuous **Troilus** is not generally used, although it has been given to Sir Laurence Olivier's grandson. Cressida has a short form, **Cressy**.

Crisiant see CRYSTAL

Crispin
Crispin or **Crispian** and his brother **Crispinian** are the patron saints of shoe-makers. Their name comes from the Latin meaning 'curly-haired'. The use of the name Crispin is probably helped by memories of the speech that Shakespeare gives to Henry V before the battle of Agincourt, where he tells his men: 'And gentlemen in England now a-bed/Shall think themselves accurs'd they were not here, /And hold their manhoods cheap while any speaks/That fought with us upon Saint Crispin's day'.

Cristyn see CHRISTINE

Crystal, Chrystal, Krystal
As a girl's name, this belongs with the JEWEL group of names, although it is worth noting that **Kristel** is a German form of the name CHRISTINE. It was particularly popular in the USA in the 1980s. The name also exists in a masculine guise, as a Scots pet form of the name CHRISTOPHER. The Welsh name **Crisiant** also means crystal, and has been in use since at least the twelfth century.

Cuddie see CUTHBERT

Curt see CONRAD

Curtis
A surname from the French for 'courteous', Curtis is now increasingly popular as a masculine first name.

Cuthbert
St Cuthbert, whose name means 'well known and famous', was a seventh-century bishop of Lindisfarne (Holy Island) whose simple holiness won him great love from the people he ministered to. He was buried in Lindisfarne, but frequent Viking raids led to his re-burial at Durham. His name was much used in the past in the north of England, where **Cuddie** became a pet form of the name.

Cy see CYRUS

Cybill see SYBIL

Cynan
An old Welsh masculine name meaning 'chief, pre-eminent', Cynon has the variants **Cynin, Cynon** and **Cymon**. **Cynyr** comes from the same root

and means 'chief hero'. It was the name of St David's grandfather, who lived c. AD 500.

Cynthia

The moon goddess Artemis or DIANA had particular associations with the Greek Mount Cynthus, and Cynthia, meaning 'of Cynthus', became one of her epithets. It was used as a name in the classical world and found in England in the seventeenth and eighteenth centuries, but did not really become popular until the nineteenth. It shares **Cindy** and **Sindy** as short forms with Lucinda (see LUCY).

Cyprian

St Cyprian was a third-century bishop of Carthage and martyr, famous as a writer and devout Christian and for his gentle good manners and willingness to consult others. The name means 'man from Cyprus' and although rare, is occasionally used.

Cyra see CYRUS

Cyril

Cyril comes from the Greek word *kyrios* ('lord'). It was the name of one of the missionaries who brought Christianity to Russia, who gave his name to the Russian Cyrillic alphabet, devised to write down the gospels. **Syril** is a rare variant. **Kyra** and **Kyrie** have been used as feminine versions of the name, although a male name **Kyree**, sometimes also spelt **Kyrie**, can be derived from the Arabic word *khayri* ('benevolent').

Cyrus

The name of a number of Persian kings, Cyrus may come from the Persian word for 'throne', although later commentators sometimes derived it from the same root as CYRIL. Its use, mainly in the United States, probably owes more to the mention of King Cyrus the Great in the Old Testament than to the rather obscure fourth-century martyr St Cyrus. It is shortened to **Cy**, and there is a feminine form, **Cyra**.

Cystennin see CONSTANCE

Dd

Daffodil

One of the less common flower names, Daffodil was used when such names were at the height of their popularity, and is still occasionally found.

Dafydd see DAVID

Dahlia

Another flower name, Dahlia seems to have had more popularity with authors – it is used by George Meredith in *Rhoda Fleming* (1865), and by P.G. Wodehouse for Bertie Wooster's favourite aunt – than with parents, although both Dahlia and **Dalia**, a form also found in France, have been recorded.

Dai see DAVID

Daisy see MARGARET

Dakota

Like CHEYENNE, this is another Native American nation, a branch of the Sioux. It is used as a first name for both sexes, but more commonly for boys. Other nations have been used as names, for instance **Cherokee**, but Dakota and Cheyenne are the two most popular.

Dale

A surname meaning 'dweller in the dale' used as a first name, Dale was once restricted to men, but is now used for both sexes, perhaps under the influence of Dale Arden, heroine of Alex Raymond's Flash Gordon adventures. **Dayle** is an alternative spelling.

Dallas, Dallin, Dalton

These three place names and surnames, now used as boys' first names, particularly in the USA, share the same sounds but not the same histories. The most popular of them is Dalton, a common English place name meaning 'farmstead or village in the valley', and transferred to several places in the USA. Dallas, the next most popular, is famous for the Texan city, probably named after George Mifflin Dallas, vice president of the United States from 1845 to 1849, but ultimately goes back to two British place names – one Scottish, meaning 'dwelling in the valley', and one English, meaning 'house in the valley'.

Dallas has been used as a first name since the nineteenth century. Another Texan city, **Houston**, named after Sam Houston (1793–1863), first president of the Republic of Texas, is also used as a boy's first name. Dallin is more obscure, and probably goes back to the English place name Dalling, meaning 'settlement of the descendants of Dalla' (an Anglo-Saxon name).

Damaris

Damaris is a biblical name, that of an Athenian woman converted by St Paul. As such it was adopted as a name by the Puritans. It seems to have been quite fashionable at the beginning of the twentieth century, and is still regularly, if quietly, used. It is probably a corruption of the Greek Damalis ('a heifer').

Damian

Damian is probably a form of the rather less common **Damon**, an old Greek name meaning 'to tame, subdue'. The story of Damon and Pythias, proverbial for loyal friendship, dates from the fourth century BC when Damon, an ardent republican, tried to assassinate Dionysius, the tyrant of Syracuse. His friend Pythias volunteered to stand surety for him while Damon went to say goodbye to his family before being executed. Dionysius was so impressed by Pythias' offer and by the fact that Damon returned rather than leave his friend to die in his place, that he pardoned them both. For the legend of St Damian see COSMO. Damon had a certain currency in the first half of the twentieth century, and is found in the authors Damon Runyon (1884–1946) and Damon Knight. Damian and its variant **Damien** were more popular in the latter part of the twentieth century, although they went into steep decline for a few years after the film *The Omen* appeared in 1976, where Damian was the name given to the child born to be Antichrist.

Dan see DANIEL

Dana

As a masculine name, Dana is from a surname meaning 'a Dane'. Use of the surname as a first name is due to various prominent Americans who bore the name, most notably Richard Henry Dana (1815–82), who, in an attempt to cure his failing eyesight, signed on as a deckhand to sail round the Horn, an experience recounted in his book *Two Years Before the Mast*, and who as a result of his experiences of the privations endured by the common sailor became a reforming lawyer. As an Irish girl's name, it is said to come from the Irish word meaning 'bold'. Outside Ireland the feminine form is probably adopted from the Scandinavian pet form of Daniella (see DANIEL).

Danaë

Danaë is a character from Greek mythology. It was prophesied that her father would be killed by her son, so to try to avoid this fate he shut her in a tower of brass. However, the god Zeus fell in love with her, visited her in the form of a shower of gold, and she had a son, **Perseus**, who fulfilled the prophesy.

Dand, Dandie, Dandy see ANDREW

Danica see DANIKA

Daniel

This name comes from the Hebrew and means 'God is judge'. Daniel, with his adventures in the lions' den, is one of the most attractive of the Old Testament prophets and it is not surprising that his name was popular from the beginning of the Middle Ages. **Dan** and **Danny** or **Dannie** are used as pet forms for both sexes, with **Dani** also used for girls, the feminine forms of the name being the French **Danielle**, the Italian **Daniella**, and more rarely **Danette** and **Danita**. In Wales, **Deiniol** or **Deinioel**, meaning 'attractive, charming' and the name of an early Welsh saint, is used as a form of Daniel. Daniel has been increasingly popular as a name for boys since the middle of the twentieth century, while Danielle has been popular since the 1980s. (See also SUSAN, DANA.)

Danika

Danika or **Danica** is a Slavic name meaning 'morning star'. Well established in eastern Europe, it is now starting to be used by English speakers.

Dante see DONTE

Daphne

Daphne is the Greek for 'laurel', and therefore the equivalent of LAURA. In mythology Daphne was a nymph with whom the god Apollo fell in love. She fled from his embraces, and when he had all but caught her, her prayers to be saved from him were answered and she was transformed into a laurel tree. Heartbroken, Apollo declared the laurel sacred to him. This story lies behind the use of the laurel wreath as a symbol of honour or achievement in the ancient world.

Dara

In Connemara, Ireland, the local patron saint of fishermen is known as Mac Dara, meaning 'son of the oak' ('oak' here indicating stoutheartedness), and the name Dara, a shortened form of his name, has spread from Connemara, first through Ireland, and then to other English speakers. It is usually male, but is now also used for girls, probably because most '-a' names are female. The name **Darragh** (occasionally **Daragh**), pronounced the same, is either a form of this or is from a related surname.

Darby see DERMOT

Darcy

The original Darcy family got their name from the fact that they came from (*de*) a French place called Arcy, and the name is occasionally found in something near the original form – D'Arcy. This surname was also used in Ireland as an anglicization of the similar-sounding surname O Dorchaidhe ('descendant of the dark one'). It is used as a first name for both sexes, with feminine forms including the variant spellings **Darcey**, **Darci** and **Darcie**.

Daria, Darius

The masculine form of this name, **Darius**, is an ancient Persian royal name meaning 'protector'. The feminine form, **Daria** (although this may owe something to **Darija**, a Russian pet form of DOROTHY), is more widely used internationally than the masculine, because it was the name of a saint martyred in 283. However, the man's name has recently become fashionable in the USA, and also appears in altered forms. **LaDarius** has been used as a Black name, combining the popular prefix La- with Darius, and the well-used name **Darian** could be seen as a development of Darius or Daria, although it could also be interpreted as from DORIAN. **Darian** is usually masculine, but occasionally feminine, and also occurs as **Darien, Darrien, Darrian** or **Dar(r)ion**.

Darlene see MARLENE

Darragh see DARA

Darren
This is a modern name of obscure origin. It has been described as an Irish surname, but this is not well documented. Whatever its source, this name and its variants **Darran** and **Darin** became immensely popular throughout the English-speaking world in the middle of the twentieth century. Its popularity is often attributed to its use in the 1960s American TV series *Bewitched*.

Daryl
Daryl is another surname used as a first name. It is French in origin, from *de Airel*, the name of someone from the Norman village of Airel. The village got its name from the Latin word for 'an open space' or 'courtyard'. **Darryl, Darrel** and **Darrell** are variants. The name started out as masculine, but is now used for both sexes.

David
The name of the killer of Goliath, and later King of Israel, is the Hebrew for 'beloved, friend'. The old short forms **Daw** and **Dawkin** have now been replaced by **Dave, Davie** or **Davy**. The Welsh form of the name is **Dafydd** (anglicized to **Taffy**), the form **Dewi** usually being restricted to the patron saint of Wales; short forms are **Dai, Deio** and **Deian**. **Davina** and **Davida**, with their short forms **Vina** and **Vida**, are originally Scots feminines. **Davita, Davinia** and **Divina** are also found. David was steadily popular throughout the twentieth century and shows no sign of falling out of favour.

DaVon see DEVON

Dawn
A modern name, Dawn was at first strongly associated with fiction and then given wider fame by several actresses. Its use may owe something to the Latin name **Aurora**, the goddess of dawn, which is occasionally used. The forms **Aurore** or **Aure** are well used in France. Dawn was particularly popular in both the USA and the UK in the 1960s and 1970s.

Dayle see DALE

Dean
As a surname, Dean has two sources, either an Old English name meaning 'dweller in a valley', or from the church office of Dean. Its success as a first name may owe something to the romance attached to film actor James Dean,

although it was well established in the United States before he sprang to fame. The feminine name **Dena** may have started as a feminine form of the name.

DeAndre see ANDREW

DeAngelo see ANGELA

Deanna, Deanne see DIANA

Dearbhail, Dearbhla see DERVLA

Deborah

This is a Hebrew name meaning 'bee'. From the account of the original Deborah in the Old Testament book of Judges, she must have been a formidable woman, for at a time when the role of women was very much that of a subordinate she was a prophetess, a Judge of the People, and even led the army. **Debra** has become a very popular variant, and **Debora** is also used. **Deb**, **Debbie** and **Debby** are short forms.

Declan

This is the name of an Irish saint who was a missionary associated with the southeast of Ireland from the earliest Christian times in Ireland, even before the coming of St PATRICK. The meaning is not known.

Dee, Dee-Dee

These are pet forms of any name beginning with the letter 'D'. **Deeann** and **Deeanna** are forms of DIANA.

Deiniol see DANIEL

Deirdre

This is the name of the great romantic and tragic heroine of Irish legend, whose beauty caused the death of several heroes. The meaning is debated: it has been interpreted as meaning 'the raging one', 'fear' or (most attractively) 'the broken-hearted'. The name was given wider currency by the publication of W.B. Yeats's *Deidre* (1907) and J.M. Synge's *Deidre of the Sorrows* (1910), both based on her legend. Variants include **Derdre** and **Deidre**, while the form **Deidra** is used in the USA.

Deja

This is a new name for which there has been a recent fashion as a girl's name in the USA. It has been suggested that it is a short form of the Spanish Dejanira, a form of the Greek Deianeira, the wife of Hercules in legend, or that it is a form of the French word *déjà*; but none of these is very convincing. The 'j' is not pronounced as a 'y', as it would be if the name came from Spanish, and there seems little reason for the use of the French. In addition, these explanations ignore the existence of Dejah Thoris, the beautiful and capable princess of Mars in the *Barsoom* novels of Edgar Rice Burroughs (1875–1950). She first appeared in print in 1912, but Burroughs was writing about Barsoom as late as 1948, and the novels are not only still read but were very influential on, and often mentioned by, later science fiction writers.

DeJuan see JOHN

Del, Dell
These are used as short forms of any name beginning Del-. A number of these are masculine and represent a fashionable use of place or surname, or of 'blends' – a mix of elements from different names. In some cases the sense of 'del' = 'of the', found in Romance languages, can still be traced. Thus we have **Delmar**, a place and surname ('of the sea'), **Delroy**, a French surname meaning '(servant) of the king', and the blend **Delbert**, 'Del + Bert'. Del is also used as a pet form of DEREK. The singer Del Shannon (1934–90), who made the name widely known, was born Charles Westover. (See also DELYTH.)

Delia
Delia means 'girl from Delos', the Greek island sacred to Apollo and Artemis. Its use as a first name is adopted from the first-century BC Latin poet Tibullus, who celebrated Delia (a pseudonym for one Plania) in his love poems, and from its use by Virgil for one of his shepherdesses. It was popular in the seventeenth and eighteenth centuries, particularly in literature, and at one time was practically synonymous with 'sweetheart'.

Della see ADELA

Delyth
This is a Welsh girl's name meaning 'pretty'. **Del** alone is also used, as is **Delun** ('pretty one') and **Delwen** ('pretty and fair'). This has a masculine form **Delwyn**. **Dilwyn** or **Dillwyn**, also masculine, is not a variant, but comes from the name of a Herefordshire village and means either 'white honeycomb' or 'petal'.

DeMarcus see MARK

Demelza
A Cornish feminine name, Demelza has reached a wider audience through Winston Graham's *Poldark* novels and the television series made from them. It is a place name, meaning 'the hill-fort of Maeldaf', and is said to be a twentieth-century introduction.

Demetrius
A name that has a certain popularity in the United States, particularly with Black Americans, Demetrius means 'follower of **Demeter**', the Greek goddess of agriculture and mother of **Persephone** (see CORINNA, CHLOË, MELANIE). Her name means either 'earth mother' or 'corn mother'. Demetrius occurs several times in the Bible, which may in part explain its use. It is also a saint's name, found in the form **Demetrios** in the Greek Church, and as **Dimitri** in Russian. **Demitrius** is another variant. The film star **Demi Moore** has made the short form of the feminine form **Demetria** (or **Demitra**) well known.

Dena see DEAN

Denholm
This is a surname, made up from the place-name elements 'valley' and 'dry land in a fen'. The similar **Denham** comes from 'valley' and 'homestead'.

Denis

Denis, with its variants **Dennis** or **Denys**, is a form of the name **Dionysius**, 'a follower of the god **Dionysos**', the Greek god of wine and poetic inspiration, whose name probably comes from the title 'son of Zeus', the king of the gods. The form Denis is the French corruption of the name of the martyr St Dionysius of Paris, who became the country's patron saint. **Den** and **Denny** are pet forms. The Greek form of the name is shortened to **Dion**, a name of growing popularity, which has the feminine **Dionne** as in the singer Dionne Warwick, and more rarely **Dione** and **Dionysia**. However, **Denise** is still by far the commonest feminine of the name.

Denzil

This is a Cornish place name of unknown meaning. Originally used as a masculine first name in the seventeenth century in a very limited way, it has now spread outside Cornwall and into more general use.

Deodatus see THEODORE

Derby see DERMOT

Derdre see DEIRDRE

Derek, Derrick, Deryck

This is the English form of the name **Theodoric** ('ruler of the people'), an unstable name since the German form is **Dietrich**, the Dutch **Dirk** and the French **Thierry** (one of the sources of **Terry**). Theodoric the Ostrogoth (c. 455–526) was an outstanding figure of his day, ruling northern Italy (by conquest) and parts of what are now Switzerland and Germany. After his death he became a figure in European folklore, which would explain the changes that happened to his name. The word 'derrick' for a crane is said to come from the name of a seventeenth-century hangman, whose name was first applied to the gallows and then used more generally to anything roughly that shape. DEL is occasionally used as a short form.

Dermot

Dermot or **Dermod** (in Irish **Diarmuid** or **Diarmaid**) is a figure from Irish mythology, a warrior who eloped with GRAINNE. There were also 11 Irish saints of the name. The name probably means 'free from envy'. It occurs in a wide variety of forms, including **Diarmod** and even **Diarmjuid**, and **Kermit** the Frog (from *The Muppets* TV show) owes his name to a regional variant. It was anglicized as **Darby** or **Derby**, and is the source of the popularity of this name in Ireland, although elsewhere it is from the surname which comes from the English place name, originally meaning 'farmstead where deer are kept'.

Dervla

This is the most usual anglicization of the Irish **Dearbhail**, meaning 'true desire', which is also found in the forms **Dearbhla**, **Derval** and **Dervilia**. It is rare outside Ireland, although the travel writer Dervla Murphy has made the name much better known.

DeShawn see JOHN

Désirée

This is the French word for 'desired, longed for', and was used for a long-awaited child from early times, originally in its Latin form **Desiderata**. **Desiderius** Erasmus (1466–1536), the Dutch Humanist, bore the masculine form of the name, which is also found as **Desideratus**.

Desmond

This is an Irish surname meaning 'descendant of one from Desmond, South Munster', used as a first name. It was also the title of the influential earls of Desmond, and it is probably because of them that the name came to be used as a first name. **Des** and **Dezzi** are used as short forms.

Destiny

This vocabulary word has come to be a popular first name for girls in the USA. The 'de-' element is quite popular at the moment, which makes it an easy word to adopt, and as 'destiny' is often linked with 'great', it is probably chosen by parents to express their hope for their child's future.

Detta see BERNARD

Devin, Devon

There is a group of names beginning Dev- that has recently become popular, particularly in the United States. In Great Britain, Devon is the one most prominently used. It is found for both sexes, and is pronounced with the stress on the first syllable, as in the county name. In the USA these names tend to be stressed on the second syllable. Devon is primarily feminine there, but sometimes used for boys. However, boys are more likely to be **Devin**, although this too can be used for girls. Other variants of these names are **Devan**, **Deven** and **Devyn**. In addition, there are two Black American boys' names that belong in this group, **DaVon** or **DeVon(n)** and **Devonte** (**Davonte**, **Devante**), which appears to be a blend of Devon and DONTE.

DeWayne see DUANE

Dexter

This is a surname used as a first name. The surname originally came from a word meaning 'a female dyer', but the name has long since lost any feminine associations.

Diamond

There has recently been a mild fashion for this jewel as a girl's first name, particularly in the USA.

Diana

Diana was the Roman goddess of the woods and wild nature, and later of the moon. She was equated with the Greek goddess **Artemis**, whose name is occasionally used as a first name. For example, the grand-daughter of the famous beauty Lady Diana Cooper was christened Artemis with reference to her grandmother. **Artemisia** ('follower of Artemis') is another rare name, probably used with direct reference either to the queen who fought at the battle of Salamis is 480 BC, or to the queen of Halicarnassus who built the

Mausoleum, one of the Seven Wonders of the ancient world, in memory of her husband. Diana occurs in a number of variants. **Diane** is the French form which also occurs as **Dianne** or **Dian**. **Deanna** is a form introduced by the film actress Deanna Durbin; and **Deeann**, **Deanne** and **Deeanna** are now also found, along with **Dyan** and **Dyanna**. Surprisingly, the enormous popularity of the Princess of Wales does not seem to have had any great influence on the popularity of the name. Other names linked with Diana as moon-goddess are PHOEBE and CYNTHIA.

Diarmaid, Diarmod, Diarmuid see DERMOT

Diccon, Dick, Dickie, Dickon, Dicky see RICHARD

Dietrich see DEREK

Dieudonné see THEODORE

Digby
This comes from the place name in Lincolnshire which means 'farm by the dyke'. As a surname it belonged to a notable family, the most prominent member of which was Sir KENELM Digby.

Diggory
This is a corruption of the name of a hero of medieval romance, Sir Degaré, 'the lost one'. The work, highly romantic and full of unlikely events, is not very highly thought of today, but the survival of the name must indicate a different opinion in the past.

Dillan, Dillon see DYLAN

Dilwyn, Dillwyn see DELYTH

Dilys
This is a Welsh word meaning 'certain, genuine', used as a first name. According to Davies it was first used by William and Jane Davis for their daughter, who was born on 11 June 1857, and they took the word from a Welsh version of the 23rd Psalm. **Dilly** is used as a short form.

Dimitri see DEMETRIUS

Dinah
Dinah is strictly speaking a separate name from the Greek DIANA, being a Hebrew word meaning 'judgement', although it is often used as a variant of Diana. The story of Dinah's abduction and the revenge taken by her brothers is told in chapter 34 of the Book of Genesis. The name is also found in the form Dina.

Dion, Dione, Dionne, Dionysia, Dionysius, Dionysos see DENIS

Dirk see DEREK

Divina see DAVID

Djamila see JAMAL

Dod, Doddy see GEORGE

Dodie, Dodo see DOROTHY

Dolly, Doll see DOROTHY

Dolores
A Spanish name meaning 'sorrow', Dolores is taken from the title of the Virgin Mary as Our Lady of the Sorrows, and was at first used for girls born on 15 September, the feast day of the Seven Sorrows of Mary. Despite the religious nature of the name, the pet forms have gained notoriety, one being attached to the adventuress **Lola** Montez, the other, **Lolita**, inescapably attached to Nabokov's novel (1955). Dolores was particularly popular in the USA in the 1930s. Other Spanish names associated with the Virgin Mary are **Mercedes**, 'Our Lady of Mercy', and **Montserrat**, a Spanish place name meaning 'jagged mountain', where there is a famous monastery with a Black Madonna, which is the patron of Catalonia.

Dolph, Dolphus see ADOLPH, RANDOLPH

Domhnall see DONALD

Dominic
Dominic comes from the Latin meaning 'of the Lord' and therefore has the same root-sense as CYRIL. It may at first have been used for those born on a Sunday, the day of the Lord, but since the thirteenth century it has been associated with St Dominic, the founder of the Dominican Order. The old-fashioned spelling **Dominick** is sometimes used, and the name can be shortened to **Dom** and **Nic**. **Dominique**, from the French, is the usual feminine form of the name, although the Latin **Dominica** can also be found.

Donagh see DUNCAN

Donald
Donald is the most usual form of the Celtic name **Donal** (**Domhnall**, **Domnall**), meaning 'world-mighty'; in eighth- and ninth-century Ireland it was regarded as a royal name. It was very well used in North America for the first three-quarters of the nineteenth century, where it was a particularly popular choice with those of Scottish descent. **Don** and **Donnie** or **Donny** are the short forms. There is no common feminine form, although **Donelle** and **Donalda** (particularly in Scotland) have been used (see also under DONNA).

Donata
The Latin masculine form of the name, **Donatus**, means 'given', and is naturalized as **Donat**. The occurrence of this rare name in Ireland may owe something to St Donatus of Fiesole, by tradition a ninth-century Irishman who

miraculously became bishop of this town outside Florence. The feminine **Donata** has been recorded more frequently than the masculine, and has also been found in the form **Donate**.

Donna

This is the Italian word for 'lady' and is a fairly recent name, not found before the 1920s. It probably derives from **Madonna**, the Italian for 'My Lady', a title often given to the Virgin Mary. This was rarely found outside the American Middle West until given notoriety by the singer. **Ladonna**, 'the lady', also came into use in the United States in the early part of the twentieth century. Donna was very well used in the USA between the 1930s and 1970s (where it is sometimes used as a feminine of DONALD), but did not become popular in the UK until the 1960s. **Donella** is an occasional elaboration.

Donovan

This is an Irish surname, originally *Donnduban*, meaning 'dark brown (person)', now used as a first name. Modern use was inspired by the Scottish-born singer Donovan Leich who, in his early career, was known only by his first name.

Donte

In the USA, Donte is the most usual form of the Italian name better known elsewhere as **Dante**, thanks to the fame of the great Italian poet Dante Alighieri (1265–1321). Both are contractions of the name **Durante**, meaning 'enduring, steadfast' from the same Latin root as the word 'durable'. Black Americans also use the name in blends such as **Devonte** (see DEVIN) and **Dontavius**, a blend of Donte and Octavius (see OCTAVIA).

Dora see DOROTHY, THEODORE

Dorcas see TABITHA

Doreen see DOROTHY

Doris

Doris means 'Dorian woman', the masculine name **Dorian** being 'Dorian man'. The Dorians were an early Greek tribe who gave their name to the Doric order of architecture. Doris seems to have come into use at the beginning of the nineteenth century, but became popular only at the end of that century, around the time Oscar Wilde (1854–1900) seems to have invented the masculine form for his *A Portrait of Dorian Gray* (1891). This story of a beautiful but corrupt youth with a portrait in his attic which shows the true ravages of time and vice does not seem to have put parents off the name, which is quietly but steadily used. Doris has been little used since the 1940s, but both Dorian and **Dorien(ne)** are now used for girls, while various elaborations and spelling variants blend names for both boys and girls into variants of DARIA and DARREN.

Dorothy, Dorothea

This name means 'gift of God'. It has long been a popular name, as is reflected in the use of the short forms **Doll** and **Dolly** for the toy – in use since the late seventeenth century, although earlier the word could mean 'a mistress'. Other short forms are **Dee, Dora, Dodie, Dodo, Dot, Dorrit** (unusual, but kept alive by Dickens), **Dorrie** and **Thea. Doreen** is probably an Irish elaboration of the name (although it has been linked with the Irish word for 'sullen') and **Dorinda** is a literary elaboration of the eighteenth century, with **Dorinne** another elaboration. There is no masculine form of the name, but a number of other names have the same meaning, including **Deodatus**, THEODORE and JONATHAN.

Douglas

Douglas, with its short forms **Doug, Dougie, Duggie**, is a Scottish surname derived from a river whose Gaelic name means 'blue-black'. In the Renaissance, the name was used for both sexes, but it is now exclusively masculine, with **Douglasina** a rare feminine. **Dougal** or **Dugald** comes from the same root and means 'black(-haired) stranger', a name given to the invading Danish Vikings; the name **Fingal**, 'fair stranger', being given to the blonder Norwegians. **Duff** has much the same meaning: 'dark-haired'. Outside Scotland, Douglas has not been particularly well used in the UK since the 1920s, but in the USA it was, like many other Scottish names, well used from the 1950s.

Dreena, Drew, Drogo see ANDREW

Drusilla

Drusilla is one of the names used by the Roman imperial family. According to Roman tradition, it was first used in its masculine form, **Drusus**, by a man who had killed a Gaulish chieftain called *Drausus* in battle, and who adopted the name to commemorate this deed. This name is said to mean 'firm, rigid'. Its introduction to England does not, however, come from this exalted source, but from a brief mention of a Drusilla in the Acts of the Apostles, thereby giving the name respectability in the eyes of the Puritans who first used it.

Drystan see TRISTAN

Duane, Dwane, Dwayne

This is an Irish surname, probably meaning 'son of the little dark one'. Its great popularity as a first name in recent decades seems to owe much to the success of the pop singer Duane Eddy in the 1950s. In recent years, the form **DeWayne**, as if combining the fashionable 'De-' prefix with WAYNE, has also appeared in the USA.

Dudley

This comes from the English town name (west of Birmingham) which became an aristocratic surname. The town's name means 'Dudda's clearing or wood'; and Dudda may be an old Saxon nickname for a dumpy man. **Dud** is a short form.

Duff see DOUGLAS

Dugald see DOUGLAS

Duke see Madoc

Dulcie

This is a nineteenth-century feminine name, based on the Latin word *dulcis* ('sweet'). It is little used today.

Duncan

This was originally a pet form of the old Gaelic name **Donagh** (**Donnchadh**), which means 'brown warrior'. However, Duncan looks more as if it is derived from the Gaelic words for 'brown head', linking it with the group of names under Douglas, and it is often understood in this way.

Dunstan

St Dunstan, whose name means 'dark hill', is one of the great Anglo-Saxon saints. He was archbishop of Canterbury, the adviser of the kings of his time, and responsible for the revival of monasticism in tenth-century England. He also devised a coronation service which is still used today.

Durante see Donte

Dustin

The spread of this surname as a first name owes much to the fame of the actor Dustin Hoffman, although there was an earlier American film actor called Dustin Farnam, after whom Hoffman is said to be named. The origin of the surname is obscure, but it may be from the French form of the Viking name that is the origin of Thurstan (see Thora).

Dwane, Dwayne see Duane

Dwight

Modern use of this boy's name is largely inspired by the respect in which American president Dwight D. Eisenhower (1890–1969), supreme commander of the Allied forces in western Europe during World War II, is held. The original use of the name seems to have been in honour of Timothy Dwight (1752–1817), an American educator, theologian and poet who had a major influence on the thinking of his contemporaries.

Dylan

Dylan is a Welsh name from heroic legend, traditionally understood as 'son of the wave'. Its spread is due to the Welsh poet Dylan Thomas, and also to the singer Bob Dylan, generally referred to by his surname. Bob Dylan is said to have been inspired in his choice of stage name by the character of US Marshal Matt Dillon in the then very popular television cowboy series *Gunsmoke*, but then to have modified it to match the poet. The spellings **Dillon** or **Dillan** are also used. The Welsh pronounce the 'y' in Dylan with a 'u' sound, but Dylan Thomas preferred the English pronunciation, so elsewhere it is pronounced with an 'i' sound.

Dymphna

Dymphna or **Dympna** is an Irish name, perhaps meaning 'befitted'. There is a St Dympna of Gheel who is the patron saint of the insane, but little is known of her, and the story of her being an early Irish princess who fled to Belgium to escape the incestuous attentions of her father owes more to folk-tale than to history.

Ee

Eachann see HECTOR

Eamon, Eamonn see EDMOND

Earl
With its variant **Erle** this is the Old English word for 'a noble', now a title, used as a first name. It is rare in the United Kingdom, but not unusual in the United States.

Earnest see ERNEST

Eartha
Although this name is hardly known in this country other than from the singer Eartha Kitt, it is one of a group of names well established among the Black population of the American South. Attempts have been made to link this name with an old Germanic earth goddess, but the name has a much more recent source. According to the 1953 edition of the journal *Names*, 'if a mother has lost two children in childbirth or shortly thereafter, she can be assured of the survival of her third child, according to popular belief, only if the second dead baby lies buried face down in its grave and the new baby is named for Mother Earth'. For boys, names such as CLAY, Clayton, ASHLEY or Sandy would be chosen. For girls, the name would be taken from the word 'earth', and included Eartha, **Ertha** and **Erthel**.

Ebenezer
Ebenezer is a biblical name, but of a rather different kind from the majority. It is not a personal name in the Bible, but first appears as a place name (I Samuel 4. 1) and later as the name of a memorial stone erected to commemorate an Israelite victory (I Samuel 7. 12). The word means 'stone of help', and Samuel sets it up as 'hitherto hath the Lord helped us'. The name was introduced by the Puritans, and it has been suggested that it was first adopted by the early American Puritan settlers with reference to Samuel's words. It is certainly more frequently used in the United States than in Great Britain, often in its short form, **Eben**.

Ebony
This is a recently introduced girl's name, particularly popular among Black

families seeking a name suggesting blackness, beauty and preciousness. **Sable** is sometimes used in the same way, although it is also used by Whites.

Ebrilla, Ebrillwen see APRIL

Eck, Ecky see ALEXANDER

Ed, Eddie see EDGAR, EDMOND, EDWARD, EDWIN

Edana see AIDAN

Edgar
Edgar comes from the common Old English name-element *ead* ('happy, fortunate') plus the common *gar* ('spear'). It remained in use after the Norman Conquest, but became obsolete in the Middle Ages, except for such uses as Shakespeare's for the virtuous brother in *King Lear*, where the names used in the play reflect the early English setting. It shares the short forms common to all the Ed- names: **Ed**, **Eddy**, **Ned**, **Neddy** and **Ted** and **Teddy**.

Edie see ADAM, EDITH

Edith
Edith is the one surviving Old English feminine name that shows the common name-element *ead* ('happy, fortunate') which is found in so many masculine names. It was the name of two English kings' daughters, one in the ninth and one in the tenth century, both of whom were canonized, and the name probably owes much of its early popularity to these two saints. The original form of the name was *Eadgyth*, the second element meaning 'battle'. Edith is sometimes shortened to **Edie**, and can be found in the Latinate form **Editha**.

Edmond, Edmund
This is an Old English name meaning 'happy or fortunate protection'. **Eamon** or **Eamonn** is the Irish form of the name, which shares the usual short forms with other Ed- names. King Edmund the Martyr was a ninth-century king of East Anglia who, according to his Old English biographer, was taken prisoner by the Vikings because he refused to fight, wishing to follow Christ's example. He was martyred by them in a way similar to St SEBASTIAN, being used as target practice for their spears until he was covered with their missiles 'just like a hedgehog's spines'. He was interred at Bury St Edmunds, where many miracles were ascribed to him.

Edna
A name of disputed origin, Edna occurs in the Apocrypha as the name of Enoch's wife and of Tobias's mother-in-law, in which case it probably comes from the Hebrew meaning 'pleasure'. However, it has also been described as a form of the name Edwina or of Edana, a form of EITHNE.

Edom see ADAM

Edred
An Old English name meaning 'fortunate counsel', Edred was made more

widely known at the beginning of the twentieth century by its use for the hero of E. Nesbit's *The House of Arden*.

Edward
This is the most popular of the Old English names beginning with the element Ed- ('prosperous, fortunate'), this time combined with the element meaning 'guard'. Its original popularity must owe much to its being the name of two canonized English kings. The first, Edward the Martyr (c. 963–78), was a boy-king assassinated for what were probably political ends (see further under ELFRIDA). The second was King Edward the Confessor (c. 1002–66), the last legitimate Saxon king of England. He had been brought up in Normandy, favoured the Normans at his court and had no children. William the Conqueror based his claim on the English throne on his having been made, so he said, Edward's heir, which would explain why this saint's name was one of the few Old English names to survive in common use after the Conquest. It shares the short forms **Ed, Eddy, Ned, Neddy, Ted** and **Teddy** with the other names in this group.

Edwin
Edwin is an Old English name meaning 'fortunate friend' and was the name of a seventh-century king of Northumbria who was an early convert to Christianity. **Edwina** is a feminine form of the name coined in the nineteenth century. The names have the same short forms as EDWARD.

Efa see EVE

Effie, Effy see EUPHEMIA

Egbert
This was a common Old English name, its users including an archbishop of York, a hermit-saint, and a tenth-century king who became overlord of the whole country. It means 'edge-bright'. Like many other Old English names it was revived in the nineteenth century, but is now rare.

Eileen
The Norman conquerors brought over with them the name **Aveline,** which developed into the surname Evelyn. This was adopted first as a man's name in the seventeenth century, but has now become predominantly feminine, although the author Evelyn Waugh (1903–66) still keeps an awareness of the masculine use very much alive. The origin of Aveline is not clear; it could be from the Old French word for 'hazel nut', or it may come from the same obscure source as AVICE. In Ireland Aveline became **Aibhilin** or **Eibhlin**. The 'bh' could either be pronounced 'v', in which case the name was anglicized as **Evelyn,** or be silent, in which case it was anglicized as **Aileen** or Eileen, with **Aily** or **Eily** as pet forms. Eileen was a very popular name in Ireland and in the UK in the first half of the twentieth century, but is not notably popular now. When it is used it is more likely to be spelt Aileen. The Evelyn form is sometimes seen as an elaboration of EVE, and has various elaborations of its own: **Evelina** is the Latinate form of the name and **Evilina, Eveline, Evaline** and **Eveleen** are variants.

Eilis, Ailis

These Irish names, often spelt phonetically in forms such as **Eil(l)ish** and **Ailish**, are usually regarded as variants of the same name, although strictly speaking Eilis is an Irish form of ELIZABETH, and Ailis of ALICE. However, as variation between Ai- and Ei- is common in Irish names (compare EILEEN and Aileen), this distinction has been lost.

Eiluned see LYNETTE

Eilwyn see ALVIN

Eimear, Eimhear see EMER

Einion, Einiona see EYNON

Eira

A Welsh feminine name meaning 'snow', Eira is also found in the form **Eiry**. There are many Welsh names from this root; among the most popular are **Eirlys** ('snowdrop') and **Eirwen** ('snow-white'). **Gwyneira** reverses the elements, giving 'white-snow'. **Eirian**, which can be used for either sex, looks as if it should belong with the same group, but is thought to come from the word *arian* ('silver').

Eirene see IRENE

Eithne

According to medieval legend, Eithne was the name of one of the divine inhabitants of ancient Ireland who was miraculously converted to Christianity. As a result, it became a popular name in religious circles, as well as a royal name. One of the early saints who bore her name is known as St **Ethenia**, and the name, which died out but was revived in the twentieth century, is also found as **Ethna, Etney** and **Ethni**. ENA and EDNA are anglicized versions of the name.

Elaine

This is an Old French form of the name HELEN. However, since it is the name of a character in the Arthurian romances – she seduces Sir Lancelot and becomes the mother of Sir Galahad – it is possible the name comes from, or has been influenced by, the Welsh name **Elain** ('a fawn'), for many of the Arthurian names have a Welsh origin, while some regard it as a short form of ELEANOR. Elaine was a popular name in the UK in the 1950s and 1960s.

Eldon see ELTON

Eldred

Eldred, with its variant **Aldred**, is an Old English name meaning 'old (thus mature) counsel'. It was the name of the last Anglo-Saxon bishop of York who died in 1069. It was revived in the nineteenth century, but is now rarely used.

Eleanor

Despite the popularity of this name throughout Europe, the meaning of Eleanor is obscure. It may well come from the same root as HELEN, and mean 'bright, shining', but it has also been derived from the Greek for 'pity, mercy'; from the Arabic meaning 'god is my light'; and from a Germanic root connected with the word for 'foreign'. It first came into English from France in the form **Alienor**, and has developed spellings such as **Eleanore** and **Elinor**. Its short forms include ELLA, **Ellen**, **Nell**, **Nellie**, **Nelly** and NORA. **Eleonora** is an Italian form of the name, which has a short form **Leonora** (sometimes **Leanora** or **Lenora**), made famous by Beethoven, while another form, **Lenore**, has been given fame by E.A. Poe (1809–49). **Annora** is said to be a northern English form of the name (see also HONORIA). ELAINE is sometimes treated as a form of the name.

Eleasha see ALICE

Elen, Elena see HELEN

Eleri
This is the name of a fifth-century Welsh woman saint, as well as of a river and valley in Ceredigion. Its meaning is not known.

Elfrida
This is an Old English name meaning 'elf strength', usually found in the history books in its old form, *Ælfthryth*. It was the name of a very forceful tenth-century queen of England, who virtually ruled the country at one time. She has been held responsible for the murder of her stepson, EDWARD the Martyr, in order to secure the throne for her own son, Ethelred the Unready; but despite this unsavoury reputation her name was revived in the nineteenth century and popular in the late nineteenth and early twentieth centuries, and some cases of **Freda** represent a short form. It is sometimes found in the form **Elfreda**. An allied name, revived at the same time but less popular, is **Elfgiva**, a Latinized form of *Ælfgifu* ('elf gift'), which was borne by a noblewoman whose family was persecuted by the same Ethelred. The family enmity led to her marriage to King Canute (c. 995–1035), who was fighting Ethelred for the English throne, and at one time she was his regent in Norway. She, too, had an unfortunate reputation, for she was deposed and 'Ælfgifu's days' became proverbial in Norway for bad times.

Eli
Eli was the name of the high priest in the Old Testament who was given the infant SAMUEL to bring up when he was dedicated at the temple. The name probably means 'high, elevated'. It can also be found as **Ely**, and the name is sometimes a shortening of **Elijah** (see below) or of **Elisha** ('God saves'). Elisha can now also be found as a girl's name, when it is probably best analysed as a blend of Elise and Alicia.

Elias
Elias is the Greek form of the name, as used in the New Testament, of the Hebrew prophet **Elijah** ('Jehova is God'). The surname **Ellis**, now used as a first name, is derived from this name, and its pet form gives us **Elliot(t)**, **Eliot** or **Eliott**.

Elinor see ELEANOR

Elisha see ELI

Elissa see ALICE

Elizabeth
Elizabeth is the English spelling of the New Testament **Elisabeth**, cousin to the
Virgin Mary and the mother of John the Baptist, who was the first person to
recognize the significance of the child that Mary was to bear (see Luke 1: 40–
45). Her role in the Bible made the name enormously popular throughout
Christendom, where it took many forms, particularly in diminutives. English
pet forms include **Eliza, Bess, Bessie, Bessy, Bet, Beth, Betsy** and **Betty; Libby,
Lisa, Liza, Lisbeth, Lizbeth, Liz** and **Lizzie.** In Scotland, the name became
Elspeth, with pet forms **Elspie, Elsie** and **Elsa.** French gives us **Babette** and
Lisette, as well as spawning a whole set of names from the form ISABEL and its
diminutives. Italy gives us **Bettina,** which has developed **Bettyne,** while the
Germanic languages give us **Elise, Ilse, Ilsa, Lise** and **Liesel. Bethan** is a Welsh
pet form of **Elisabeth** (the Welsh spelling) and the popularity of **Bethany** may
have been influenced by this, although it is also linked with Mary of Bethany,
one of Christ's female disciples in the New Testament. Bethan has also been
linked with the Celtic name **Bethia,** meaning 'life', itself also a biblical place
name. (See also EILIS.)

Elke, Elkie see ALICE

Ella
A Norman French name derived from the German word for 'all', Ella is also
used as a pet form of ELEANOR and **Isabella** (see ISABEL). It has been a popular
choice in the UK in recent years.

Ellen see HELEN, ELEANOR

Ellicia, Ellie see ALICE

Elliot, Eliott, Ellis see ELIAS

Elmer
This is a form of the Old English name *Æthelmær* ('noble and famous'), which
also gives us **Aylmer.** It is principally an American name and probably best
known nowadays from the cartoon character Elmer Fudd, the implacable
enemy of Bugs Bunny. Its popularity in the United States is due to the fame of
the brothers Ebenezer and Jonathan Elmer who played an important part in the
American Revolution. **Elma** looks like a feminine version of the name, but is a
pet form of such names as Wilhelma (see WILLIAM).

Elmo see ERASMUS

Eloisa, Eloise see HELOISE

Elroy see LEROY

Elsa, Elsie see ALICE, ELIZABETH

Elshender see ALEXANDER

Elspeth, Elspie see ELIZABETH

Elton
Popularized through the stage name of the singer Elton John, this is a surname coming from an Old English place name meaning 'Ella's settlement'. Similarly, **Eldon** means 'Ella's mound' – 'Ella' here is a short form of an Old English name containing the same element, meaning 'elf', found in ALFRED and ELFRIDA.

Eluned see LYNETTE

Elvira
This is a Spanish name of debated meaning, possibly meaning 'noble and true'. Its associations are mainly with the arts, as it is rare in real life except for those of Spanish descent. It is familiar through the character in the Don Juan or Giovanni story; as the ghost in Noel Coward's *Blithe Spirit* (1941); and through the film *Elvira Madigan*.

Elvis
Elvis Presley was lucky enough to be given his father's middle name as a first name, a name so rare and striking that there was no need for him to use a stage name. Its origin has been much debated, but Dunkling is probably right in identifying it with the Irish saint's name **Ailbe** or **Ailbhe**, usually anglicized as **Alby**, **Elli** or **Elly**. The feminine form is usually anglicized as **Elva**, and there is a place called St Elvis in Dyfed. The name is not unique to the Presley family, but was rarely found before the singer made it famous. An alternative interpretation is that, as southerners, the Presley family would have been exposed to the local traditions of creating new names for their children, and that the name is a creation, based on a name such as ALVIN.

Ely see ELI

Elysia see ALICE

Emanuel
Hebrew for 'God with us', Emanuel is the term used in the Old Testament for the Messiah. **Emmanuel** is a variant and **Manny** the short form. The name is popular with Spanish speakers in the form **Manuel**. There are feminine forms **Emanuela** or **Emmanuela** from Italian, while **Emanuelle** is the French form.

Emblem see AMELIA

Emer
In Irish legend, Emer was the wife of the great hero Cuchulainn, notable for the self-sacrificing devotion she bore him. The name is occasionally spelt **Emir**, and occurs in Scots Gaelic as **Eimear** or **Eimhear**.

Emerald see ESMERALDA

Emery, Emory
These are forms of the old Germanic name **Almeric**, formed from elements meaning 'labour' and 'rule'. Modern uses come from the surname, which in turn derived in the past from the old first name.

Emily
Emily comes from the Roman family name of the Æmelii. The Renaissance Italian writer Giovanni Boccaccio named one of his heroines **Emilia** in the *Teseida* (c. 1339), and when Chaucer translated this work as 'The Knight's Tale' he introduced the name as **Emily**. **Emmy**, **Emmie** and **Em** are used as short forms. (See also EMMA and AMELIA.) Emily has been one of the most popular choices for parents on both sides of the Atlantic in recent years.

Emir see EMER

Emlyn
Emlyn is a Welsh man's name, traditionally said to derive from the Roman name Æmelius, the same source as EMILY; in fact, it is more likely to come from a place name in Dyfed.

Emma
Emma started life as a short form of names containing the Germanic element *ermin* ('universal, entire'), such as **Ermyntrude** ('universal strength'). It was introduced in the eleventh century, has remained in use ever since, and in recent years has been one of the most popular girl's names. It shares the same short forms as EMILY, for which it is sometimes used as a pet form. The German names **Irma** and **Irm(e)gard** ('universal protection') come from the same root.

Emmeline see AMELIA

Emrys see AMBROSE

Emyr see HONORIA

Ena
Ena is a name with a number of different sources. It can be a pet form of names ending -ena or -ina (also giving INA), such as Eugenia or Helena, and it can be an anglicization of EITHNE. However, its popularity in the past came from Queen Victoria's granddaughter, Princess Victoria Eugénie Julia Ena, always known as Ena, who became Queen of Spain. Her last name was to have been Eva, but at her christening the handwritten notice of her names was misread, and she became Ena.

Enat see AIDAN

Eneas see ANGUS

Enid
This is a Celtic name, probably from the Welsh *enaid* ('soul'). In medieval literature it is the name of one of the outstanding heroines in the Arthurian stories, distinguished for her loyalty and patience, and it was brought back to

the public's attention by Tennyson when he told her story in his *Geraint and Enid* (1859). In Ireland, it can be an anglicization of Enat (see AIDAN).

Enoch
This is a rare name, made famous by the politician Enoch Powell. It was adopted by the Puritans from the Bible, where Enoch is an early descendant of Adam who has a particularly close relationship with God. According to tradition, he lived for 365 years and was then translated to Heaven without experiencing death. The meaning of the name is disputed, and it is possible that the name and stories about Enoch go back to a Babylonian sun-god.

Enola
This is a name from the French-speaking area of Louisiana which gained notoriety when the United States bomber 'Enola Gay', named after the captain's mother, dropped the atom bomb on Hiroshima in 1945. It appears to be one of the many names from the United States invented by blending together sounds from other fashionable names.

Eoghan see EUAN

Eoin see JOHN

Ephraim
In the Bible Ephraim is a son of JOSEPH and founder of one of the 12 tribes of Israel. The name means 'fruitful'.

Eppie see EUPHEMIA

Erasmus
Erasmus comes from the Greek meaning 'desired, beloved' and was the name of an early Christian martyred in southern Italy. As Ermo or **Elmo**, he became the patron saint of sailors in the area, and it is after him that the strange phenomenon of St Elmo's fire is named. Gerhard Geerts (1466–1536) adopted the name Desiderius Erasmus in the mistaken belief that this was the Greek translation of his Dutch name, and the name Erasmus is now most closely associated with this great scholar. **Erastus** is a less common name from the same root and with the same meaning. **Rasmus** and **Rastus** are the short forms of these names.

Eric
Eric is a Viking name, the second element of which means 'ruler', with the first coming either from a word meaning 'one, alone' or one meaning 'ever, always'. After the Viking age it was little used until the middle of the nineteenth century when Dean Farrar wrote the improving book *Eric, or Little by Little*, a moral tale approved of by parents but the bane of generations of children. **Erica** is a feminine form, interpreted by some as a flower name as it is the Latin for 'heather'. **Rick** and **Ricky** are used as short forms for both sexes. In recent years it has been more popular in the USA than in the UK.

Erin
A poetic term for Ireland, Erin is used in many a sentimental poem about the country. It was turned into a first name in the USA, spread to Canada and

Australia, and then to England; it has been particularly popular since the 1970s, but is rarely used in Ireland itself.

Erle see EARL

Ermin, Ermine, Erminia see HERMAN

Ermyntrude see EMMA

Ernest

This German name was introduced into England by the followers of George I when he came over from Hanover to become king. It has the same ultimate root as the English adjective 'earnest' and the name is sometimes spelt **Earnest** under its influence. However, the original meaning of the name came from a word that did mean 'seriousness', but which could also be used to mean 'a battle to the death'. **Ern** or **Ernie** are short forms; **Ernestine** is a feminine form which was fairly fashionable around the end of the nineteenth century, but which is little used now.

Errol

This name, made famous by the film star Errol Flynn and in steady use ever since, has been given a variety of origins. Some have linked it with a Scottish earldom and surname; some have claimed that it is a variant of HAROLD or EARL, while others have linked it with the Welsh name **Eryl**, used for both sexes, meaning 'a look-out post'. As many men's names come from aristocratic surnames, this would seem to be the most probable source of the name, but the main source of the name may be literary. In Frances Hodgson Burnett's *Little Lord Fauntleroy* (1886) the hero, who stands up for fairness and democracy, is called Cedric Errol, and this has probably popularized the name.

Ertha, Erthel see EARTHA

Erwin see IRVING

Esau see JACOB

Esmé

This name comes from the French word meaning 'esteemed', but was early on confused with the verb *aimer* ('to love'), whence the variants **Aimé** or **Aymé** (see also AMY). These were introduced as masculine names in the sixteenth century in Scotland, where they were used in the family of the dukes of Lennox, and spread from there. The name is now mainly feminine and has variants **Esme**, **Esmée**, **Esmee** and **Esma**.

Esmeralda

Esmerelda is the Spanish for **Emerald**, which is also occasionally found as a first name. Use of this name owes much to the heroine of Victor Hugo's *The Hunchback of Notre Dame* (1831).

Esmond

Esmond started off as an Anglo-Saxon name, probably a compound of elements meaning 'grace' and 'protection'. It became a surname in the Middle Ages, and was re-adopted as a first name in the middle of the nineteenth century when so many Old English names were revived, in this case perhaps under the influence of William Thackeray's *The History of Henry Esmond* (1852).

Estella, Estelle see STELLA

Esther
Sometimes spelt **Ester**, Esther is said in the Old Testament to be a translation of a Hebrew name meaning 'myrtle', although it may actually be a Persian name meaning 'star'. The biblical Esther was a Jewish orphan of outstanding grace and beauty who replaced VASHTI as the queen of King Ahasuerus (Xerxes to the Greeks). When the jealous Haman plotted the death of all Jews, Esther was able to use her influence to save her people. **Hester** is an alternative form of the name which has been in use since the Middle Ages, and the names are shortened to **Ess, Essie** and **Hetty**.

Esyllt see ISOLDA

Etain
An Irish name, this is the name of the most beautiful woman in ancient Ireland, whose troubled love life was told in the 1914 opera *The Immortal Hour* by Rutland Broughton. The success of the opera led to a brief fashion for the name.

Ethan
This is the name of several minor figures in the Old Testament, the most important of whom is revered for his wisdom. It has a longer history of use in the United States than in Britain, probably after Ethan Allen (1738–89), who fought the British in the American Revolution, and has recently come back into fashion on both sides of the Atlantic. The name means 'firmness'.

Ethel
This was originally a short form for a number of Old English names starting with the common name-element *æthel* ('noble'). It came into use as a name in its own right in the middle of the nineteenth century as a part of the revival of Old English names (see AUDREY and ALBERT).

Ethelbert see ALBERT

Etheldred, Etheldreda, Ethelthryth see AUDREY

Ethenia, Ethna, Ethni see EITHNE

Etta see HENRY

Euan
The history of this name is rather muddled. In the original Scots Gaelic it is **Eoghan**, which was anglicized as Euan (currently the most popular spelling), **Ewen, Euen,** or occasionally **Evan**. In Irish, it is **Owen** and in Wales, **Owain** or

Owen. These have long been thought of as the Celtic forms of EUGENE, and this may be the case, but some commentators think that this is a later rationalization of an earlier name, perhaps meaning 'son of the yew', which may indicate a memory of ancient tree worship, or perhaps from *eoghan* ('youth').

Eugene

Deriving from the Greek and meaning 'well born', Eugene was the name of a number of saints, the most prominent of whom was Eugenius, bishop of Carthage, who died an exile because of his faith in AD 505. The name is frequently shortened to **Gene**. The feminine form of the name, **Eugenia**, belongs to an early saint of whom little is known, but who has acquired a highly melodramatic legend in which she figures as a reformed fallen woman, who, disguised as a man, becomes abbot of a monastery; when accused of breaking vows of chastity, she proves her innocence by revealing her true gender. The French form of the name, **Eugénie** (often spelt without the accent), became popular in the UK out of admiration and sympathy for the French Empress Eugénie (1826–1920), who spent the last 50 years of her life in retirement in England. Eugénie was the name chosen by the Duke and Duchess of York for one of their daughters, which has led to a slight increase in its use. The pet form of Eugenia is one of the sources of the name ENA.

Eulalia

This is a Greek name meaning 'sweetly speaking', but the saint who spread the use of the name was Spanish. It is difficult to separate fact from fiction in her legend, but she seems to have been a 12-year-old girl who was martyred c. AD 304 after trying to stop the local magistrate persecuting Christians. It is said that after her death a dove appeared to fly from her mouth and a fall of snow covered her body. Her cult spread to Anglo-Saxon England, where several writers refer to her. Although it is a rare name, both Eulalia and the French form **Eulalie** can be found.

Eunice

Eunice is a Greek name meaning 'good victory'. The Puritans borrowed it from the New Testament where it is the name of the mother of TIMOTHY, a Jew married to a Gentile, who had introduced him to Christianity and given him a careful religious training (II Timothy 1. 5. and Acts 16. 1). The name was originally pronounced with three syllables, 'you-nice-see', but this is now very rare, and the phonetic spelling **Unice** reflects the modern form.

Euphemia

Euphemia, whose name means much the same as EULALIA, was a saint martyred just a few years later, c. AD 307. Her legend, also highly fictionalized, tells of her survival through various attempts to put her to death, until she was thrown to the wild beasts. It was particularly popular as a name in Scotland, and was much used by the Victorians and at the beginning of the twentieth century, but is rarely found in its full form. **Effie** is by far the most common short form, but **Eppie**, **Phemia** and **Phemie** are also used, and Euphemia is also one of the sources of the name PHOEBE. **Effy** and Effie were used in Scotland to anglicize the Celtic name **Oighrig**, which developed into AFRIC.

Eurfron

A Welsh feminine name meaning 'gold breast', Eurfron is one of a large number of Welsh names beginning with the element *eu* meaning 'gold', such as **Eurwen** ('gold' + 'fair, white') and **Euryl** ('gold').

Eustace

Eustace comes from the Greek word meaning 'good harvest' and was the name of a saint who was popular in the Middle Ages but who is probably fictional. His legend has many connections with that of St HUBERT; it involves the loss of possessions, wife and children and their miraculous recovery, in a form found elsewhere in medieval romance. The name is not common now, but its pet form is one of the sources of the increasingly popular **Stacy**. **Eustacia** is a feminine form.

Eva see EVE

Evadne

Evadne is a Greek name of unknown meaning, borne by two women in Greek legend. One of them features in the tale of *The Seven against Thebes* as so devoted a wife that, when her husband is killed in battle, she throws herself on to his funeral pyre in order not to be parted from him.

Evaline see EILEEN

Evan see EUAN, JOHN

Evangeline

This name means 'good news' and is from the same root as the word 'evangelist'. The Italian form of the name is **Evangelista**, and Henry Wadsworth Longfellow seems to have created Evangeline by given this a French form for his poem of this name in 1847. Charlotte M. Yonge, writing in 1863, describes it as an American name, but it soon spread to the UK, in both the basic form and as **Evangelina**.

Eve

Eve is the English, **Eva** the Latin form of the name given by ADAM to the 'Mother of Mankind', probably from the Hebrew for 'life'. This meaning led early Greek writers to translate the name as ZOE. In Ireland, Eve has been used to translate the Celtic name AOIFE. It takes the form **Efa** in Welsh. **Evie** is used as a pet form and **Evelina**, **Eveleen** and **Evaline** are used as elaborations of both Eve and Evelyn (see EILEEN).

Eveleen, Evelina, Eveline see EILEEN

Evelyn see EILEEN

Everard

Everard comes from a Germanic root via Norman French and means 'brave as a wild boar'. The surname **Everett**, occasionally used as a first name, is a variant and **Ewart** is the Scottish form of the name. For female names from the same root, see APRIL.

Everild, Everilda see APRIL

Evonne see YVONNE

Ewen see EUAN, JOHN

Eynon
This is a Welsh masculine name meaning 'anvil', said to symbolize stability and endurance. **Einion** is a variant and a feminine form **Einiona** has been recorded.

Ezekiel
Ezekiel was an Old Testament prophet whose name means 'God strengthens'. The name is rarely found in its full form, although it appears to be mildly fashionable in the USA, but the shortened **Zeke** is sometimes used.

Ezra
Ezra was another Old Testament prophet, whose name means 'help'. The name is chiefly associated with the poet Ezra Pound (1885–1972).

Ff

Fabian

The Roman patrician house of the Fabii, whose name comes from the Latin for 'bean' (presumably because some ancestor grew or sold them), gave Rome a number of eminent fighters and generals. Indeed, according to legend, at one point the family was all but wiped out fighting for their native city. The most famous of these was Quintus **Fabius** Maximus, nicknamed *Cunctator* ('the delayer'), who successfully wore down HANNIBAL and his invading forces by harrying them but refusing a direct engagement which he knew he would lose. It is after him that the Fabian Society (founded 1884) is named. A descendant of the family called Fabian was a martyred pope in the second century, thus giving the name Christian respectability. There are several feminine forms: a French direct feminization, **Fabienne**; the Latin **Fabia** and **Fabiana**, and **Fabiola**. The last was the name of an energetic and enterprising member of the Roman family, active on behalf of the Church in the fourth century and later canonized; but it is better known today as the name of Dona Fabiola de Mora y Aragon, the popular Spanish-born queen of the Belgians.

Faith

As one of the three great Christian virtues along with HOPE and CHARITY, Faith was popular with the Puritans. It seems probable that the twentieth-century name **Fay** or **Faye** comes from a short form of Faith, rather than from the synonym for 'fairy'. Although the French have a masculine name **Foy**, meaning 'faith', in most other languages the adjective rather than the noun is used, as it is with John Bunyan's character **Faithful**, which has been recorded as a real name. Thus we find Beethoven's *Fidelio* (1805), while **Fidel** Castro illustrates the Spanish form. The mainly Irish feminine name **Fidelma** seems to be an elaboration of Fidel, possibly combined with MARY. (See also VERA.)

Fallon

Fallon is an Irish surname, originally O *Fallamhain* ('descendant of the leader'), used as a first name. It came to prominence in the 1980s as the name of one of the more sympathetic female leads in the television series *Dynasty*, and has been used quietly ever since.

Fanny see FRANCIS

Farall, Farrel see FERGUS

Fatima

While Fatima is primarily a Muslim name, popular because it was the name of the Prophet's daughter (its meaning is unknown), it is occasionally found used in honour of Our Lady of Fatima, a Portuguese village where visions of the Virgin Mary occurred.

Fausta, Faustina, Faustine, Faustus see FELICITY

Fawn

The word for the young of the deer is occasionally used as a girl's first name, presumably on account of its connotations of large-eyed innocence. **Bambi**, the name of a fawn in a book by Felix Salten, published in 1921 and turned into a highly successful cartoon film in 1942, is also used, but usually as a nickname.

Fay, Faye see FAITH

Feargal, Fearghas, Fearghus see FERGUS

Fedor, Fedora see THEODORE

Felicity

The Romans worshipped *Felicitas*, the embodiment of happiness or good fortune, as a goddess. The name Felicity comes from this and was also the name of several saints, an appropriate name as they were deemed to be happy in having found their martyr's crown. **Felice**, still to be found, was the medieval form of the name, and was used for the faithful and pious wife in the Guy of Warwick legends. **Felicia** is another form of the name, currently popular in the United States, while **Felicitas**, the Latin word for 'happiness', is a rare alternative.

The masculine form of the name is **Felix**. This was first adopted as a name by the Roman dictator Sulla (138–78 BC), who believed that he was especially blessed with luck by the gods: not only did he fight his way to wealth and power, but he was one of the few dictators fortunate enough to be able to divest himself of power in old age and die a private citizen. Sulla had twin children whom he named **Faustus** and **Fausta**, from an adjective with the same meaning as Felix, thus introducing another new name. **Faustina** was later also used by the Romans. The French form **Faustine** was given fame by the poet Algernon Swinburne (who also wrote a poem to **Félice**), although the notoriously 'decadent' and sensual poem of that name was only written to settle a bet as to who could find the most rhymes for the word. In Ireland Felix has been used as an English form for the name **Felim** (**Felimid, Felimy, Phelim**), which means 'ever good'. The traditional use of Felix as a name for a cat is based on the similarity of the name and the Latin word for 'a cat' (*felis*).

Fenella

This is the anglicized form of the Celtic name **Fionnuala**, also found as **Fionnghuala** and **Fionola**. This is shortened to **Finola**, and the two Celtic forms of the name produced further shortenings to **Nuala** and **Nola**, which are used as names in their own right. The form Fenella became well known in Britain as a result of Sir Walter Scott's use of it in *Peveril of the Peak*. **Fiona** comes from the same root, being the Celtic for 'white, fair' with a Latin ending.

The name was invented by the Scottish poet James Macpherson, and made well known by William Sharp (1855–1905), a Scottish poet who used it for his pen name of Fiona Macleod.

Feodor see THEODORE

Ferdinand
When the Visigoths invaded Spain in the sixth century, they took with them a name based on the words *farth* ('a journey') and *nand* ('brave'); this developed into the Spanish name **Fernando** or **Hernando**, which in turn became Ferdinand in English. Short forms are **Ferd**, **Ferdie** and, rarely nowadays, **Nandy**.

Ferelith
This Scottish name is strangely neglected by books on names for, although by no means common, it is no rarer than many that appear regularly in the books, and is quite well represented in the public eye – dog-lovers may be familiar with it from the work of Ferelith Hamilton, there is a book illustrator called Ferelith Eccles Williams, and Ferelith Lean is prominent in the world of the performing arts. It is a traditional name in the Hamilton and Ramsey families, who regard it as meaning 'perfect princess', derived from the Old Irish words *fir* ('true, real, very') and *flaith* ('lady princess'). It appears to be the same name recorded in Scotland in the thirteenth century as *Forveleth*, and in eighth-century Ireland as *Forbflaith*, which one modern book on medieval Irish names glosses as meaning 'overlordship, sovereignty'. However, the form Ferelith makes it highly unlikely that it has been in continuous use since then, for the way Irish is pronounced has changed radically since the Middle Ages. The related Irish name **Gormlaith** (also found in early texts as *Gormflath*), which means 'illustrious lady' and is in current use in Ireland, has an alternative form **Gormla** (**Gormelia** in Scotland), which reflects its pronunciation, and the modern Irish pronunciation of *Forbflaith* would be something like 'furla'. Ferelith is thus probably a scholarly revival, perhaps of the nineteenth century, of an otherwise obsolete name.

Fergus
Spelt **Fearghus** in Irish and **Fearghas** in Scots Gaelic, this is a Celtic name meaning 'man of vigour'. Traditionally it was brought from Ireland to Scotland in the fifth century by Fergus mac Erca, who led his people to settle in Scotland. Whatever the truth of that, it was certainly in use by the fifth century, for it is recorded as the name of St Columba's grandfather (see MALCOLM). From the same root comes the name **Fergal** (**Feargal** in Irish) ('man of strength'), also an early Irish name, for it was the true name of the man known as St VIRGIL of Salzburg (d. 784), in his day a highly controversial academic as well as a missionary. Fergal was sometimes anglicized as **Farrell** or **Farall**, which became a surname, now occasionally found as a first name.

Fern
One of the newer plant names, Fern was introduced in the twentieth century. The variant **Ferne** is also found.

Ffion
This Welsh feminine name is an old word for the foxglove. In medieval Welsh

love-poetry it is a typical word used to describe the colour of a lovely girl's cheek. It has also been spelt **Fionn**, while forms such as **Ffiona** blend into the unrelated name Fiona.

Ffleur, Fflur see FLORA

Fidel, Fidelma see FAITH

Fifi see JOSEPH

Finbar, Finbarr see FINLAY

Fingal see DOUGLAS, FINLAY

Finlay
Finlay comes from a Scottish surname meaning 'fair hero' (traditionally given as the name of Macbeth's father), used as a first name. The variants **Findlay** and **Finley** are also found. It is one of a collection of masculine names based on the Celtic element *fionn* ('fair', 'white'). The simplest is **Finn** (sometimes **Fynn**), the name of one of the great heroes of Celtic legend. In folklore he is the giant Finn Mac Cool who builds the Giant's Causeway, but in mythology he is a hero fighting in Scotland, where he was known as *Finn na Gael* ('Finn the Foreigner'), which became **Fingal**, a form of the name well established by the fourteenth century, but made famous by the poems of James Macpherson (1736–96), purportedly by Finn's son OSSIAN. **Fintan** is a diminutive of Finn. Two Irish saints bear names from the same root: the fifth- to sixth-century St **Finbar** or **Finbarr** ('fair head' (ie hair)) whose name is one source of BARRY, and the sixth-century St **Finian** or **Finnian** ('the fair'). For feminine names from the same root, see under FENELLA.

Finola, Fiona, Fionola, Fionnghuala see FENELLA

Flann
Flann is an ancient Irish name meaning 'blood red'. It is probably best known from Flann O'Brien, one of the pen names of Brian O'Nolan (1911–66). The surname **Flannery**, occasionally found as a first name, comes from the same root, having originally been a nickname meaning 'red eyebrows'.

Flavia
This comes from an old Roman name, at one time the family name of the Roman emperors. The name would have started as a nickname, for it means 'golden yellow' or 'flaxen' and would have been used to describe someone of that colouring. Someone with tawny or dark yellow hair must have been the founder of the family which gave us the name **Fulvia**, the best known Roman holder of which was the wife of Mark Antony, who fought actively on his behalf in the civil war, even though at the time he was neglecting his own interests in order to dally with Cleopatra. The masculine forms of these names, Flavian or Flavius and Fulvius, do not seem to be used.

Fleur see FLORA

Flip see PHILIP

Flora
The name of a Roman goddess of fertility and flowers, Flora was later seen as symbolic of spring. **Florrie** is used as a diminutive. The name has been fashionable throughout the British Isles in recent years, but in the past it was particularly associated with Scotland, no doubt in memory of Flora Macdonald (1722–90), who helped Bonny Prince Charlie escape. **Fleur**, the French word for 'flower', seems to have spread from its use by John Galsworthy in *The Forsyte Saga* series of novels, and it is said to have been more widely used after the successful TV version of the books, first shown in 1967. However, the similar Welsh form of the name, **Ffleur** or **Fflur**, has been in use since the mid-twelfth century. **Flower** and **Blossom**, the English translations of these names, are also found.

Florence
Florence Nightingale (1820–1910), who made Florence such a popular girl's name, was so-named because she was born in the city of Florence. This city in its turn got its name from the Latin for 'to flower, flourish', so that the name really belongs with the FLORA group. In the Middle Ages Florence or **Florent** was quite a common name, but mainly a masculine one, which has long been obsolete except in Ireland, where it is said to be used to 'translate' FLANN. When Miss Nightingale got her name it was a most unusual one. Florence is shortened to **Flo**, **Florrie**, **Flossie** and **Floy**.

Flower see FLORA

Floyd see LLOYD

Forrest
There has been a recent fashion in the USA for using this surname as a first name. The surname would originally have been given either to someone who was a forester, or who lived in a forest. The form **Forest** is also used.

Francis
In the fifth century a group of Germanic tribes who called themselves the Franks invaded and took over Romanized Gaul. From these rulers the country took its new name of France via the Latin *Francia*; and since only these people were fully free, the word **Frank** soon came to mean 'free'. Similarly, in England **Franklin** was firstly a title given to a free landowner, then a surname which can also be used as a first name. In the twelfth century, when France already held an important cultural position, a young Italian called Giovanni Bernardone (c. 1181–1226) was considered by his contemporaries to be so Frenchified that he was given the nickname **Francesco** ('the little Frenchman'), which became **Francisco** in Spanish. It was in honour of this man, better known as St Francis of Assisi, that the name Francis became used in various forms throughout Europe. Frank is used as a short form of Francis as well as a name in its own right, as are **Fran**, **Francie** and **Frankie**. **Frances** is the feminine, which has **Fanny** as a pet form in addition to those used for Francis. The French **Francine** can also be found, while the Italian form **Francesca** has now become quite popular.

Fraser, Frazer

These, along with **Frasier and Frazier**, are variants of a Scottish surname of unknown meaning, which are used as first names. The family name is associated with the strawberry because the strawberry plant – *fraisier* in French – was adopted as a punning heraldic symbol.

Fred, Freddy see ALFRED, FREDERICK, WILFRED

Freda see ALFRED, ELFRIDA, FREDERICK, WINIFRED

Frederick

Frederick is a Germanic name meaning 'peaceful ruler'. Although it was used by the Normans, its modern use is due to its reintroduction by the Hanoverian rulers of Britain. It is sometimes spelt **Frederic** in the French fashion and is shortened to **Fred, Freddie** or **Freddy**, and more rarely to **Rick** and **Ricky**. **Frederica** is the usual feminine form of the name which shares the masculine short forms. In addition it has **Frieda**, a German spelling, and **Freda**, shared with ELFRIDA and WINIFRED, as short forms which are also used as independent names.

Freya

Freya was the name of the Norse goddess of fertility, so lovely that the Scandinavian myths are full of stories of the plots made to win possession of her. She also had some of the attributes of the Valkyries, and fallen heroes were feasted in her palace in Asgard. It has been quite a fashionable name in recent years in the UK.

Frieda see FREDERICK

Fulvia see FLAVIA

Gg

Gabriel

In the Bible the Archangel Gabriel ('strong man of God') acts as God's messenger. It is he who announces to the Virgin Mary that she is to have a child. Although it is by no means common, it has had steady use as a man's name, and in recent years has been popular in the USA. Feminine forms are also well used: **Gabrielle** is from the French feminine, while **Gabriella** or **Gabriela** is from the Italian. Both sexes have **Gabe** and **Gabby** as short forms, and the latter is sometimes further shortened to **Abby** (see ABIGAIL) for girls.

Gaenor see JENNIFER

Gaia see GEORGE

Gail, Gale, Gayle see ABIGAIL

Gaius see CAIUS

Galfrid see GEOFFREY

Gareth

The name of an Arthurian hero, introduced by the fifteenth-century writer Sir Thomas Malory, Gareth is probably a corruption of the name of an earlier hero, but it has been linked with the Welsh word *gwared* ('gentle'), and is usually taken to mean that. **Gary** or **Garry** is often used as a pet form of this name, but Gary Cooper, the film star who made the name world famous, took his stage name from his home town of Gary, Indiana. **Garth** is also sometimes thought of as a pet form of Gareth, but this again is also an independent name, based on a northern English word for an enclosure or small cultivated area. Gary was popular in the USA from the 1940s to 1960s, but only became popular in the UK in the 1960s, its popularity lasting through to the 1980s, when Gareth was also popular. The similar-sounding Garret (see GERALD) is not related to these names.

Garfield

A surname used as a first name, Garfield probably came into use in honour of J.A. Garfield (1831–81), the 20th president of the United States. The surname is Old English and usually interpreted as meaning 'field of spears', but the alternative of '(someone who lives by a) gore-shaped field' has been suggested. The cricketer Sir Garfield Sobers (b. 1936) illustrates the use of **Gary** (see GARETH) as a pet form of Garfield.

Garmon see GERMAINE

Garret, Garrett see GERALD

Garry, Garth, Gary see GARETH

Gaspar, Gaspard see JASPER

Gavin
Gavin is the Scots form of the Arthurian hero Sir **Gawain**, which appears in early Welsh literature as *Gwalchmai* ('hawk of the plain'), a hawk being used as a symbol of a heroic warrior; but Gawain may come more directly from a form with *gwalch* ('hawk') + *(g)wyn* ('white'). This name became Gauvin in medieval French literature and was adopted as Gavin in Scotland, which in the Middle Ages had closer cultural ties with its ally France than with its enemy England. The use of the name was for a long time limited to those with Scottish connections, but the name has now spread throughout the English-speaking world, and was well used by parents in the 1980s.

Gay
Gay, with its alternative form **Gaye**, is a modern name based on the vocabulary word. It has hardly been used since the general introduction of the word 'gay' as a synonym for 'homosexual' in the 1970s, and is unlikely to survive.

Gayle see ABIGAIL

Gaynor see JENNIFER

Geena see GINA

Gemma
This is an old Italian name, meaning 'gem'. The poet Dante's wife was Gemma Donati, but the most famous bearer of the name was St Gemma Galgani (1875–1903), a poor orphan who went into domestic service and suffered from ill-health all her short life, but who nevertheless experienced remarkable visions and showed on her body the marks of Christ's crucifixion. Her canonization in 1940 probably led to the steady rise in popularity of the name, either in its original form or in the spelling **Jemma**. In the 1980s it was one of the most popular girl's names in the UK, but is little used in the USA.

Gena see GINA

Gene see EUGENE

Generys see NERYS

Genevieve

Geneviève (c. 422–512) is the name of the patron saint of Paris. As a young girl living with her grandmother in Paris, Geneviève devoted her life to prayer and good works and vowed to eternal virginity, while none the less managing to play a prominent part in the affairs of the city. When it was threatened with attack by Attila the Hun, she persuaded the citizens to stand fast, and when the expected attack failed to materialize this was put down to her prayers. When the city was later besieged by the Franks, it was Geneviève who led the convoy that broke the blockade and brought food to the starving citizens. **Ginette** and **Ginetta** are pet forms, and the occasional use of **Geneva** as a first name may come from her name rather than from the Swiss city, perhaps influenced by **Ginevra**, the Italian form of Genevieve.

Geoffrey

Geoffrey is a Germanic name which was very popular with the Normans. While the second half of the name is clearly from the word *frith* ('peace'), the meaning of the first half is not clear, and it seems likely that it represents the falling together of a number of different names. **Jeffrey** was an early variant, and is now probably the more common spelling. **Geoff** or **Jeff** are used as short forms. The name was sometimes written in the old Latin chronicles as *Galfridus*, and this led to a nineteenth-century pseudo-antique name **Galfrid**.

George

George comes from the Greek word for a farmer, made up of the elements *ge* ('earth'), from the same root as the name of the earth goddess **Gaia**, a name currently having a certain popularity with feminists, and *ergein* ('to work'). Despite St George's role as the patron saint of England from the fourteenth century onwards, the name was not in common use until the eighteenth century, with its four successive kings of that name. **Georgie** or **Georgy** is one short form; in the north of England we find **Geordie**, while the Scots are said to use **Dod** and **Doddy**. There are a number of feminine forms: **Georgia**, **Georgianna**, **Georgette** and **Georgina**, all of which use **Georgie** as a short form; Georgina is one source of GINA.

Geraint

Yet another name from Arthurian legend, Geraint was also in use in real life from a very early date, for a king of Cornwall with that name was killed in battle in AD 530. He may well be the original of the fictional character, for he was both noble and praised for his skill in battle. The name comes from the Latin (ultimately Greek) name **Gerontius**, meaning 'old'.

Gerald

Gerald comes from a Germanic name made up of elements meaning 'spear' and 'rule', by way of Norman French. It is shortened to **Gerry** or **Jerry** and **Ger**, and has the variants **Gerold**, **Gerrold** and **Geralt**. In the Middle Ages the name **Gerard** (from 'spear' and 'brave') was rather more popular than Gerald, and it is not always possible to distinguish the history of the two names. In Ireland the name Gerard developed into **Garret** or **Garrett** (see also JARED); these names share the same short forms as Gerald. Ireland was also the source of the feminine form of Gerald, **Geraldine**. Prominent in the Norman invasion of Ireland was the FitzGerald ('sons of Gerald') family, also known collectively as the Geraldins, and it was a member of this family, Lady Elizabeth Fitzgerald, who was addressed in poetry by the sixteenth-century earl of Surrey as 'The Fair Geraldine', thus creating a new name.

Gerda
Best known as the name of the girl in the fairytale 'The Snow Queen' Gerda was one of the Old Norse goddesses, the wife of Freyr (the brother of FREYA), and, like him, a fertility deity.

Germaine
Germaine is probably best known to English speakers from the Australian writer Germaine Greer, but the name was most in use around the end of the nineteenth century. It was the name of the sixteenth-century St Germaine of Pibrac, a deformed child and a victim of what would now be called child abuse, who was none the less outstanding for her piety and about whom miracles were manifested both before and after her early death. Her canonization in 1867 gave a boost to the name. The masculine form, **German** or **Germain**, is rare in Great Britain, even though St Germanus of Auxerre (c. 378–448) is one of the few early saints associated with Britain. St Germanus was twice sent to Britain to counter the spread of the Pelagian heresy (see MORGAN), and is said to have won a notable victory on behalf of the British against the invading Picts and Scots. He arranged the troops in a strong and well-hidden position, and on a given signal they all cried 'Alleluia!'. The invaders are supposed to have been so taken by surprise that they fled without a blow being exchanged. 'The Alleluia victory', as it became known, was accounted a miracle. Germain's name is, however, used more in the USA, usually in the form **Jermaine**. The name is found in Welsh in the form **Garmon**.

Geronimo see JEROME

Gerontius see GERAINT

Gerry see GERALD

Gertrude
Gertrude is a Germanic name meaning 'strong spear'. It is thought that it was introduced from the Netherlands, where the seventh-century St Gertrude of Nivelles was widely venerated. She seems to have been remarkable more for being a capable and devout administrator of her abbey than anything else, but a large body of folklore grew up around her. Her emblem is a pastoral staff with a mouse running up it. The name's short forms are **Gert**, **Gertie** and **Trudy** or **Trudie**.

Gervase, Gervais
This was the name of a martyr of unknown date and history, whose remains were exhumed in Milan in AD 386 after a 'presentiment' by St Ambrose that they would be found. Despite his obscurity, Gervase was widely revered and his cult spread through western Europe. **Gervas**, **Jervis** and **Jarvis** are variants and there is a feminine form **Gervaise**. The meaning of the name is obscure, but may come from the same root, meaning 'spear', found in other Gar- and Ger-names.

Gethin
This is a Welsh masculine name that would have started out as a nickname, as it means 'dark, swarthy'.

Geunor see JENNIFER

Ghislaine see GISELLE

Giana, Gianna, Gianni see GINA

Gideon
A Hebrew name probably meaning 'having a stump for a hand', Gideon was the name of one of the great Old Testament leaders who liberated his people from the domination of their enemies. To help him, the Lord manifested a number of signs, including a miracle when dew fell only on a fleece laid on the ground, and not on the earth, and vice versa. The fleece became the symbol of Gideon, which led in the Middle Ages to a curious association of Gideon and the classical hero JASON.

Gilbert
Gilbert comes from Germanic words meaning 'pledge' and 'bright'. **Gib**, at one time proverbial as the name for a cat, is probably now obsolete as a short form, but **Gil**, **Gillie** or **Gilly** (with a hard 'g') and **Bert** are still used. Gilbert is somewhat out of fashion at the moment, but it was a popular name in the Middle Ages, no doubt influenced by the fame of St Gilbert of Sempringham, the founder of the only specifically English religious order, who died, aged over 100, in 1189. His order took a special interest in caring for orphans and lepers. There seems to be no English feminine of the name, but the French use Gilberte, which is the true name of the girl known as **Gigi** in Colette's novel. Gigi came into use as a first name after 1958, when a highly successful film was made of the musical based on the novel.

Giles
This name has come a long way from its original form of **Aegidius**, a Greek name derived from the word for the goat skin that this Athenian saint used to wear. He is said to have fled to France (where his name was shortened to Giles, now sometimes **Gyles**), in order to escape publicity, and to have become a hermit there. He became the patron saint of Edinburgh, and for a time **Aegidia** or **Egidia** was used as a feminine form in Scotland; often these were only the official written forms of the name, and girls, too, were called Giles when spoken to.

Gill see JULIA

Gilleasbuig, Gillespie see ARCHIBALD

Gillian see JULIA

Gina
Gina, now widely used as an independent name, was originally a short form of names such as Georgina, Eugena and Regina. The Italian actress and

photographer Gina Lollobrigida, who helped spread the name among English speakers, gets her name as a shortening of **Luigina**, a feminine form of **Luigi**, the Italian form of LEWIS. The actress **Geena** Davis, who has made an alternative spelling well known, has Virginia as her given name. **Gena** is another spelling, as in **Jean(n)a**, which makes the name seem a derivative of Jean (see JANE). These variant forms merge imperceptibly into forms such as **Giana** or **Gianna**, strictly the Italian equivalent of Jane, being feminines for **Gianni**, itself a pet form of **Giovanni**, the Italian form of JOHN.

Ginette, Ginetta see GENEVIEVE

Ginevra see GENEVIEVE

Ginny see VIRGINIA

Giovanni see GINA

Giselle
This French form of a Germanic name derived from the word for 'a hostage or pledge', it can also be spelt **Gisèle**. The name **Ghislaine** (the 'g' is hard and the 's' silent), far more common in France than in England, seems to come from an Old French pet form of the name.

Gladys, Gwladys, Gwladus see CLAUDIA

Glenda
Glenda comes from the Welsh and is made up of words meaning 'holy, fair' and 'good'. **Glenys** comes from the same source, being *glan* ('holy, fair') plus a feminine ending. It is also spelt **Glenis** and **Glennis**. However, there is a rather grey area where the names listed under GLENN overlap with those coming from *glan*, and forms such as **Glinda** show how much the two groups of names have merged.

Glenn, Glen
This is a name based on the Celtic word for 'a valley', also spelt **Glynn** or **Glyn**, the first form being more obviously Scottish, the other Welsh. Glenn is predominantly a masculine name, but is also used for women along with the more obviously feminine **Glenna** and **Glenne**. The feminine of Glynn is **Glynis** or **Glinys**.

Gloria
The Latin word for 'glory' used as a first name, Gloria seems, like CANDIDA, to have been introduced by George Bernard Shaw, this time in his play *You Never Can Tell* (1898). However, **Gloriana** was well known as a poetic title given to Queen Elizabeth I, and this is occasionally used as a first name, sometimes transformed to look like a blend of Gloria and Anna in forms such as **Glorianna** and **Gloranna**. **Glory** is occasionally used as a name in its own right.

Glyn, Glynn, Glynis see GLENN

Godfrey

The Anglo-Saxons had a name **Godfrith**, formed from elements meaning 'God' and 'peace', but with the Norman Conquest this was more or less superseded by the Norman form of the same name, Godfrey. Nevertheless, some of the Old English names with God- did survive, such as **Godric** ('God' and 'rule'), the name of an Anglo-Saxon saint still used in his native East Anglia, and **Godwin** ('God' and 'friend'), the name of the father of the last Saxon king of England, HAROLD.

Gordon

A Scottish surname, Gordon is derived from a place name possibly meaning 'spacious fort'. It seems to have become a first name only in the nineteenth century, used in honour of General Gordon of Khartoum (1833–85).

Gormelia, Gormla, Gormlaith see FERELITH

Goronwy

This ancient Welsh name also occurrs in such forms as **Gronwy**, **Gronw**, and **Grono**. The first part of the name means 'hero', but the second element is not understood.

Gotlieb see THEODORE

Grace

Grace, one of the names introduced by the Puritans, is based on a word with strong Christian associations (see also HOPE, FAITH). It is popular with British parents at the moment, particularly as a second name. **Gracie**, made famous by the singer Gracie Fields ('Our Gracie'), is a pet form. The name is ocasionally spelt **Grayce**, and the Spanish form **Gracia** and the Italian **Grazia**, with its pet form **Graziella**, are sometimes found.

Graham

This Scottish clan name used as a first name comes from the town of Grantham in Lincolnshire, a place name which is spelt *Graham* in the Domesday Book and probably means 'homestead on a gravel outcrop'. A certain William de Grantham was given lands in Scotland by King David I in the twelfth century, and thus the family name was transferred north of the border. The name is also spelt **Grahame** and **Graeme**.

Grainne

Grainne and its anglicized, phonetic form **Grania** is an Irish name which comes from the word for 'love'. In Irish legend Grainne eloped with DERMOT, one of the followers of her betrothed FINN Mac Cool. The name was regularly translated as GRACE, and the pirate raider Grace O'Mally (c. 1530–1600), who gave the Elizabethan authorities in Ireland so much trouble, was actually a Grainne.

Grant

This comes from a surname, in origin a French nickname, *le grant*, given to a tall person. Its popularity in the USA may owe something to General Ulysses S. Grant (1822–85), 18th president of the country.

Granville
With its variants **Grenville** and **Greville**, this was originally a surname for someone coming from Granville ('large town') in Normandy.

Grazia, Graziella, Grayce see GRACE

Gregory
This is actually a Greek name meaning 'to be awake' or 'watchful', but since the Latin form of the name, Gregorius, was more familiar in the Middle Ages, it was often interpreted as if from this language. Thus Caxton's translation (1483) of *The Golden Legend* tells us, in the life of Pope Gregory – the man responsible for the conversion of the Anglo-Saxons to Christianity and who made the name famous – 'Gregory is of [the Latin] Grex, which is to say a flock; and of gore, which is to say a preacher. Then Gregory is to say as a preacher to an assembly or flock of people.' Its commonest short form is **Greg**. There is a Scots form **Gregor**.

Grenville, Greville see GRANVILLE

Greta, Gretchen, Gretel, Grethel see MARGARET

Griffith
Griffith, with its alternative forms **Gruffydd** and **Gruffudd** and derivative **Griffin** are all forms of an early Welsh name used by a number of the independent Welsh princes. Its meaning is uncertain, but it probably means 'lord' or 'strong warrior'. **Griff** is a frequent short form.

Griselda
A Germanic name, Griselda means 'grey battle-maiden', an inappropriate meaning for a name which has become so inextricably associated with the word 'patient' after Chaucer's account of the long-suffering wife in 'The Clerk's Tale'. In Scotland the name can take the form **Grizel** (or **Grizzel**, **Grissel**, **Grisell**), but much more fashionable is the short form **Zelda**, made notorious by the antics of F. Scott Fitzgerald's wife.

Grono, Gronw, Gronwy see GORONWY

Gruffydd, Gruffudd see GRIFFITH

Gudrun
This is a very common name in Norse saga and German epic. One character of that name is very important in the stories that Wagner later turned into the *Ring Cycle*, and another Gudrun is central to the thirteenth-century *Laxdale Saga*, one of the best of the Icelandic sagas. In England the name is probably best known from Gudrun Brangwen, one of the main characters in D.H. Lawrence's *Women in Love* (1920). The name is made up of elements meaning either 'God' or 'good' + 'rune, wisdom'.

Guenevere, Guinevere see JENNIFER

Gus, Gussie see AUGUSTUS

Guy

The old Germanic form of Guy is *Wido*, a name of uncertain origin, possibly meaning either 'wide' or 'wood'. There was a tenth-century Belgian saint of this name about whom very little is known, but who appears to have taken to the life of a wandering pilgrim after becoming a bankrupt. The name became all but impossible to use in Britain after the capture of Guy Fawkes, but was revived again in the nineteenth century. It continued to be popular well into the twentieth century, but since then does not seem to have been much used by parents until recently, when there has been some evidence of it coming back into fashion.

Gwen

Gwen is an important Welsh feminine name-element, a feminine form of the word *gwyn* meaning 'white, fair, blessed'. It has been used as a name in its own right since the fifth century, is either the first element or the final one in many Welsh names, and a short form of many such names. The most common of the compound names outside Wales is **Gwendolen** (also spelt **Gwendolyn, Gwendolyne, Gwendoline, Guendolen**), the second element of which means 'bow' and 'ring'. The name may have been that of an ancient moon-goddess, and is traditionally the name of Merlin's mother. (See also SABRINA.) **Gwenda** is a combination of *gwen* and the word for 'good', although it is also used as a short form of Gwendolen. **Gwenfrewi** (*gwen* combined with the word for 'reconciliation') was the name of the seventh-century saint known in English as WINIFRED. **Gwenfron** ('white breast') is the reversed form of the name BRONWEN; **Gwenhwyfar** is the Welsh source for JENNIFER; while **Gwenllian** (rarely, **Gwenlian**) means 'fair and flaxen' and was in use in twelfth-century princely houses. **Gweno** is the Welsh form of JUNO and with **Gwennie** is used as a pet form of all these names, but the modern name **Gwenith** is actually the word for 'wheat'. **Gwyn** is the masculine form of the name, which is anglicized to **Wyn** or **Wynn**. It too has many compounds, the best known of which is **Gwynfor** (*gwyn* combined with *mor*, meaning 'great'), anglicized as **Wynford**.

Gwil, Gwillym, Gwilym see WILLIAM

Gwyn see GWEN

Gwyneira see EIRA

Gwyneth

Gwyneth is often associated with the names in the GWEN group, but more probably comes from the Welsh for 'bliss, happiness'.

Gwynfor see GWEN

Gwythyr see VICTORIA

Gyles see GILES

Hh

Haden see HAYDN

Hadrian see ADRIAN

Haidee see HEIDI

Hailey see HAYLEY

Hal see HAROLD, HENRY

Haley, Hallie see HAYLEY

Hamish see JAMES

Hank see HENRY

Hannah see ANN

Hannibal

This is a Phoenician man's name, meaning 'mercy of Baal'. It is said to have been particularly used in Cornwall, which has traditional, but unproved, links with Phoenician traders. The historical Hannibal was a third-century BC Carthaginian whose father brought him up from childhood to hate Rome. As an adult, Hannibal invaded Italy via the Alps, and for many years ravaged the country and almost brought about the destruction of Rome, but was finally defeated, more by force of circumstances than by superior skill. (See also FABIAN.)

Harlan, Harley

Harlan is a surname, from a place name meaning 'hare-land', used as a first name, particularly in the USA. Although it was in use in the nineteenth century, modern use may be influenced by respect for Supreme Court judge John Marshall Harlan (1833–1911). Harley, another surname used for both sexes, but commonly a girl's name, can have a similar meaning ('hare-clearing'). For girls it can also be spelt **Harlee, Harleigh** and **Harli**.

Harmony see MELODY

Harold

This is the name of the last king of England before the Norman invasion; he was part Danish and bore a Scandinavian-influenced name. Harold is a typical Germanic compound made up of elements meaning 'army' and 'power'. It died out after the Norman Conquest, but was revived along with other Old English names in the nineteenth century. **Hal** is sometimes used as a short form. Harold was popular on both sides of the Atlantic in the first three decades of the twentieth century, but is now an unusual choice.

Harriet, Harrison, Harry see HENRY

Harvey

This is a form of the French name Hervé, a Breton saint whose name meant 'battle-worthy'. Little is known about the saint's life, although according to the somewhat fantastical legends about him, he was a wandering monk and minstrel. Until the French Revolution a Breton church kept his supposed cradle as an object of veneration. The Normans brought the name over to England, and from there the name spread to the rest of the English-speaking world.

Hatty see HENRY

Havelock see OLIVER

Haydn

This name, thought of as typically Welsh, is actually the surname of the composer Josef Haydn (1732–1809), used as a first name. It is sometimes spelt **Hayden** or **Haydon** or even **Haden,** in which case it can be construed as from an Old English place name meaning 'hay valley'. Although once restricted to men, it is now appearing as a feminine name.

Hayley, Haley

This is a surname meaning 'hay field', now used as a first name. It owes its currency to the film actress Hayley Mills, who was named after her mother Mary Hayley Bell. The name caught the public's attention and has been very popular throughout the English-speaking world. Hayley is the usual spelling in the UK, followed by **Hailey,** but in the USA it is most usually Haley, with a wide range of other variants. **Hallie** is probably not one of these variants, but a revival of an old pet form of Harriet (see HENRY), where the 'r' has become 'l' in the same way that Hal became a pet form of Henry.

Hazel

The name of this small nut-bearing tree does not seem to have been used as a first name before the end of the nineteenth century, when plant names in general were very popular.

Heather

Like HAZEL, Heather seems to have come into fashion in the late nineteenth century along with a number of other plant names for girls. It has been most popular in the USA in recent years, and is also well used in Scotland. **Heath,** also a surname, is a synonym for the same plant and is sometimes found as a boy's name. (See also HEDLEY.)

Hebe

In classical Greek mythology, Hebe was the goddess of youth (which is the meaning of her name) and cupbearer to the gods. Fairly popular in the nineteenth century, the name is rarely used now. As it is also the name of a group of plants, it may be thought of as one of the flower names.

Hector

Hector was the great warrior of Troy who, until he was killed in battle by the Greek hero **Achilles**, was the chief defender of the city in the Trojan War. It is therefore appropriate that his name means 'holding fast', which should probably be understood as 'defender, support'. The name can be shortened to **Heck**. It has been particularly popular in Scotland, where it was used as an anglicization of the Gaelic name **Eachann**, which means 'lord of horses'. Since the Trojan Hector is depicted by HOMER as fighting from a horse-drawn chariot, this, as much as similarity of sounds, may lie behind the association of the two names.

Hedda see AVICE

Heddwen, Heddwyn

These are Welsh names, the first feminine, the second masculine, coined at the beginning of the twentieth century from elements meaning 'peace' and 'blessed, fair, holy'.

Hedy, Hedewig, Hedwige see AVICE

Hedley

This is a man's name which comes from a place and surname meaning 'a clearing where HEATHER grows'. It was popular at the beginning of the twentieth century, but is now little used.

Heidi, Haidee

These are two distinct girls' names, although they may sometimes be used as variants. The first is Austrian, the second Greek: both owe their use to literary sources. Heidi, the more common of the two names, owes its introduction to the popularity of Johanna Spyri's book *Heidi*. It is a pet form of the name **Adelheid**, the German form of Adelaide (see ADELA). **Haidee** is probably a form of the Greek name Haido ('to caress') and came into fashion after its introduction by Lord Byron in *Don Juan* (1819). In this poem, the adolescent Juan and Haidee fall deeply in love, and the depiction of combined innocence and passion forms some of Byron's most memorable writing.

Helen

Like HECTOR, Helen is a name from Homer's *Iliad*. Helen, the wife of the Greek Menelaus, was the most beautiful woman alive, and her abduction, or seduction, by the Trojan prince PARIS, led to the long siege of Troy described in Homer's epic. The name means 'the light, the bright'. However, the popularity of the name throughout Europe probably owes more to St Helen or **Helena**, empress and supposed finder of the True Cross. Tradition makes her a British princess, but in fact she was born in Asia Minor of humble parents, traditionally described as innkeepers. There are many variants and short forms of the name. **Ellen,** sometimes ELAINE, and **Elena** are early forms of the name, the last giving **Lena.** These are now used independently. **Nell, Nellie, Nelly** are pet forms. **Ilona,** sometimes found in this country, is a Hungarian form of the name, as is **Ilana,** while **Elen** is Welsh and Elena the Spanish form. See further under ELEANOR.

Helga see OLGA

Heloise
Abelard and Heloise were two twelfth-century lovers whose real-life story, preserved in the letters they wrote to each other after they were parted, rivals anything to be met with in fiction. Despite the fact that Abelard had secretly married Heloise, he was castrated by her guardian for having seduced her, and they each ended their lives as the heads of learned religious institutions, only to be reunited in death, when Heloise's body was buried next to Abelard's grave. Heloise is also spelt in the French manner **Héloise** or **Héloïse,** and is frequently found in the form **Eloise** or **Eloïse,** or more rarely **Eloisa.** The origin of the name is disputed. Some derive it from an old German name **Helewise,** used in England until at least the thirteenth century; others argue that it is a form of the name Louise (see LEWIS), via the Provençal form **Aloys, Aloyse,** which may also have been an influence on LOIS.

Henry, Henrietta
Henry comes from an old Germanic name meaning 'home-rule'. It was brought to England by the Normans in the French form *Henri*, and the nasalized French pronunciation is reflected in the form **Harry** which comes from it, and which was the normal English form of the name until the seventeenth century; it is currently the more popular given form in the UK: possible influences include Prince Harry, and the leading pupil at Hogwarts School of Witchcraft and Wizardry, Harry Potter, in the popular *Harry Potter* series of novels by J. K. Rowling. Use of 'Harry', and the pet form **Hal,** is well illustrated in Shakespeare's *Henry IV.* **Hank** is a pet form more often met with in North America. **Harrison,** the surname meaning 'son of Harry', has shown a recent increase in popularity as a first name.

   The feminine forms of the name do not seem to have been used until after the marriage of Charles I in 1625 to the French princess **Henriette** Marie, who became known in this country as **Henrietta** Maria. These names were soon anglicized to **Harriet,** and developed the short forms **Hatty, Hetty** and **Etta.** (See also HAYLEY.)

Hephzibah
This is a Hebrew name meaning 'my delight is in her'. In the Bible it is mentioned as the name of the mother of one of the kings of Judah, but more importantly is used by the prophet Isaiah as a symbol of Jerusalem. The name is more often found in the United States than in Britain, as is the name **Beulah** ('married'), which occurs in the same verse of Isaiah. The name is usually pronounced, and sometimes spelt, **Hepzibah,** and has a short form **Hepsie.** It is probably best known in this country through the pianist Hephzibah Menuhin.

Herbert

Herbert is a Germanic name meaning 'army-bright'. It is found very early in the form of Charibert, king of the Franks from 561 to 567, whose daughter BERTHA married the pagan king of Kent. It was she who welcomed St Augustine of Canterbury to convert the English (see AUGUSTUS). The name more or less died out in the Middle Ages, but was revived again in the nineteenth century, possibly in connection with the aristocratic surname of Herbert. It shares **Bert** and **Bertie** as short forms with other names ending -bert, and **Herb** and **Herbie** are also used.

Hereward see HOWARD

Herman

This is a Germanic name meaning 'army man'. It is sometimes spelt in the German manner, **Hermann**. The French form of the name is **Armand**, and from this come the unusual feminine names **Armine** and **Arminel(le)**, the latter regarded as a local name in Devon and Cornwall. **Hermine**, another unusual feminine name, also found as **Ermin**, **Ermine** or **Erminia**, comes from the same Indo-European root, but via the Latin family name of *Herminius*, although it has no doubt been influenced by the Germanic forms.

Hermione

This is a Greek name, meaning 'dedicated to the god Hermes'. The best-known Hermione in Greek legend was the daughter of HELEN; she was first unhappily married to Achilles' son Neoptolemus, and then to her cousin Orestes. The Athenian tragedian Euripides wrote a play on the subject, and the name probably became more widely known in the seventeenth century through the French playwright Racine's *Andromache* (1667), which adapted Euripides' work. In the twentieth century, the name was given publicity by two comic actresses, Hermione Baddeley and Hermione Gingold. Shakespeare used Hermione in *A Winter's Tale* and he introduced another form of the name, **Hermia**, in *A Midsummer Night's Dream*, but this name has not been much used by parents. Hermione has recently had new publicity in the popular *Harry Potter* series of novels by J. K. Rowling, as the name of Harry Potter's friend at Hogwarts School of Witchcraft and Wizardry.

Hernando see FERDINAND

Hester see ESTHER

Hetty see ESTHER, HENRY

Heulwen

This is a Welsh girl's name, well used at the moment. It means 'sunshine'.

Hew see HUGH

Hieronymus see JEROME

Hilary

Hilary means 'cheerful' and was the name of St Hilary of Poitiers, a theologian and writer of the fourth century. Since his feast day falls in mid-January, his name was given to the 'Hilary Term' of the Law Courts and some universities, which begins at about that time. The name is used for both sexes, although there is also an uncommon feminine form, **Hilaria**. The author **Hilaire** Belloc (1870–1953) shows the French masculine form of the name. In the United States the spelling **Hillary** is usual, but in Great Britain the original spelling is the norm.

Hilda

An Old English name meaning 'battle', Hilda was the name of a Northumbrian princess who founded the monastery at Whitby where the seventh-century cowherd **Cædmon** is supposed to have written the first religious poetry in English. Hilda was a much respected woman who acted as an adviser to both kings and bishops. The name died out after the Conquest along with other Anglo-Saxon names, but was revived in the nineteenth century. It is occasionally spelt **Hylda**. From the same root comes the German saint's name **Hildegard**. There has recently been a revival of interest in the work of St Hildegard of Bingen (1098–1179), who was a visionary, theologian, writer on science, poet and very fine composer, and took an active part in the controversies of her day. This name has always been more common in the United States, particularly among those of German descent, than in Great Britain.

Hillary see HILARY

Hiram

Hiram is a Hebrew name meaning 'brother of the exalted one'. It was the name of a king of Tyre who was an ally of King DAVID and his son SOLOMON, and who sent building materials for the Temple at Jerusalem. It was one of the biblical names which became popular in the seventeenth century, was taken over by early settlers to America, and also had a certain popularity in the nineteenth century.

Hodge see ROGER

Holly

Holly is a plant name which only came into use at the beginning of the twentieth century. It is sometimes chosen because a child was born around Christmas, and was particularly popular in the UK in the 1990s.

Homer

This is the name of the great Greek poet used as a first name. It is rarely found in the UK, but is well used in the United States, where there is a long tradition of naming after heroes of the past. The British have not been reluctant to name their children after classical writers such as HORACE and TERENCE, but for some reason Homer has never caught on.

Honoria

Honoria means 'honour, honourable'. *Honorius* was a title given to Emperor Theodosius the Great, and his niece was named Honoria. The name is also found in the forms **Honor** and **Honora**. In England a form **Anora**, **Annora(h)** or **Anorah** developed, while in Ireland, where the name was particularly popular, it became NORAH. In Welsh the masculine form of the name developed into **Emyr** and **Ynyr**.

Hope
One of the abstract nouns that were introduced as names by the Puritans, Hope was originally used for both sexes but is now confined to women. NADIA has the same meaning.

Horace
Horace is the name of the great first-century BC Latin poet, used as a first name. It was introduced during the Renaissance revival of interest in all things classical. In the form **Horatio** it was the name of Admiral Nelson, but, surprisingly, even his fame did not make this form widely used. However, **Horatia**, the name given to his daughter by Lady Hamilton, and also used for his god-daughters, did have a certain vogue.

Hortensia
This is the feminine form of another Latin family name meaning 'gardener'. **Hortense** is widely used in France, and the name has sometimes been used elsewhere in this form.

Houston see DALLAS

Howard
The aristocratic surname Howard was one of many adopted by parents as a first name in the nineteenth century. The origin of the surname is confused. In some cases it may be a form of the occupational term 'hayward', a man whose job it was to make sure that the hedges were kept cattle-proof; in others it may be an old Germanic name meaning 'heart-protector'. In the past it was also derived from the Old English name **Hereward**, famous as the name of one of the few to mount a guerrilla campaign against the invading Normans in 1066, but this is not now accepted. **Howie** is the most usual short form.

Howel, Howell see HYWEL

Hubert
Hubert comes from a Germanic root and means 'bright-mind'. It is the name of an eighth-century saint who is the patron of hunters, having, according to his legend, been converted to the devout life as a young man by a vision of a stag with a crucifix between its antlers. The stag is his emblem in art. (See also EUSTACE.)

Hugh
Hugh comes from the Germanic word for 'mind' or 'thought', also found in the name HUBERT, and was introduced by the Normans. The city of Lincoln can boast two St Hughs. One (c. 1135–1200) was a remarkable bishop of Lincoln, famous as much for his bold fights for justice for the common man as for his pet swan, which was reputed to be so fierce that no one else could come near him, but which was so affectionate towards Hugh that it would nestle with its head up his sleeve. The other, 'Little St Hugh', is probably apocryphal, and the

sensational story of his 'martyrdom' at the hands of the local Jews was used as an excuse for much anti-Semitism. **Hew** and **Huw** are Welsh forms of the name, and the Latin form **Hugo** is not uncommon. Pet forms are **Hughie, Huey** and **Hughy**. The Irish name **Ulick** may well come from the same source – from the Viking name *Hugleik* ('mind' + 'reward'), although it has also been explained as a pet form of Uilliam, the Irish form of WILLIAM. In Ireland Ulick is sometimes anglicized as ULYSSES.

Humphrey

Humphrey is another Germanic name popularized by the Normans. The meaning of the first element of the name is uncertain, but the second element means 'peace'. **Humph** and **Hump** are used as short forms. **Humbert** is thought to come from the same unknown root as Humphrey, the second element meaning 'bright'.

Hunter

An occupational surname used as a first name, Hunter seems to have come into use first in Scotland, and is currently quite fashionable in the United States.

Huw see HUGH

Hyacinth see IRIS

Hylda see HILDA

Hywel

This is a Welsh name meaning 'conspicuous, eminent'. It is also spelt **Howel** or **Howell**, which reflect its pronunciation. Its pet form is **Hywyn** and there is a feminine **Hywela**. It is found as early as the ninth century, and King **Hoel** of Brittany, King Arthur's relative and ally in the legends, is probably the same name. It has become well known to the general public through the actor Hywel Bennett.

Ii

Iago see JAMES

Iain, Ian see JOHN

Ianthe see VIOLET

Ianto see JAMES

Ib, Ibby see ISABEL

Ibrahim see ABRAHAM

Ida

Ida is a girl's name which was very popular in the nineteenth century and the first part of the twentieth, as part of the revival of medieval names. Tennyson used it in the middle of the century as the name of the heroine of his poem mocking female pretensions to education, 'The Princess' (1847), and the name was given further currency by the adaptation of this work by Gilbert and Sullivan as *Princess Ida* (1870). It is a Germanic name, but its meaning is obscure. It probably has some connection with a word meaning 'work'. In Ireland, in the forms Ida, **Ita** or **Ide**, it comes from the Irish word for 'thirst', and was the name of a sixth-century Irish saint renowned for her austerity.

Idonea

This unusual name is associated with the north of England. It has been suggested that it comes from a Latin adjective meaning 'fit, suitable', but, since the name is not used in countries where the language is descended from Latin, this seems unlikely. A much more attractive idea is that it is a form of the name of the Norse goddess Iduna, the guardian of the Apples of Youth, the eating of which kept the gods young. When she was abducted by the giants, the gods experienced the effects of age for the first time, although their youth was restored when they won her and the apples back. It also appears in the form **Idony**, and the rare name **Idina** may come from it or be a form of IDA.

Idris

This is one of the more popular Welsh names, and has a long history. The name, meaning 'ardent or impulsive lord', was held by Idris the Giant, who was killed in 632. He has entered Welsh legend as an astronomer and magician, and one of the highest mountains in Wales, Cader Idris ('Idris's Chair'), was supposed to have been his observatory. From the same root comes **Idwal** (a combination of words meaning 'lord' and 'rampart'), probably signifying 'defender', another ancient name, having been held by two tenth-century kings of Gwynedd.

Ieasha, Iesha see AISHA

Iestin, Iestyn see JUSTIN

Ieuan, Ifan see JOHN

Ifor see IVO

Ignatius

This old Latin name means 'fiery', but its use is almost entirely in association with the Spanish saint Ignatius Loyola, who founded the Jesuit order in the sixteenth century. The Spanish form of the name is **Inigo**, and this was the form given to the Catholic architect Inigo Jones (1573–1652). The association of 'Jones' with Wales has led to Inigo being claimed and used as a Welsh name. Inigo, long out of use among English speakers, has begun to reappear as a given name outside Wales.

Ike see ISAAC

Ilana see HELEN

Illtyd, Illtud

St Illtyd was an outstanding Welsh saint of the fifth to sixth centuries, famous as a scholar and teacher, the founder of a school where numerous other Welsh saints studied. Legend credits him with introducing the plough to the Welsh, who hitherto had only used spades to turn the soil. His name is made up of elements meaning 'multitude' and 'land, people'.

Ilona see HELEN

Ilsa, Ilse see ELIZABETH

Imelda

The name of a medieval saint, Imelda is the Italian form of the Germanic name **Irmhild**, meaning 'universal battle'. It has never been a particularly common name, although not unpopular in Ireland.

Imogen

The heroine of Shakespeare's *Cymbeline* owes her name to a misprint. The name first seems to appear in the eleventh-century *History of the Kings of Britain* by Geoffrey of Monmouth as *Ignoge*, wife of Brutus, the mythical first king of Britain. She reappears in Spenser's *Faerie Queene* as 'fayre Inogene of Italy'. Shakespeare seems to have used the 'n' spelling, for in a contemporary description of the play the name is spelt Innogen, but the form Imogen is found in the First Folio, the earliest printed text of the play. The form **Imogene** is occasionally found.

Ina
This was originally a pet form of various names ending -ina, such as Georgina, Edwina, and so on, which has since come to be used as a name in its own right. In Ireland it is the name of two saints, and probably represents a local form of the name AGNES.

India
This is simply the name of the country used as a girl's name. It may owe its use to the appearance of a character of that name in Margaret Mitchell's *Gone With the Wind* (1936), and it was the name given to the model India Hicks, granddaughter of Lord Mountbatten, the last Viceroy of India. Its spread may also be connected with the interest in India and its culture of the Hippy generation of the 1970s. The name India comes from the Sanskrit word for river, and is connected with the name of the sacred river of India, the Indus. **China**, often respelled **Chynna**, is similarly recorded as a girl's name. The place name China ultimately comes from the word *Qin*, the name of the dynasty that ruled China from 221 to 206 BC.

Ines, Inez see AGNES

Ingrid
This is a Scandinavian name with connections with the pagan past. Ing was a Scandinavian god of peace and plenty, known also to the Anglo-Saxons. Ingrid has been explained in two ways: either it means 'Ing's ride or steed', probably a reference to the sacred golden boar associated with the god, or else it means 'beautiful under the protection of Ing'. The fame of the actress Ingrid Bergman undoubtedly played a large part in turning this into an international name. **Ingeborg** and its diminutives **Inge** and **Inga** (also used for Ingrid) come for the same root and mean 'Ing's protection'.

Inigo see IGNATIUS

Innes see ANGUS

Ioan see JOHN

Iolanthe see VIOLET

Iolo
This is the more widely used pet form of the Welsh name **Iorwerth**, formed from elements meaning 'lord' and 'value, worth'. For some unknown reason it has been used in the past as the Welsh equivalent of Edward, although there is no known connection between the names. There is a less common feminine form, **Iola**.

Iona
The Hebridean island of Iona was already an ancient religious site when St Columba (see MALCOLM) settled there in 563 and founded its famous

monastery, which formed a base for the spread of Christianity through Scotland and the north of England. The island is still an important religious centre as well as a popular place to visit for its beauty and ancient ruins, so it is not surprising that a place name with so many associations, and with a form that fits in so well with other female names, should have come into use, at least by the beginning of the twentieth century. Attempts have been made to link the name with other names beginning Ion- from the Greek root meaning VIOLET; but, although these may have helped in the acceptance of the name, the island seems a much more likely source. Its name seems to have come from a misreading of the original Celtic name which meant 'yew island', although the current form of the name in Gaelic just means 'island'.

Ione see VIOLET

Iorwerth see IOLO

Ira
A Hebrew name meaning 'watchful', Ira is found in the Bible as the name of one of King David's priests. It is little used in the UK, possibly because it is so easily mistaken for a feminine name, but is a part of the Puritan heritage of biblical names in the USA. The best-known modern holder is probably Ira Gershwin, lyricist to so many of his brother George's best tunes.

Irene
The old three-syllable pronunciation of this name comes from the original Greek, where the word means 'peace'; the shorter, two-syllable form is a modern pronunciation based on the spelling. Irene was the name of an early fourth-century martyr whose legend, probably embroidered, tells of her being confined, but unmolested, in a brothel before being burnt. It was also the name of a number of Byzantine empresses, one of whom, in the eighth century, managed to reign in her own right, even though holding on to the throne meant putting out the eyes of her son. The name is also spelt **Eirene**, while **Irena** reflects the Slavic form. **Renie** is a pet form.

Iris
In Greek mythology Iris is a goddess who acts as messenger for the gods. She uses the rainbow as her bridge between the heavens and earth. It is from the colours of this rainbow that the flower gets its name. The Romans used the name **Hyacinth** for what we would call an iris. In myth Hyacinth was the name of a particularly beautiful boy, accidentally killed by the god Apollo, and then transformed into a flower. It has been used as a boy's name in the past, but is rarly found now. It is, however, sometimes used as one of the flower names for girls. In France and Spain Hyacinth became **Jacinthe** and **Jacinth** (with **Jacinth** and **Jacinta** as variants), which again were originally boys' names, but are now mainly feminine. These are rare names, but are sometimes found in Ireland.

Irma, Irm(e)gard see EMMA

Irving
This Scottish surname comes from the place and river name meaning 'west

river'. It is also found in the forms **Irvin** and **Irvine**. The very similar-sounding **Irwin** or **Erwin** technically come from a different root, an Anglo-Saxon name meaning 'boar-friend' (and hence possibly linked to the sacred role of the boar mentioned under INGRID), but in practice the two names are often treated as variants of each other.

Isa see ISABEL

Isaac
We are told in the Old Testament that when Abraham was 100 years old, and his wife Sarah was 90, God told him that they would have a son. Abraham's reaction to the idea of having a child at their age was to laugh, and when a son was born he was named Isaac, which is Hebrew for 'he laughed'. In Britain the name has tended to be associated with the Jewish community, but in the United States it has been more widely used, and there has been something of a revival of the name, in its pet form, **Zac** (but see also ZACHARY). **Ike** is another pet form, but the use of Ike as a nickname for President Dwight D. Eisenhower is unconnected with the name Isaac. The seventeenth-century fishing enthusiast **Izaak** Walton, author of *The Compleat Angler* (1653), illustrates another spelling of the name.

Isabel, Isobel
These properly belong with ELIZABETH, with which Isabel was interchangeable from the twelfth until at least the sixteenth century. Short forms are **Bel**, **Bell**, **Belle**, **Ella** and **Izzy**. In France the name, often in the forms **Isabelle** or **Isabeau**, all but replaced Elizabeth, while **Isabella** was the form adopted in Spain. The Old Alliance between France and Scotland against the English may have helped Isabel become particularly popular in Scotland, where it developed a wide variety of pet forms including **Ib**, **Ibby**, **Isa**, **Belag**, **Tib**, **Tibbie** and **Tibby**. In Gaelic the name became **Iseabel**, from which comes the form **Ishbel**, and which led to such wild variations as Easabell, Easybell and Eysie. Forms such as **Ysabel** are sometimes found.

Isadora, Isadore see ISIDORE

Isaiah
This is a Hebrew name meaning 'salvation of the Lord', and the name of one of the great prophets of the Old Testament. It has recently become fashionable in the USA, sometimes in the form **Isaias**.

Iseabel see ISABEL

Iseult see ISOLDA

Ishbel see ISABEL

Isidore, Isidora
This ancient Greek name has been interpreted as meaning 'gift of Isis', an Egyptian goddess who was widely worshipped in the Mediterranean region in late classical times. It is a name particularly associated with Spain, thanks to St Isidore of Seville (c. 560–636), who wrote one of the first ever encyclopaedias –

a fascinating combination of knowledge from the classical world, some of which would otherwise have been lost, and arrant nonsense – which formed the basis of much medieval learning. **Isodor** and **Isadore** are variants of the masculine form of the name, and it is shortened to **Izzy**. **Isadora** Duncan made the alternative spelling of the female form widely known through her innovative dancing and scandalous personal life.

Isla
This is a Scottish river name that means 'swiftly flowing'. However, the Hebridean island of **Islay** is also used as a first name (for both sexes, although Isla is only used for girls), and since Isla represents the normal local pronunciation of Islay (the 's' is silent in both cases), it may be that in origin Isla is, like IONA, an island name.

Isleen see ASHLING

Isobel see ISABEL

Isodor see ISIDORE

Isolda
This name occurs in numerous different spellings and forms including **Iseult, Isold, Isolde, Isolt, Ysold, Ysolda, Ysolde, Yseult, Yseut** with **Esyllt** as the Welsh form; the variety reflecting the fame of the name through Europe. Its exact meaning has been much debated, without any convincing result. In the medieval love-tragedy of *Tristan and Isolda*, she is the heroine torn between her duties as a wife and queen and her unquenchable love for TRISTAN brought about by the accidental drinking of a love potion. Thus she becomes a symbol of undying and unhappy love. The name was popular until the sixteenth century, then went into a decline until a mild revival from the end of the nineteenth century, due in part to Celtic nationalism and in part to the success of Wagner's opera. (See also BRONWEN.)

Ivan, Iwan see JOHN

Ivor, Ivo, Ifor
This is a confused and confusing group of names. Strictly speaking Ivor is interpreted as a Teutonic name probably connected with the god Ing (see under INGRID), Ivo is the Latinate form of Yves (see under YVONNE) and Ifor is the Welsh for 'lord'. However, these three names have become inextricably tangled, each influencing the other from an early date, and it is not really possible to draw any hard lines between the three.

Ivy
One of the plant names introduced in the nineteenth century, and popular through to the 1920s in the UK, Ivy is not much used today. Its introduction may have been helped by a feeling that there was a gap left by there being no female equivalent of the Ivor group of names, although there is a rarely found name **Iva**, which may be a feminine of IVOR or of Ivan (see JOHN).

Izaac see ISAAC

Izzy see ISABEL, ISIDORE

Jj

Jabez

According to the Old Testament Jabez was so-called by his mother 'because I bare him with sorrow'. He is a minor character in the Bible, with a reputation for being an honourable man.

Jacalyn see JAMES

Jace see JASON

Jacinta, Jacinth, Jacintha, Jacinthe see IRIS

Jack see JOHN

Jackeline, Jackelyn see JAMES

Jackie, Jacky see JAMES, JOHN

Jacob

Jacob may actually go back to an ancient Babylonian name meaning 'God rewards', but it is understood in the Bible to mean 'supplanter', from the story that Jacob got his elder twin brother **Esau** to sell him his birthright for 'a mess of pottage'. **Jake**, which has recently become more popular than its original in the UK, is a pet form, which is found as **Jaikie** in Scotland. There is a rare feminine **Jacoba**; and the form **Jacobina** was in the past a popular name for the daughters of Scottish Jacobites. JAMES is a form of the same name.

Jacqueline, Jacques see JAMES

Jacquetta, Jacqui see JAMES

Jacy see JAY

Jade

Although there is a long tradition of using jewels as girls' names, this one seems to have been in use only in the last 30 or so years. It may have been popularized by its use by the singer Mick Jagger for his first daughter. The word 'jade' comes from the Spanish word *jada* meaning 'colic', because it was anciently believed to help cure that condition. **Jayde** is an occasional variant, and **Jadene** may be an elaboration. (See also under JEWELL.)

Jago see JAMES

Jaikie see JACOB

Jake see JACOB, JESSE

Jamal

This Arab name, meaning 'beautiful', has been popular in recent years in the USA, particularly among Black Muslims. It appears in a wide variety of spellings, most prominently the original Jamal, **Jamel** and **Jamil**, and has developed a variant **Jamar**. Although it can be used for both sexes, **Jamil(l)a** is the most usual feminine form, which can also appear in the North African form **Djamila**.

James

In Latin the name JACOB occurs in two forms: *Jacobus*, from which we get Jacob, and *Jacomus*, from which we get James. The two forms have proved useful for distinguishing the Old Testament patriarch Jacob from the New Testament saints James the Less, the brother of Jesus, and James the Great, the son of ZEBEDEE. The shrine of St James the Great at Santiago de Compostella in Spain was one of the most popular places of pilgrimage throughout the Middle Ages, and this has resulted in James, in its various forms, being one of the most widely spread names in western Europe. In the British Isles alone it occurs as **Hamish** in Scotland; **Shamus** or **Seamus** in Ireland, with the form **Seumus**, or less commonly **Seumas**, popular with Scots Gaelic speakers; as **Iago**, with its pet form **Ianto**, in Wales; and **Jago** in Cornwall. **Jim** (**Jimmie**, **Jimmy**) and **Jamie** are the commonest pet forms of James, while **Jem** and **Jemmie** were common in the past.

The name has also been productive of feminine forms, although these are mostly derived from the French form of James, **Jacques**. **Jacqueline** is the most usual one; it is found in a very wide variety of spellings including **Jackeline**, **Jackelyn**, **Jacalyn**, **Jaqueline**, and shortened to **Jackie**, **Jacky**, **Jacqui**, and so on. **Jacquetta** is another form of the name, known in this country since at least the fifteenth century when Jacquetta of Luxemburg was bigamously married to Humphrey, Duke of Gloucester, then *de facto* ruler of England, as part of her long, brave, but ultimately unsuccessful attempt to inherit her duchy in her own right rather than have it pass to a distant male relative. By yet another marriage she was grandmother to the Princes in the Tower. Shakespeare uses a further form of the name, **Jacquenetta**, in *Love's Labour's Lost*, but this has never really caught on. From the male form of the name comes the Scottish **Jamesina**, while since the 1960s **Jamie** has been popular as a girl's name, particularly in the USA, but is as likely to be found used of boys in the UK. **Jamesha** (**Jamisha**, **Jameisha**, etc) is a development of the name in use among Black Americans, perhaps a blend of Jamie with AISHA.

Jan see JOHN, JANE

Jane, Jean, Joan

All the names in this large group are feminine forms of the name JOHN, the first two coming from the early French form *Jehane*, the third from the Latin *Johanna*. All three have developed a large number of variants and pet forms. **Joan** seems to have been the earliest form of the name. It gives us the forms nearer to its Latin root such as **Johanna** and **Joanna**; is sometimes spelt **Joanne** and has the pet form **Joanie**. **Jane** seems to have come into use in the fifteenth century and developed into **Janet**, **Janette**, **Janetta**, with pet forms **Netta** and **Nettie**. In the twentieth century all sorts of variants have become popular, such as **Janine** and **Janina**, **Janice** and **Janis**, **Jana** (particularly in Ireland), **Jan** and **Jancis**, which was made better known through its use for a character in Mary Webb's highly successful novel *Precious Bane* (1924). Pet forms include **Janie**, **Janey**, **Jen** and **Jenny** (see also JENNIFER), and the name is also spelt **Jayne**. **Jean** started life as the Scottish form of Jane or Joan, and has given rise under French influence to **Jeanette** or **Jeanet** and **Janetta**. **Jeannie** is the usual pet form, but in Scotland **Jess**, **Jessie**, **Jessy** (see also JESSICA) are used, as well as **Jinty**, **Janny**, **Jancey** and **Jinsie**. The Spanish form of the name **Juanita** and its pet forms **Nita** and **Juana** are also found, mostly in the USA. More recently still, elaborations such as **Janelle**, **Jonelle** and **Janessa** have made their mark.

The Celtic languages have also adopted this group of names, in forms in which the 's' is pronounced as a 'sh', the nearest the Celtic languages come to a 'j' sound, giving us **Sian** (**Sîan**) in Welsh, with pet forms **Siani** or **Shani** (although this can also be a name that bearers derive from an African word meaning 'wonderful') for Jane; **Sheena** (also spelt **Sine**) with its variant **Shona**, in Gaelic for Jane and **Sinead** as the Irish, **Seonaid** as the Scottish Gaelic form of Janet, and **Siobhan** for Joan. Even in Ireland, Siobhan can have a variety of spellings, such as **Shivaun**, while in the United States it appears in a bewildering range of forms, most often **Shavon**, but including forms such as **Chavon** and **Chivonne**. In Welsh Joan becomes **Siwan**. Siwan was the name given to the illegitimate daughter of King John of England, the wife of Llywelyn the Great of Wales in the early thirteenth century. This Siwan was the subject of a play written by Saunders Lewis and performed in Welsh in 1954, and later translated and performed in English. This led to a great revival of the name in Wales.

Jared

In the book of Genesis Jared is the father of ENOCH, but the only information we are given about him is that he lived for 962 years. The name probably means 'a rose' and is therefore unusual in being a masculine flower name. It was used by the Puritans, but then went into decline and was used only occasionally until a revival in the 1960s. In recent years it has become very popular in the United States and Australia. **Jarrad**, **Jareth**, **Jarrath**, **Jered** are variants, with the forms **Jarett** and **Jarrod** also being used, although technically these come from surnames derived from Garret (see GERALD).

Jarvis see GERVASE

Jasmine

The name of the sweet-scented jasmine flower can be traced back to ancient Persia, where scented oil was made from the plant. The Arabic forms of the name, **Yasmin** and **Yasmine**, are also sometimes used. **Jessamy** is an old form of the word, which was once synonymous with a fop; and **Jessamine**, with a pet form **Jess**, was also found. Nowadays **Jasmin** and **Jasmina** are the most likely variants.

Jason
Jason is the Greek form given to the Hebrew JOSHUA. There are at least four Jasons in the Bible, and it is also the name of the reputed author of the Old Testament book of *Ecclesiasticus*, so that when it was adopted in the seventeenth century it was thought of as a biblical name. However, it is highly unlikely that when the name came back into fashion in the 1960s, parents associated it with anyone from the past other than the hero of Greek myth, leader of the Argonauts and winner of the Golden Fleece. The name means 'healer'. **Jace** is a pet form sometimes used as an independent name.

Jasper
Jasper is the English form of the traditional name of one of the three Magi (the others being **Balthazar**, which is very occasionally found, and **Melchior**) and as such comes appropriately from the Persian meaning 'master of the treasure'. **Caspar**, **Casper** or **Kasper** are the German forms of the name, and **Gaspar** and **Gaspard** the French.

Javon, Javonne see YVONNE

Jay, Jaye
Now established as an independent name, in the past this was often just a pet form of any name beginning with J. It can also be derived from the surname, which in its turn was originally a nickname, implying that the person so-called was a chatterer, from the noise made by the bird. It is used for both sexes, but is most frequently male, with **Jaya** an occasional feminine variant. The recent girl's name **Jacy** looks and sounds as if it is from a similar source, the initials J.C., but may be a development of Jace, the short form of JASON, for which there is otherwise no feminine form.

Jayde see JADE

Jayne see JANE

Jean see JANE

Jeana see GINA

Jeanet, Jeanette, Jeannie see JANE

Jeanna see GINA

Jedidiah
This is another Old Testament masculine name adopted by the Puritans and more commonly used in the United States. It means 'beloved of the Lord'. **Jedediah** is an alternative spelling, while the short form **Jed** seems to have become a stock name for minor characters in Westerns.

Jeff, Jeffrey see GEOFFREY

Jem see JAMES

Jemima
The biblical Jemima was the eldest daughter of JOB. She was born after her father's return to prosperity, so escaped the calamities which befell him. We are told that 'in all the land were no women found so fair as the daughters of Job', which would support those who want to interpret the name as meaning 'fair as the day' rather than the more usual 'dove'. **Mima** is an occasional short form. (See further under KEZIAH.)

Jemma see GEMMA

Jemmie see JAMES

Jen, Jennie see JANE, JENNIFER

Jennifer
This is the Cornish form of **Guenevere** or **Guinevere**. The Welsh form of the name is **Gwenhwyfar**, meaning 'fair' or 'white' and 'smooth, yielding'. This was shortened in Wales to forms such as **Gaenor, Gaynor** and **Geunor**, which then spread to England. In Scotland it became **Vanora**, and in Cornwall Jennifer or **Jenifer**. Although it is possible to find examples of the name being used, for example, at the end of the nineteenth century, it was for a long time a rare name, regarded as strictly local, until it became fashionable in the 1930s, possibly as a result of its use for characters in plays by George Bernard Shaw and Noel Coward. It has remained popular ever since. Short forms are **Jen, Jennie** and **Jenny**, which was earlier used as a pet form of JANE and Janet. The recent popularity of **Jenna**, another Cornish form of the name, can no doubt be attributed to the exposure given to it on the TV 'soap' *Dallas*, while **Jenae** is a new name which has the appearance of a blend between Jenny and a name like Renée but which may just be a respelling of Jenny.

Jenny see JANE, JENNIFER

Jered see JARED

Jeremy
Jeremy is the English form of **Jeremiah**, the Old Testament prophet whose dire warnings and reproofs to the people of his times gave rise to the term 'jeremiad'. **Jeremias**, the Greek form of the name, is occasionally found. The pet form **Jerry** is shared with a number of other names. **Jerrica**, used for girls in the USA, looks like a blend of Jerry and Erica (see ERIC), while the new masculine name **Jerrell** or **Jerryl** looks like a blend of Jerry and **Daryl**.

Jermaine see GERMAINE

Jerome
This comes from a pre-Christian Greek name meaning 'sacred name', which was adopted by Christians in honour of St Jerome (c. 342–420), the hermit and great

Bible scholar whose translation of the Bible into Latin was used by the Catholic Church until recently. The Latin form of St Jerome's name was **Hieronymus**, as in the painter Hieronymus Bosch, while the Native American chief **Geronimo** shows another form of the name. **Jerry** is used as a short form of Jerome.

Jerrell, Jerryl, Jerrica see JEREMY

Jerry see GERALD, JEREMY, JEROME

Jervis see GERVASE

Jess see JANE, JASMINE, JESSE, JESSICA

Jessamine, Jessamy see JASMINE

Jesse

In the Bible Jesse, whose name means 'God is', is the father of DAVID. He is regarded as the founder of the family which culminated in Jesus Christ, and 'Jesse windows' can sometimes be found in medieval churches showing this descent. **Jess** (and occasionally **Jake**, although this is more usual for JACOB) are used as pet forms.

Jessica

Jessica is a difficult name. There have been at least half a dozen different attempts to derive it from different Hebrew words, of which the most convincing is that it means 'God is looking'. A recent researcher has suggested that it is in fact a name made up by Shakespeare for the character in *The Merchant of Venice*, based on a name such as JESSE, and that while the first part of her name is Jewish, the ending is Venetian, a transition which reflects her role in the play. Whatever its origin, the name has been very popular on both sides of the Atlantic since the 1980s. **Jess** and **Jessie** are used as pet forms.

Jessie, Jessy see JANE, JESSICA

Jesus see JOSHUA

Jet see JEWELL

Jethro

This is another biblical name, that of the father-in-law of Moses, meaning 'preeminence, excellence'. It belongs with the other Old Testament names introduced in the sixteenth century. Its most outstanding holder was Jethro Tull, the eighteenth-century agricultural reformer whose name was adopted by a 1970s pop group.

Jewell

Also spelt **Jewel** and **Jewelle**, this name came into use in the 1920s when exotic precious stones for women's names came into fashion; some women, such as **Emerald** Cunard, even went so far as to change their names to suit the fashion. Jewell is now rarely used, but there has been something of a revival of precious names, such as AMBER, particularly in fiction. A number of stone names will be found under their own entries, but unusual ones that have been recorded include **Opal, Amethyst, Jet, Onyx** and **Topaz.**

Jill, Jillian, Jilly see JULIA

Jim, Jimmie, Jimmy see JAMES

Jinny see VIRGINIA

Jinsie, Jinty see JANE

Jo, Joe
As a masculine name this is a pet form of JOSEPH; for women, it is a form of names such as Joanna (see JANE) and Josephine (see JOSEPH). It is also well used in blends and compounds such as **Billy-Joe** (for both sexes) and **Jolene** or **Joleen.**

Joan, Joanna, Joanne see JANE

Job
Job is interpreted as the Hebrew for 'persecuted', reflecting the afflictions, ranging from the deaths of his family to a plague of boils, sent by God in the Old Testament *Book of Job* to test this 'perfect and upright' man. He is eventually restored to greater prosperity than ever. It has pet forms **Joby, Jobie, Joabee, Jobey.**

Jocelyn, Joscelin
Experts try to distinguish between the two forms of this name, deriving Jocelyn from the Latin for 'sportive' and Joscelin from the Latin for 'just', the same root as for JUSTIN. The name has also been derived from the word for 'a Goth'. In practice the two forms are so confused that it is pointless to try to distinguish them. Jocelyn or **Jocelin** was a common name for men in the Middle Ages, as in the chronicler Jocelin de Brakelond, but the name is now uncommon for men. The form **Joycelin** is also found, possibly through combination with the name JOYCE.

Jock, Jockie see JOHN

Jodi(e), Jody see JUDITH

Joe, Joey see JO, JOSEPH

Joel
The name of one of the Old Testament prophets, Joel means 'Jehovah is God'. It was introduced into England by the Puritans and taken by them to North America, where it has been more used than in Great Britain. A recent increase of interest in the name may owe something to the success of the actor Joel Grey. In France a feminine form **Joelle** is also used.

Johanna see JANE

John

Derived from the Hebrew meaning 'the Lord is gracious', John has remained one of the most popular names for boys since the early Middle Ages. It is the name of numerous saints, notably John the Baptist and John the Divine. As in the case of the feminine form JANE, the name has developed a wide variety of forms in the British Isles, the number being multiplied by duplicate forms derived from both the Latin form of the name *Johannes* found in the Bible, and the Norman-French form *Jehan* (modern French *Jean*) adopted from the Norman conquerors.

In Wales the name is found as **Ieuan, Ioan, Ifan** and **Iwan,** the latter two being anglicized to **Evan** and **Ewen,** and there is also a form which reflects the Welsh pronunciation of the English name, **Sion.** The Scots form of the name is **Ian** or **Iain,** as well as the archetypal **Jock** and **Jockie.** Ireland gives us **Sean,** with its various phonetic spellings **Shaun, Shawn** and **Shane** (which in turn have spawned feminine forms **Shauna** and **Shawndelle,** although the masculine forms are also now used for girls, and a feminine formed directly from Sean, **Seaneen,** has also been recorded), as well as the less frequent **Eoin,** which comes directly from the Latin. In the USA the name **DeShawn** has been a fashionable development among Blacks.

From further afield the Russian **Ivan** is sometimes used (although this can also represent a spelling of the the Welsh Ifan); **Jan** is a Germanic form of the name as well as being the traditional West Country pronunciation; and **Juan,** the Spanish form, is well used in the United States, and has also been elaborated into **DeJuan.**

Jack (derived via the old pet form **Jankin**) is a common pet form, and at the time of writing the most popular name for boys in the UK. **Johnnie** and **Jackie** are further pet forms. The spelling **Jon** is also used, although this properly belongs to the related JONATHAN. Sometimes a child is named directly after one of the saints and called **St John,** in which case the name is pronounced 'sin-jn'.

Joi, Joie see JOY

Joleen, Jolene see JO

Jolly, Jolyon see JULIA

Jon see JOHN, JONATHAN

Jonah, Jonas

The Old Testament Jonah, meaning 'dove, pigeon', has become such a byword for bad luck that only the most dismal of Puritans would want to saddle their child with such a burden. Consequently the New Testament Greek form of the name, Jonas (the father of Simon Peter), has always been much the commoner.

Jonathan

Jonathan means 'gift of God'. In the Bible Jonathan is the son of King Saul and loyal friend of David, whose lament on the death of Jonathan is justly famous. In the eighteenth century 'Brother Jonathan' was as widely recognized a reference to Americans as 'Uncle Sam' is today. The short form is **Jon** and the name is sometimes spelt **Jonathon.** The name seems never to have developed a feminine form, but DOROTHY and THEODORA have the same meaning.

Jonelle see JANE

Jonquil
One of the flower names introduced in the twentieth century and briefly popular in the 1940s and 1950s, Jonquil is little used for children today.

Jordan
It is hardly surprising that the name of the River Jordan, which means 'flowing down', with its strong associations with baptism, became a Christian name. It is recorded as a man's name from the thirteenth century onwards, but is now well used for both sexes. It can also be spelt **Jourdan**, **Jordin** or **Jordyn**, and there is a feminine form **Jo(u)rdana**.

Joscelin see JOCELYN

Joseph
This is a Hebrew name meaning 'increase, addition (to the family)'. In the Old Testament Joseph is the best beloved of the twelve sons of the patriarch JACOB, by whom he is given the coat of many colours. In the New Testament, Joseph is the husband of the Virgin Mary. In the USA the Spanish form, **José**, is well used. The feminine form of the name, **Josephine**, owes its popularity to Napoleon's wife, the Empress Josephine. Other feminine forms are **Josepha** and **Josephina** or **Josefina**. The pet forms **Jo** or **Joe**, **Jojo**, **Josie** or **Josey** are used for both sexes, but **Joey** is usually restricted to the masculine. **Fifi** is a French pet form of Josephine, **Pepita** the Spanish. **Josette** is another feminine form.

Joshua
A Hebrew name meaning 'the Lord is my Salvation', Joshua was the name of the great general who led the Israelites in the conquest of the Promised Land. **Josh** is used as a pet form. **Jesus** is the Greek alternative form of the same name, popular with Spanish speakers. Joshua has been a particularly popular name in recent years.

Josiah
Josiah was the name of one of the kings of Israel and means 'may the Lord heal'. Its most famous British holder was probably Josiah Wedgwood (1730–95), the founder of the china firm. The Greek form of the name, **Josias**, is also found, and pet forms are **Josh** and **Jos**.

Josie see JOSEPH

Josse see JOYCE

Jourdan, Jourdana see JORDAN

Joy
An abstract noun used as a first name, Joy therefore has connections with the name JOCELYN. It is found as early as the twelfth century, but did not come into its own until the nineteenth. The French spellings **Joie** and **Joi** are sometimes found, and **Joya** is an elaboration.

Joyce

This name is of disputed, or perhaps mixed, origin and is used for both sexes. Some derive it from a Breton St **Jodocus** (giving the French name **Josse**), others from the same root as JOY. It has been in and out of fashion over the centuries, and is now very rare as a man's name, although the author Joyce Cary (1888–1959) shows its survival into the twentieth century.

Joycelin see JOCELYN

Juan see JOHN

Juana, Juanita see JANE

Jude

This has never been a particularly popular name, although its use was given a boost by the Beatles song *Hey Jude*, and it is known in literature through Thomas Hardy's *Jude the Obscure* (1896), a story not likely to increase the name's popularity. **Yehudi** Menuhin shows the Hebrew form of the name, which means 'praise'. It is found in the Bible as **Judah**, and the Hellenized form of the name is found in Judas Iscariot. Jude was the form of the name used for the apostle who was elected to replace Judas, but neither this nor the attractive fact that St Jude is the patron saint of lost causes, has been enough to displace the taint to the name of the treacherous Judas. As a girl's name it is usually a short form of Judy.

Judith

Judith means 'a Jewess' and Judith is one of the great heroines in the Bible. When the Israelites are under attack she gets herself invited to spend the night with the enemy general Holofernes, but instead, after getting him drunk, she cuts his head off with his own sword. Inspired by her return to her native city with the head, the Israelites then fall upon the enemy and are victorious. Pet forms of the name, often used as names in their own right and currently more popular than the full form, are **Judy** or **Judie**, **Jodi**, **Jodie** or **Jody**.

Julia, Julian

The ancient Roman clan of the Julii claimed direct descent from **Venus** or **Aphrodite**, the goddess of love and generation, through her son Aeneas (see under ANGUS). We are told by the poet VIRGIL that Aeneas' son **Ascanius** had his name changed to *Iulus*, meaning 'the first down on the chin', because he had not yet reached the age of a full beard when he killed his first man. From him the Julii derived their name. Modern scholars have doubted this story, and have suggested that the name might be from the Latin *deus* ('god'). Julia is the feminine form of the name, and **Julie** is both its pet and the French form of the name, now as much used in its own right. **Juliet** and **Juliette** reflect the Italian form of the name, and their use derives from Shakespeare's heroine.

Julius, the masculine form of the name, is rarely found, but **Julian**, from the Latin adjective meaning 'connected with the Julii', is now quite common, sometimes shortened to **Jule** or **Jools** (influenced by the French form **Jules**). **Jolyon** is a form of the name from the north of England, given publicity by Galsworthy's use of it in his *Forsyte Saga* novels along with its pet form **Jolly**. **Juliana** is the feminine form of Julian, and this was corrupted in the Middle

Ages to **Gillian** or **Jillian**, which later developed into **Jill** or **Gill** and its pet form **Jilly**. In the nineteenth century Juliana or **Julianne** developed in France into **Lianne** with its many variants such as **Leanne, Lian, Lean(n)a** and **Lianna**, although some parents prefer to interpret this as a blend of the names LEE and ANNE.

June
This is the name of the month used as a first name. It may be given because a girl is born in that month, or because of the happy feelings associated with the beginning of summer. It has only been used as a name since the twentieth century, but the name for the month is very old, going back to the Latin meaning 'month sacred to JUNO'.

Juno
Juno was the Roman queen of the gods and a goddess with special responsibility for the lives of women. There is disagreement over the meaning of her name, which may mean simply 'goddess or divine one' (which links the name to JULIA) or may signify 'young woman'. It is not in common use as a first name, but can be found in Ireland, as in Sean O'Casey's play *Juno and the Paycock* (1924), where it is used as an English equivalent of the Irish UNA. The Welsh form is **Gweno** (see GWEN).

Justin
Derived from the Latin word meaning 'just', Justin was the name of a Christian martyr and theologian who died c. AD 165. **Justus** and **Justinian** are rare forms of the name. In the form **Iestyn** or **Iestin** it has been used in Wales since at least the sixth century. **Justina** is the older feminine form, but since the success of Lawrence Durrell's novel *Justine* (1957) and of the film made from it, this has been the more frequently used form. Occasionally the masculine form of the name is found used for a woman.

Kk

Kady
A recent girl's name, Kady appears to be a development of Kay, or to derive from the initials K.D., in the same way that Jacy relates to JAY. It is also found as **Kaydee** and **Kadi**, and with a spelling beginning with 'C'.

Kai see CAIUS

Kaine see KEENAN

Kaitlyn see CAITLIN

Kalie see KAYLEIGH

Kalin see CALEB

Kami see CAMILLA

Kane see KEENAN

Kanisha
A recent Black American name, blending the fashionable elements Ka- and -isha. It is also found as **Kaneesha**, **Kaneisha** and in forms such as **Kenisha**, when it may be thought of as a feminine equivalent of KENNETH.

Kara see CARA

Karel see CHARLES

Karen see CATHERINE

Karenza see KERENSA

Kari see CAROLINE

Karin, Karina see CARA, CATHERINE

Karl see CHARLES

Karla see Carol

Karol, Karoline see Carol

Kasia see Keziah

Kasimir see Casimir

Kasper see Jasper

Kate, Katharine see Catherine

Katelyn, Katelynn see Caitlin

Katerina, Katherine, Kathleen, Kathryn, Kathy, Katrina, Katrine see Catherine

Katia, Katie, Katja, Katy see Catherine

Kay see Catherine, Caius

Kaydee see Kady

Kayla
This name, very popular in the USA and in growing use in the UK, is probably a development of Kay, the pet form of Catherine, although it has been suggested that it could come from a shortening of Michaela. As a look at these pages will show, there has recently been a growth in names beginning Kay-.

Kayleigh
This girl's name is probably best analysed as a blend of Kay and Leigh, although it has been suggested that it comes from the Irish surname Kayley, which ultimately comes from the word *caol* ('slim'), just as the name **Kaylyn** has been derived from the Irish *Caelainn* ('slender lady'), rather than the more obvious blend of Kay and Lyn, while **Keely** (also **Keylee**, **Keeley** and **Keelie**) is derived from *cadhla* ('graceful'). As with so many recently fashionable names, the sound of these names is probably more important than the sense, for they complete a set with the other recently fashionable names Kelly and Kylie. Kayleigh is found in numerous spellings, such as **Kaylee**, **Kalie**, **Caley** and **Caleigh**. Use of the name seems to have grown after the group Marillion had a hit with a song called Kayleigh in 1985.

Kayne, Kean see Keenan

Keanu
Virtually unknown before the actor Keanu Reeves made the name famous, this is a Hawaiian name meaning 'cool breeze over the mountains'.

Keefer see Kiefer

Keelan see KILLIAN

Keelie, Keeley Keely see KAYLEIGH, KELLY

Keenan
The Irish surname **Keenan** comes from **Kenan**, the pet form of the name **Cian** ('ancient'), which is usually anglicized as **Kean** but also found as **Kian**. Variations of these names are not always easy to sort out from **Kane** (also found as **Kaine** and **Kayne**), which was popular in Australia in the 1960s and which usually comes from the Irish name *Cathan* meaning 'warrior', although as a surname Kane can also indicate someone from the French town of Caen.

Keesha see KEISHA

Keir
This is a Scottish surname and place name, meaning 'a fort'. It is occasionally used, in honour of (James) Keir Hardy (1856–1915), one of the founders of the Labour Party.

Keira, Keiron see KIERAN

Keisha
The origin of this modern name is not known. It has been suggested that it could be from the Bobangi language of Central Africa, where the word *nkisa* means 'favourite', or that it is a blend of the fashionable K- beginning of a name with **Aisha**. However, it is spelt in a wide variety of ways, one of which is **Keshia**, which is also recorded as a form of **Keziah**, so Keisha could also be a development of that. Other spellings of the name include **Keesha**, **Kiesha** and **Kesha**, and it is often found prefixed with La- to give forms such as **LaKeisha**.

Keith
Keith is a Scottish place and surname, meaning 'a wood'. It was not adopted as a first name until the twentieth century. It was popular in the mid-twentieth century, and is back in fashion in the USA at the moment.

Kelly
This is an Irish surname, which probably means something like 'war, strife', used as a first name for both sexes, but now more commonly for girls. In the form **Kelley** it was well established in the American Bible Belt by the 1950s, but the form Kelly seems to have come into use rather later in the UK. The name **Keeley** is a variant that lies somewhere between Kelly and the fashionable KAYLEIGH and KYLIE.

Kelsey
Although the best-known bearer of this fashionable name, the actor Kelsey Grammer who plays *Frasier* on television, is a male, it is currently being given to more girls than boys. The surname from which it comes derives from a place name in Lincolnshire meaning 'Cenel's Island', Cenel being a personal name derived from the Old English word for 'fierce'. Spellings such as **Kelsie** and **Kelsee** are also found.

Kelvin

Attempts have been made to link this name with the Old English name **Kelwin**, meaning 'keel-friend', but it is far more likely that a bearer of this Scottish first name has connections with Glasgow, through which the river Kelvin flows, and which has a Kelvingrove Park, a Kelvin Hall and a benefactor in the scientist Lord Kelvin (1824–1907), who chose the river name as his title. The exact meaning of the river name is debated, but probably means either 'wooded river' or 'narrow river'. The name is sometimes shortened to **Kel**.

Kenan see KEENAN

Kendall

This is a surname used as a first name for both sexes, particularly in the USA. The surname comes from either of two place names in the north of England, one meaning 'valley of the river Kent', the other 'valley with a spring'.

Kendra, Kendrick

Kendra is a blend of one of the many names beginning Ken- with the ending found in names such as Sandra. Some commentators regard it as the feminine version of the name Kendrick. This comes from a surname which has various sources depending on whether the original holder was English, Welsh, Scottish or Irish.

Kenelm

An Old English name meaning 'brave-helmet', Kenelm was the name of an Anglo-Saxon saint. It is not a common name, but had a famous bearer in Sir Kenelm Digby (1603–65), who in his varied life was a diplomat, privateer, writer and a scholar who left behind a magnificent collection of important manuscripts, as well as being the devoted husband of VENETIA Stanley. The name is said to have remained traditional in his family.

Kenneth

The Gaelic name **Cinaed**, meaning 'born from fire', was a common one in the MacAlpine family and when one of their clan became the first king of Scotland in the ninth century the name was anglicized to Kenneth. There was another Gaelic name, **Coinneach**, meaning 'fair-haired', from which the MacKenzies get their surname, which was also anglicized as Kenneth. Short forms are **Ken**, **Kennie** and **Kenny**. **Cenydd** is the Welsh form of the name.

Kent

Kent is a masculine name which comes from the surname, which is in turn derived from the county name. This in its turn means 'coastal district'.

Keon see KIANA

Keren

This is the short form of **Kerenhappuch**, one of the three daughters of JOB (see also JEMIMA and KEZIAH). The name means 'horn [i.e. container] of antimony', which refers to the kohl used even then to enhance the eyes. Although not a common name, it has been used quietly but steadily since at least the seventeenth century, and there are even recorded cases of three daughters being given the names of Job's three. Keren may sometimes be used as an alternative form of **Karen** (see CATHERINE), although the names are unrelated.

Kerensa
A traditional Cornish girl's name meaning 'affection, love', Kerensa is also found in the forms **Kerenza** and **Karenza**.

Keri see CERI

Kermit see DERMOT

Kerry
The Irish county name is the obvious source of this name, but its popularity may have been helped by the existence of the Welsh name CERI (pronounced in the same way) and by the fact that Kerry has been used, particularly among the Boston Irish, as a pet form of CATHERINE. The name first became popular in Australia in the 1940s, when it was primarily thought of as a masculine name, as in the case of the businessman Kerry Packer, but it is now mainly used as a feminine name. It can also be found in forms such as **Keri**, and **Ker(r)yn** should probably be thought of as an elaboration or as a blend of Kerry and Karen.

Kesha, Keshia see KEISHA, KEZIAH

Kester see CHRISTOPHER

Keturah
This is the name of the second wife of Abraham and was adopted by the Puritans. It has been used regularly since then, although more frequently in America than Britain, but it declined in popularity in the twentieth century. The name means 'fragrance' or 'incense'.

Kevin
Kevin was the name of a seventh-century Irish saint who founded an important school at Glendalough, which became equally famous for its learning and the beauty of its situation. The name was restricted to Ireland until the 1920s, but in the second half of the twentieth century it became enormously popular throughout the English-speaking world and has now even conquered France. Kevin means 'comely birth'. The spelling **Kevan** is often treated as a variant, but strictly speaking is a separate name meaning 'little handsome one'.

Keziah, Kezia
This is the Hebrew word for 'cassia', a type of shrub much admired for its fragrance. It was the name of the middle of Job's three beautiful daughters, the others being Jemima and Kerenhappuch (see KEREN). The fame of these three must have been great, for, unusually for the Bible, we are given his daughters' names, but not his sons'. Keziah was the name of one of John Wesley's sisters, who was known by the pet form **Kissy**. She took the name to America, where along with WESLEY it became a popular Black name. It is also found as **Keshia** (see KEISHA) and **Kasia** (although this is also a Polish form of the name CATHERINE) and has the further pet forms **Kizzie**, **Kissie** and **Kezie**.

Kian see KEENAN

Kiana, Kiara, Kierra

Kiana, well used in the USA for girls, appears to be a respelling of the trade name Qiana, the brand name of a type of silk-like fabric. This in turn was chosen from a computer-generated list, so has no further significance. More significant, perhaps, is the sound of the name. It not only uses the immensely fashionable k- sound, but fits in with other new names, not just those listed under KEISHA and on the surrounding pages, but particularly with Kiara, which appears to be a respelling of the Italian Chiara (see CLARE) and Kierra, an apparent blend of Kiana or Kiara with SIERRA. All these names are subject to a wide variety of spellings. It has been suggested that the boy's name **Keon** or **Kion** is the masculine equivalent of Kiana.

Kiefer

This has come into use, sometimes spelt **Keefer**, as a result of the fame of the actor Kiefer Sutherland. In origin it is a German surname either meaning a barrel-maker, the equivalent of the English surname Cooper, or else it comes from the German word for 'a pine tree'.

Kieran

Derived from the Irish word *ciar* ('black') Kieran means 'little dark one'. There are as many as 15 Irish saints of this name, one of whom, St Kieran of Saighir, is said to have been a missionary in Ireland even before St Patrick got there. Another, St Kieran of Clonmacnoise, is said to have used parchment made from the skin of his favourite cow to write down the great Irish national epic of *The Tain*. A twelfth-century copy of this sixth-century manuscript has come down to us as *The Book of the Dun Cow*. The Irish form of the name is **Ciaran**, although the K- form is commoner elsewhere as it makes the pronunciation clearer. The name can also be spelt as **Kieron** or **Keiron** and there are feminine forms **Ciara**, **Kiera** and **Keira**. However, in the USA Ciara is a name taken from a brand of perfume, given a soft 'c', and often pronounced identically with SIERRA. **Kira**, popular for some years in the USA, and no doubt set to grow since its use for an attractive character in the Star Trek spin-off *Deep Space Nine*, is probably also a form of the name, although it can also be seen as a form of Kyra or a feminine of CYRUS.

Kierra see KIANA

Kiesha see KEISHA

Killian, Kilian

Killian is an Irish saint who went as a missionary to Germany in the late seventh century and was martyred at Würzburg, where a cathedral was later built in his honour. The survival of the name into modern times may owe something to its use by Sir Walter Scott in *Anne of Geirstein* (1829). The name is a diminutive of the Irish word meaning 'strife' and is spelt **Cillian** in Irish. **Keelan** is another variant, and **Killie** is used as a short form.

Kim, Kimberly

The name Kim comes primarily from Rudyard Kipling's novel of that name, published in 1901. His child hero, the 'little friend of all the world', was known as Kim in the Indian bazaars, but his full name was **Kimball** O'Hara. The success of the book led to Kim being used occasionally as a boy's name, and more often as a pet name, but the full form of the name does not seem to have been used. Within a few years Kim was being used for girls, and has remained predominantly a female name. The spy 'Kim' Philby (real name Harold) is an example of the name used as a masculine nickname. When he got to Russia, Philby would have found that the name is also in use there as a quite common masculine name, invented in post-revolutionary fervour from the initial letters (in Russian) for 'Communist Youth International'.

Kim is also used as a short form of **Kimberly**, the commoner spelling as a first name for **Kimberley**, the South African diamond town. This came into use at about the same time as Kipling's book was published. Soldiers used to have a custom of naming their children after the garrison in which they were born, or after battles, and at the turn of the century there were many British soldiers around Kimberley, fighting in the Boer War. (This custom is well illustrated in Kipling's short story 'Daughter of the Regiment', where Colour-Sergeant McKenna's children are called Colaba, Muttra and Jhansi from the cantonments where they were born). Kimberley was at first mainly masculine, and is still sometimes used as a man's name, but is now predominantly female. It was well established in America by the 1950s and has been very popular ever since, often shortened to **Kimmy**.

Kira see KIERAN

Kirk
Kirk is a Scandinavian name meaning 'a church'; it was brought to public notice by the film star Kirk Douglas. It is sometimes spelt **Kirke**.

Kirsta, Kirstie, Kirsty, Kirsten, Kirsteen, Kirstine see CHRISTINE

Kissie see KEZIAH

Kit see CHRISTOPHER, CATHERINE

Kittie, Kitty see CATHERINE

Konrad see CONRAD

Kristel see CRYSTAL

Kristin, Kristina see CHRISTINE

Krystal see CRYSTAL

Kurt see CONRAD

Kyle
This is the name of a district in Scotland, used first as a surname, then as a first name, mainly for men, but occasionally for women, although **Kyla** is usually used for girls. It has been in use since at least the later part of the nineteenth century, and is popular at the moment. Tradition links the district of Kyle with

the name of Old King Cole, but less romantic place-name experts derive it from the river Coyl, which means 'narrow'.

Kylie

This name has been popular in Australia for a number of years, but it burst upon the rest of the English-speaking world with the success of *Neighbours* actress and singer Kylie Minogue. According to Leslie Dunkling, it is a Western Australian Aboriginal word meaning 'curl' or 'boomerang', but it probably owes its success to being thought of as a feminine version of KYLE, or as a variant of KELLY.

Kyra, Kyree, Kyrie see CYRIL

LI

Lacey

Lacey is a surname, originally belonging to someone from the village of Lassy in Normandy, used as a girl's first name. However, the fashion for the name probably owes much to the attractive associations it has with lace, particularly as the name is also spelt **Lacy**.

Lachlan

This Scottish Highland name comes from the Gaelic name for Norway, *Lochlann*. It is the origin of the surname MacLachlan. It can also be spelt **Lachlann** and **Lachunn**, and has pet forms **Lachie**, **Lachy** and **Lauchie**. Its recent popularity in Australia may perhaps owe something to a memory of General Lachlan Macquarie, who was an exceptionally liberal governor of New South Wales (1809–21), and whose encouragement of building projects led to the local late-Georgian style of architecture being called Macquarie style.

LaDarius see DARIA, LAETITIA

Ladonna see DONNA

Laetitia, Letitia

This is the Latin word for 'joy, delight', used as a girl's name. It has been in use in England since the twelfth century, and was early on anglicized to **Lettice**. It is shortened to **Lettie** or **Letty**, and **Laeta** is an alternative form of the name. Another shortening, **Tiesha**, **Teesha** or **Ticia** is used as a name in its own right. It is probably this name that lay behind the explosion of names beginning La- among Black Americans since the 1970s, although names based on the French forms of 'the', *la* and *le*, did already exist. Laetitia became the more phonetic **Latisha** (shortened to **Tisha**), and from this developed names such as **Latasha** (as if La + Natasha), **LaToya** (perhaps from **Toya**, a Mexican pet form of Victoria), an increase in the use of **Larissa** (see LARA) and even some boys' names such as **LaDarius**.

Laila, Lailah see LEILA

LaKeisha see KEISHA

Lalage

This come from the Greek word for 'to babble, prattle'. The name was used in the first century AD by the Latin poet Horace for the woman addressed in his love poems, and has been similarly used by a number of English poets since then. **Lallie** or **Lally** are short forms.

Lamar

A surname from the French for 'the pond', Lamar is used as a masculine name in the United States. Use was probably inspired by either Mirabeau Buonaparte Lamar (1798–1859), 2nd president of the Republic of Texas, or Lucius Quintus Cincinnatus Lamar (1825–93), Confederate politician and associate justice of the US Supreme Court.

Lambert

This is an old Germanic name meaning 'land-bright', which should perhaps be interpreted as 'pride of the nation'. It was the name of a seventh-century saint and was popular in the past, but is rarely used today, although a knowledge of the name is kept alive by the fame of Lambert Simnel, the pretender to Henry VII's throne.

Lana see ALAN

Lance, Launce

These are both used as independent names from the surname and as short forms of **Lancelot** or **Launcelot**, the great knight of King Arthur's court. Despite his fame, we do not really know where the name comes from. Lancelot first appears in French Arthurian literature, and the name may come from the words *L'ancel*, diminutive *L'ancelot*, meaning 'the servant' (perhaps a reference to his humility or to his time spent learning from the Lady of the Lake).

Lanna see ALAN

Lanty see ATALANTA

Lara

This is the pet form of the Russian **Larissa**, which is from the Latin *Hilaria* (the source of HILARY). Lara is the tragic heroine of Boris Pasternak's *Doctor Zhivago* (1957), and the name became widely known as a result of the success of the 1965 film of the novel. Some parents may use it as a variant of LAURA.

Laraine, Larraine see LORRAINE

Larissa see LARA

Larry see LAWRENCE

Latasha, Latisha, LaToya see LAETITIA

Launce, Launcelot see LANCE

Laura

The Latin equivalent of the Greek DAPHNE, Laura comes from the word for a laurel tree. To be crowned with a wreath of laurels was an honour given in the ancient world to those triumphant in war, sport and the arts; a vestige of it survives in our term 'poet laureate'. Although the name comes from Latin, the Romans did not use it; but it was in use in the Middle Ages, probably with the idea that the bearer was of such excellent qualities or beauty that she deserved the laurel crown. In the fourteenth century, the Italian poet Petrarch gave the name fame by using it for the name of his beloved in his sonnets. The name is also spelt **Lora**, and has pet forms **Lori** and **Lolly**. It has a number of derivative forms, the most widely used of which at the moment is **Lauren**, a name that seems to have been coined for the film actress Lauren Bacall. The alternative form **Loren** is used for both boys (see under LAURENCE) and girls. The plant name **Laurel** is also used, along with diminutives **Lauretta** or **Loretta**, as well as such elaborations as **Lorana** and **Lorinda**. **Lowri** is the Welsh form of the name. These names may sometimes be used as feminine forms of LAURENCE.

Lauraine see LORRAINE

Laurence, Lawrence

This name shares with LAURA a derivation from the word for a laurel, probably via the name of the Roman town of *Laurentium*. It came into use because of the popularity of the third-century saint who was martyred by being roasted on a grid-iron because he would not hand over the money which had been entrusted to him to distribute to the poor. The pet form **Larry** is sometimes used as a name in its own right. Other short forms are **Laurie** and **Lawrie**, and in Scotland **Lowrie**. **Laurent** is the form of the name used in France and sometimes found here (confusingly, Laurence is the French feminine form), and **Lorenzo**, the Italian and Spanish form of the name, is sometimes used in the USA. This gives a short form **Loren**, which is not uncommon. In Ireland Lawrence became popular because of St Lawrence O'Toole, bishop of Dublin and a man deeply involved in caring for his people at the time of the twelfth-century Norman invasion of Ireland. In his case, Lawrence was used as a substitute for the native Gaelic name **Lorcan** ('little fierce one').

Lavinia

In Roman mythology, Lavinia was the daughter of the king of Latium, and wife of Aeneas (see ANGUS), the Trojan who became the founder of the Roman people. It was not used by the Romans as a name, but was taken up in the fifteenth century with the Renaissance revival of interest in things classical. It was particularly popular in the eighteenth century after the success of a poem by James Thomson called 'Lavinia and Palemon' (basically a retelling of the biblical story of RUTH and Boaz), but is now only quietly used. **Vina** is a short form of the name, and there is a variant, **Lavina**.

Layla see LEILA

Lea see LEE

Leah

Leah is the name of one of the more hard-done-by women in the Bible.

According to the story (Genesis 29), Jacob fell in love with his cousin RACHEL and served her father Laban for seven years to win her, but her elder sister Leah was secretly substituted on the wedding night. Although Jacob was later given Rachel to be Leah's co-wife, he hated Leah, but God compensated her with numerous sons. **Lia**, the Italian form of the name (also used as a short form of various names ending with those letters), and **Léa**, the French, are sometimes used as variants.

Leala see LEILA

Leana, Leanne see JULIA

Leander
In mythology, Leander swam the Hellespont every night in order to be with his beloved, Hero, until one night he was caught in a storm and drowned. In 1810 the Romantic poet Byron, who was always keen to show that his club foot did not prevent him being a sportsman, proved it was possible to swim this strait between Europe and Asia, but only at the cost of making himself ill. Afterwards he wrote a set of verses in which he wondered how on earth Leander had managed the swim *and* spent the night with his lover. He concluded cynically, 'Ye mortals, how the gods do plague you!/ He lost his life; and I've the ague'. Leander comes from the Greek meaning 'lion-man', which perhaps answers Byron's question. It has also been used for girls, and there is a feminine form, **Leandra**. Some parents may use these names as an elaboration of LEE and ANNE.

Leanna see JULIA

Leanora see ELEANOR

Lee, Leigh, Lea
Lee comes from the common surname, which means 'a meadow'. Its popularity in the southern United States probably stems from the once common practice of naming children after people admired by the parents, in this case after the Confederate general Robert E. Lee (1807–70). From there it spread, developing variant forms, throughout the USA, and then to other English-speaking countries. Use seems to be equally divided between the sexes.

Leila
Leila is a Persian name meaning 'darkness' or 'night' and thus a type of dark beauty. She is the heroine of a popular romance called *Leila and Majnun*. The name was made widely known in England by Lord Byron, who used it both for the Turkish child brought to England in *Don Juan* and for the tragic heroine of *The Giaour* (1813). It was subsequently used by other writers as a name for Eastern beauties. Variant forms are **Laila**, **Lailah**, **Leala**, **Leilah**, **Leyla**, **Lila** and **Lilah**, and, after Eric Clapton used it for his 1972 hit, **Layla**.

Len, Lennie, Lenny, Lennard see LEO

Lena see HELEN, MADELINE

Lenore, Lenora see ELEANOR

Leo, Leonard, Leonie
There is a large group of names containing the element 'Leo' meaning 'lion'. Leo was the name of 13 popes, and was popular in the Middle Ages; but, although still used it is now more common as a short form of various Leo-names. It took the form **Leon** in France and from there it spread to this country. Leonard, sometimes spelt **Lennard** (and **Leonardo** in both Spanish and Italian), is an old Germanic name meaning 'brave as a lion', and is shortened to **Len**, **Lennie** or **Lenny**. **Lionel**, the name of one of King Arthur's nobler knights, also belongs in this group since it means 'little lion'. **Leopold** looks as if it also belongs with the lion names; in fact, it comes from the Old German name *Leutpold*, formed from words meaning 'people' and 'bold', but it changed its form under the influence of Leo- names. (See also LLEWELLYN.)
   The feminine forms of the name mostly come from the French Leon. They include Leonie, **Leontia**, **Leontine**, **Leola** and **Leona**. **Leonora** is not a lion name, but a form of ELEANOR.

Leroy
The old French for 'the king', Leroy may have been used originally as a surname used to describe those who were servants to the king of France. It is a name particularly associated with the United States, and is sometimes found in the form **Elroy**.

Leslie, Lesley
This name comes from the Scottish place and surname, which probably means 'garden of hollies'. From the evidence of Robert Burns's poem to 'Bonnie Lesley' it seems to have come into use as a girl's name before being used as a boy's in the second third of the nineteenth century. This is a reversal of the usual pattern of boys' names becoming girls'. There used to be a careful distinction made between Lesley as a feminine form and Leslie as the masculine, but the distinction is no longer made, at least for girls. It can also be found in spellings such as **Lezlie**.

Lester
This is a modified spelling of the place name Leicester, meaning 'dwellings on the river Legra'. It has been used for the last 100 or so years, well-known holders being the Canadian statesman Lester Pearson and the jockey Lester Piggott.

Letitia, Lettice, Letty see LAETITIA

Levi
In the Bible, this is the name of the third son of LEAH and JACOB, whose descendants were to become the priests of Israel. His name means 'joined, attached'. However, in many people's minds the name is most strongly associated with jeans. There are records of the name being used for girls as well as the usual boys.

Lewis, Louis, Louise
When the barbarian Franks invaded France in the Dark Ages, they brought with them a name meaning 'famous battle' that was written down by the literate, but

conquered, Gauls as *Hludowig* or *Chlodowig*. This name developed into **Clovis**, the name of the first Merovingian king (481–511), and later lost its first sound to become **Louis**, a name almost synonymous with French kingship. **Ludovic** comes from the Latin form of the name, and **Aloys** and **Aloysius** – the name of a Spanish Jesuit saint, but probably best known as the name of Sebastian Flyte's teddy-bear in Evelyn Waugh's *Brideshead Revisited* (1945) – was a form which developed in Provence, and spread to Spain and Italy. The English form of the name is **Lewis**. **Luis** is the usual Spanish form of the name, well used in the USA. Pet forms of the name include **Lou**, **Louie**, **Lew** and **Lewie**.

The feminine forms of the name, **Louise** and **Louisa** and occasionally the Spanish form **Luisa**, with their pet forms **Lou**, **Louie** and **Lulu**, are at the moment more popular than their masculine counterparts. Clovis has recently developed the feminine form **Clova**, although this may owe something to the flower name **Clover**, found in Susan Coolidge's 'Katy' books.

Lex, Lexie see ALEXANDER

Lia see LEAH

Liam see WILLIAM

Lian, Lianna, Lianne see JULIA

Libby, Liesel see ELIZABETH

Lila, Lilah see LEILA

Lilian, Lillian, Lillias see LILY

Lilith
A name from Jewish mythology, Lilith has been variously interpreted as 'a serpent', 'a screech-owl' or 'a vampire'. According to legend, she was the first wife of Adam, before the creation of Eve, but refused to submit to him, and as a result was expelled from the garden of Eden. She became an evil spirit particularly dangerous to new-born children, and one tradition says she took her revenge by becoming the serpent of the Tree of Knowledge. The name is rarely given to children, but in recent years Lilith has been used as a symbol by some sections of the feminist movement.

Lily
Use of this flower name as a first name may owe something to Christian symbolism, both to the association of the Madonna lily with the Virgin Mary as a symbol of purity, and to the recommendation of the Sermon on the Mount to 'consider the lilies of the field'. Historically, it has also been used as a pet form of ELIZABETH (German **Lili** is still used in this way), and it is impossible to distinguish between these two uses. The name is also spelt **Lilly**. **Lilian** (or **Lillian**) comes from the Spanish form of the name, **Liliana**, and in Scotland this was transformed into **Lilias**, **Lillias** or **Lillas**. Lilian may have influenced the development of the name Lianne (see JULIAN). Very occasionally, as in the case of the French national-team footballer Lilian Thuram, Lilian is used for a man. SUSAN is the Hebrew equivalent of Lily.

Lina
This is a short form of a number of names ending in -lina, such as Angelina and Selina, which has come to be used as a name in its own right.

Linda
Linda started life as a short form of names ending -linda, such as BELINDA. These were old Germanic names where the -*linda* means 'serpent'. However, a much more obvious meaning for *linda* is the Spanish adjective meaning 'pretty', and most users of the name probably think of it in this sense. It is also found in the forms **Lynda** and **Lindy**. The shortenings **Lyn** and **Lin** are shared with a number of other names.

Linden
Used for both sexes, this appears to be the old English word for the lime tree, and is thus another plant name; but use, particularly for girls, owes much to the popularity of other Lin- names. The water is further muddied by the surname **Lyndon**, which is sometimes used as a first name, most prominently by the American president Lyndon Baines Johnson (1908–73). This comes, ultimately, from the same root, being from a place name meaning 'the hill with linden trees'. **Lynden** is an alternative form.

Lindsay
An aristocratic Scottish surname used as a first name, Lindsay probably comes from family connections with the district of Lincolnshire called Lindsey. When used for men it is usually in the form Lindsay, but for girls, now the more frequent use, it also occurs as **Lindsey**, **Linsey**, **Linsay** and various other spellings including **Linzi**.

Linette see LYNETTE

Linus
A Greek name meaning 'flax', Linus is found in the New Testament (II Timothy 4. 21), where St Paul sends greetings from Linus and CLAUDIA. There is an unsubstantiated tradition that these two were brother and sister, and British, and invited some of the first missionaries to Britain. There is, coincidentally, a Welsh feminine name **Llian**, which also means 'flax'. Linus is probably best known as the name of a cartoon character in the *Peanuts* cartoon, but the name is used in real life, as in the double Nobel Prize-winning scientist Linus Pauling, and the actor Linus Roach.

Linzi see LINDSAY

Lionel see LEO

Lisa, Lisbeth, Lise, Lisette see ELIZABETH

Lito see ANGELA

Livia, Livy see OLIVER

Liz, Lizzie, Liza, Lizbeth, see ELIZABETH

Lleucu see LUCY

Llewellyn
This is a Welsh man's name, traditionally interpreted as meaning 'lion-like', but which probably derives from the word for 'a leader'. It is also spelt **Llywelyn**, and is shortened to **Llew**, **Llelo** and **Lyn**, which last is often used as a name in its own right. It has been anglicized to **Leoline** or LEWIS.

Llian see LINUS

Llinos, Llio see LYNETTE

Lloyd
This is a Welsh name usually described as meaning 'grey', but in fact the word covers a range of colours including browns and greys. The correct Welsh spelling of the name is **Llwyd**, and it is also found as **Lhuyd**, **Loyd** and, particularly in America – as in the case of the boxer Floyd Patterson – as **Floyd**.

Llywelyn see LLEWELLYN

Logan
This surname is currently in fashion in the United States as a boy's name. It comes from a number of Scottish and Irish place names which come in turn from the Gaelic for 'little hollow'. A famous earlier holder of the name was the American-born British writer Logan Pearsall Smith (1865–1946).

Lois
Lois is another New Testament name: she was the grandmother of TIMOTHY, and is praised in St Paul's second Epistle to Timothy for her great faith. The name came into fashion, along with other biblical names, among the Puritans, and they took it to America, where it is still more common than elsewhere. The name is thought to be Greek, but its meaning is not known. The use of the name has been reinforced by Lois also being a form of HELOISE, via a contraction of the Provençal form **Aloisa** or **Aloys**. The name is probably best known as the name of Superman's girlfriend, Lois Lane.

Lola, Lolita see CAROL, DOLORES

Lolly see LAURA

Lora, Lorana see LAURA

Lorcan see LAURENCE

Loren see LAURA, LAURENCE

Lorenzo see LAURENCE

Loretta, Lori, Lorinda see LAURA

Lorna

Lorna was invented by R.D. Blackmore for the heroine of his novel *Lorna Doone* (1869). He probably based it on the Scottish place and family name of Lorn or Lorne, but the name also has associations with the old English word 'lorn' as in 'forlorn', meaning 'lost, forsaken', which would be appropriate for the state of his kidnapped and isolated heroine. The form **Lorne** has been used as a feminine name, but is more frequently found as the male equivalent of Lorna. The Canadian actor Lorne Green was a well-known holder. Lorne was the name of a king of the Dalriada Scots c. AD 500, one of three brothers (the others being FERGUS and ANGUS) who founded the kingdom there. His name may come from a Celtic root meaning 'a fox'.

Lorraine

This comes from the district of France of this name, its use possibly influenced by Joan of Arc, who was known as the Maid of Lorraine as well as the Maid of Orleans. The name is not used in France, but has been used in England and America since the nineteenth century. There are numerous variants of which the most common are **Loraine**, **Laraine**, **Larraine** and **Lauraine**.

Lothair see LUTHER

Lottie see CAROL

Lou see LEWIS

Louanne, Louella see LUELLA

Louis, Louisa, Louise see LEWIS

Lowena

Lowena or **Lowenna** is a Cornish name, meaning 'joy', that is being increasingly widely used.

Lowri see LAURA

Lowrie see LAURENCE

Loyd see LLOYD

Luca, Lucas see LUKE

Lucasta

This was a name coined by the seventeenth-century poet Richard Lovelace for his poems addressed to LUCY Sacheverell. It is said to have been formed from the Latin *lux casta* ('chaste light'). His poem 'To Lucasta, Going to the Wars', contains the famous lines: 'I could not love thee (Dear) so much,/ Lov'd I not honour more.' (See also ALTHEA.)

Lucretia

In Roman traditional history, Lucretia was a model of feminine virtue and modesty. According to the story, Lucretia is raped by Sextus, the son of

TARQUIN, the despotic king of Rome. Unable to live with the shame, she summons her husband and her father, and, begging them to take vengeance, commits suicide in front of them. The outrage of her family and all who heard of what had happened is said to have led to the overthrow of the kings and the foundation of the Roman Republic. Shakespeare tells the story in his poem *The Rape of Lucrece* (1594). **Lucretius**, the male form of the name, was occasionally used in the past in honour of the great first-century BC poet and philosopher of that name.

Lucy

Lucy comes from the Latin word *lux, lucis*, meaning 'light'. It is because of this association with light that St Lucy, the fourth-century virgin martyr, is invoked against blindness and eye trouble. (St CLARE, whose name means 'bright, clear', is invoked against eye trouble for the same reason.) **Lucia** is the Latin and Italian form of the name, and **Lucilla** and **Lucille** Latin and French diminutives. **Lucinda** is another diminutive, particularly popular for fictional characters in the seventeenth and eighteenth centuries. Its pet form **Cindy** or **Sindy** is now a name in its own right. The Welsh name **Lleucu**, generally regarded as a translation of Lucy, can also be interpreted as from the word for 'light' combined with *cu* ('dear').

The masculine name **Lucius** comes from the same root. **Lucian** or **Lucien** are often used as variants, but come from a Greek name of unknown meaning, made famous by the first-century AD satirist.

Ludovic see LEWIS

Luella

A blended name formed from LOUISE and ELLA, Luella is also spelt **Louella**. Similarly, **Louanne, Luanne, Luana** are formed from LOUISE and ANNE.

Luigi, Luigina see GINA

Luis, Luisa see LEWIS

Luke

The fame of St Luke the Evangelist has made this a steadily popular name since the Middle Ages. St Luke was a physician and was also traditionally supposed to have been a painter and to have made portraits of the Virgin Mary, and he is the patron saint of both professions. He was a Greek, and his name simply means 'man from the district of Luciana'. The Greek form of his name, **Lucas**, is occasionally used, and the Italian form, **Luca** (or **Lucca**), has been recorded used as an English feminine equivalent.

Lulu see LEWIS

Luned see LYNETTE

Luther

The use of Luther as a first name is due to the fame of the sixteenth-century religious reformer Martin Luther, although its use has probably been given a boost in honour of the civil rights campaigner named after him, Martin Luther

King (1929–68). The name is a form of the German first name **Lothair**, meaning 'famous army' or 'warrior'.

Lydia

Lydia simply means 'woman of Lydia' (now western Turkey). It has strong literary associations. There is an anonymous Latin poem, once thought to be by VIRGIL, lamenting a lost love, addressed to a Lydia, and the name is given respectability by a brief mention in the Acts of the Apostles. Greater fame was given to it by its use by Ariosto in *Orlando Furioso* (1532) for a beautiful but cruel daughter of the King of Lydia, and it was a popular literary name in the eighteenth century, as in the case of Lydia Languish in Sheridan's *The Rivals* (1775).

Lyn see LINDA, LYNETTE, LLEWELLYN

Lynda see LINDA

Lynden, Lyndon see LINDEN

Lyndon see LINDEN

Lynette

Lynette comes from the Welsh name **Eluned** or **Eiluned**, which means 'idol, icon', so the name probably has some connection with ancient religion. **Luned** is the short form of Eluned, and this became **Linet** or **Linette** in the medieval French Arthurian romances in which she features as a heroine. The name was given what is now its commonest form, Lynette, by Tennyson in his story of 'Gareth and Lynette' in the *Idylls of the King*. Lyn, Lynn, Lynne are used as short forms. The name is only coincidentally like that of a bird, the linnet, although some parents may have used it for that association, and **Linnet** has been used as a first name. There is also a Welsh name **Llinos** or **Llio**, which means 'linnet', the bird being used as the symbol of a pretty woman.

Lynn, Lynne see LYNETTE

Mm

Mabel

This name started life as a pet form of **Amabel**, meaning 'loveable' (see AMY), but has all but replaced its original. In its turn it developed into such forms as **Maybelle** and **Maybelline**, although these can also be thought of as developments of MAY; in turn, May, along with **Mab** and **Mabs**, is sometimes a pet form of Mabel. There is a Welsh form, **Mabli**, and Mabel can also be spelt **Mable**.

Macy

This has recently come into fashion as a girl's name in the USA, sometimes in the form **Maci(e)** or **Macey**. Although chiefly associated with the department store, it is a surname that comes from a French place name originally meaning 'Maccius' estate'. Its rise most probably owes something to the popularity of MASON as a boy's name.

Madeline

Madeline, with its various spellings such as **Madeleine**, **Madaline**, **Madaliene**, **Madaleine** and **Madalain**, comes from St Mary Magdalen, the reformed sinner who anointed Christ with costly perfume and washed His feet with her tears and hair. Her second name means 'woman of Magdala', a village on the Sea of Galilee. Other forms of the name include **Magdalen(e)**, shortened to **Magda**, and **Madelena** or **Madalena**, shortened to **Lena**. From the old pronunciation of the name, **Maudlin** (which also gives us the adjective, from her tears of repentance), comes the occasional short form **Maude** or **Maud**, which properly belongs to MATILDA. **Madge**, properly belonging to MARGARET, can also be found as a pet form. **Maddie** or **Maddy** is, however, the usual short form.

Madge see MARGARET, MADELINE

Madison

Madison has become a popular first name for girls in the USA, and is beginning to appear in the UK. As a surname it can either mean 'Matthew's son' or 'Maud's son', but its appeal as a first name must owe something to the fame of New York's Madison Avenue.

Madoc, Madog

This Welsh masculine name means 'fortunate, good'. A certain Madog ap Owain Gwynedd is supposed to have discovered America ahead of everyone else from Europe in about 1150, and from this story come legends of blue-eyed, Welsh-speaking Native Americans. The name **Marmaduke**, with its short form **Duke**, is said to derive from the Irish *Maelmaedoc* ('servant of Madoc'). Marmaduke has strong associations with Yorkshire, where the name has always been more common than in the rest of the country. The name is often described as obsolescent, but Marmaduke Hussey, former chairman of the BBC, has shown this to be incorrect.

Madonna see DONNA

Maelmor see MILES

Mae see MAY

Maeve
Maeve, also spelt **Meave** and **Maev**, comes from Irish mythology, where she appears in two forms; one as the powerful and forceful queen of Connacht; the other as the queen of the fairies, the origin of Shakespeare's Queen Mab. The name probably means 'she who intoxicates'. **Meaveen** is a pet form.

Magda, Magdalen, Magdalene see MADELINE.

Maggie, Mags see MARGARET

Magnus
Stories of Charlemagne, whose name means 'Charles the Great', the king of the Franks and defender of the Christian faith against the heathen, were popular throughout Europe in the Middle Ages. The name translates into Latin as *Carolus Magnus*, and the second half of the name was given to the son of St Olaf, king of Norway (995–1030), a convert from paganism. This Magnus later became king of Norway and Denmark and Magnus became a traditional royal name, whence it spread to the general population. Among the Viking settlers of Ireland the name was softened to **Manus**. Although the television appearances of Magnus Magnusson and Magnus Pyke have made the name better known, it is still not often found outside Scotland and Ireland.

Mahalia
Best known from the singer Mahalia Jackson, this is a form of the Hebrew name **Mahala** ('tenderness').

Mai, Maia see MAY

Mair, Maire see MARY

Maisie see MARGARET

Malachy
An Irish name, Malachy was used by two high kings of Ireland and by a popular saint, and early on it became identified with the Old Testament prophet **Malachi** ('messenger'). The name is not usually found outside Ireland.

Malcolm

Malcolm is a Scottish name, from the Gaelic *Mael-Colum*, 'follower of St Columba', also known as **Colmcille**. St Columba, whose name means 'dove', was an Irish noble who founded the monastery on IONA in 563 which became the centre for Celtic Christianity and the base for the conversion of Scotland. The Gaelic form of his name gives us the popular names **Calum, Callum, Colm**.

Mallory

This surname, originally meaning an unlucky person, has become a fashionable girl's name in the United States. Use seems to have spread after a character called Mallory Keaton appeared in the television series *Family Ties*.

Malvina

In the mid-eighteenth century, Europe was swept by an enthusiasm for the poems of OSSIAN. Supposedly ancient Gaelic epics, they were in fact largely the work of James MacPherson (1736–96). MacPherson seems to have invented the name Malvina (which may be meant to represent the Gaelic for 'smooth brow') for the name of the betrothed of the hero OSCAR. Many of the poems are dedicated to her. The enthusiasm for things Ossianic was particularly strong in Scandinavia, and it may be immigration from this area that led to the name being more common in the United States than in other English-speaking areas. Variants are **Melvina** and **Malvena**. (See also MELVIN.)

Mamie see MARY

Mandy see AMANDA

Manny, Manuel see EMANUEL

Manon see MARIAN

Manus see MAGNUS

Marc, Marcel, Marceline, Marcella, Marcelle, Marcelline, Marchell, Marcia, Marcine, Marcus, Marcy see MARK

Maredudd see MEREDITH

Margaret

Margaret comes from the Latin word for PEARL. However, the French form **Marguerite** is also French for 'a daisy', and the name **Daisy** started life as a pet form of Margaret. Margaret owes its early popularity throughout Europe to the fame of St Margaret of Antioch, a legendary early martyr who was swallowed alive by Satan in the form of a dragon, but on making the sign of the cross burst through the monster's side, thereby saving her life and killing the dragon. In Scotland, this popularity was reinforced by another saint who was queen of Scotland (1070–93). The name was so popular in Scotland that it took on a number of different forms: **Margery** (**Marjory, Marjorie**, pet forms **Marge, Margie, Madge**), **Maisie, Mysie** and MAY. Pet forms of Margaret include **Maggie, Mags, Meg** and **Meggie**, and by alteration of the first letter **Peg, Peggie** or **Peggy**. MEGAN (or **Marget**) is the Welsh form of the name. From the Continent we get **Margarita**, **Marghanita**, **Margaretta**, **Margoletta** and pet forms **Greta**, **Gretchen**, **Grethel** or **Gretel**, **Meta** and **Rita**. **Margot** is the French pet form; the variant **Margaux** has recently come into fashion as an alternative, but the model Margaux Hemingway, who probably started the fashion, was named after the wine.

Mari, Maria, Mariah, Mariam, Mariamne see MARY

Marian

Originally a pet form of Mary, Marian came to be analysed as a combination of MARY and ANN, hence the variants **Marianne** and **Mary-Ann**. **Manon** is a French pet form of the name. The form **Marion** is also used in the United States as a man's name (it was, for example, the true first name of the actor John Wayne). In this case it comes from the surname with the same etymology as the first name, and probably owes its use to Francis Marion (d. 1795), who won fame fighting in the American War of Independence.

Marie, Mariel, Mariella, Marietta, Mariette see MARY

Marigold

A marigold was the symbol of the Virgin Mary, the name coming from Mary + gold, the flower originally being simply called 'a gold'. Because of its healing properties, the flower was also chosen as the symbol of the apothecaries and can still be seen in use as a symbol by many herbalists. It was particularly popular as a girl's name at the turn of the nineteenth and twentieth centuries.

Marilyn see MARY

Marina

This is the name by which St MARGARET of Antioch is known in the eastern Mediterranean. Although it may not be the true derivation, Marina is usually taken to come from the Latin meaning 'of the sea'; and in this sense was used by Shakespeare for the sea-born heroine of *Pericles*. The name became more popular in England after 1934, when Princess Marina of Greece became the Duchess of Kent. She became so popular that her favourite shade of blue-green became known as 'Marina blue'.

Marion see MARIAN

Marisa, Marissa see MARY

Marjorie, Marjory see MARGARET

Mark

Mark is the English form of **Marcus**, a Latin name probably derived from the Roman god of war, Mars. **Marc**, the French spelling of the name, has become popular in recent years, while in the United States Marcus has been elaborated into **DeMarcus**. The Latin pet form **Marcellus** became the French **Marcel**. The feminine forms of the name do not come directly from Marcus, but from this French form or from the related Latin name *Marcius*. From the latter we get **Marcia**, often found in the phonetic spelling **Marsha**. From the French come a number of forms: **Marcelline**, **Marceline** and their short form **Marcine**, **Marcella** and **Marcelle**. **Marchell** is the Welsh form, and is one of the earliest names borrowed into Welsh. **Marcy** is used as a short form of these names. (See also MARTIN.)

Marlene

A German pet form of Mary Magdalen (see MADELINE), Marlene was introduced into this country by the film star Marlene Dietrich and by the popularity with the troops on both sides of the German song 'Lili Marlene' in World War II. The variant form **Marlena** reflects the German pronunciation, but the name is now usually pronounced 'marleen' by English users. The -lene ending has been adopted for other, newly created names such as Charlene (see CAROL) and **Darlene**. A shortened form, **Marlee**, can also be found as a first name.

Marlon

Something of a mystery, this name has not been found before its use by the actor Marlon Brando (and his father who bore the name before him), and its spread is entirely due to him. It is assumed to be a surname used as a first name. Similar names have been found earlier, however. A Mahlon Pitney (1858–1924) was a member of the US Supreme Court, and there was a seaman called Marlin Ayotte present at Pearl Harbor, so time may throw more light on the history of the name.

Marmaduke see MADOC

Marquis

Marquis is the latest aristocratic title to have become fashionable as a boy's name in the USA, following in the steps of EARL, Duke and the less common King and Prince. Curiously **Marquise**, the French feminine form of the rank, is a not uncommon variant for boys.

Marsha see MARK

Marshall

This comes from the surname, which derives from German via French and originally meant a farrier or one who looked after horses. Its use as a first name may have been helped by the fact that the name of the Latin poet Martial (c. AD 40–104) has the same sound in standard English pronunciation.

Martha

Martha is the name of the biblical woman who worked so hard to cater for Jesus and his disciples, only to be told that her sister had chosen the better course by sitting at His feet. Hence the name became popular from the sixteenth century onwards with those who wanted their daughters to grow up to be diligent housewives. Short forms shared with MATILDA are **Mat**, **Mattie** or **Matty**, and by a change in first letter (also found in other pet forms in 'm'), **Pattie** or **Patty**, although this is also used for Patricia (see PATRICK). The name is Aramaic for 'lady'. The French form **Marthe** and the Spanish **Marta** are also occasionally used.

Martin

An old Roman name, Martin comes from Mars, the Roman god of fertility and war (see also MARK). Nowadays it is also spelt **Martyn** and has the short form **Marty**. It became part of the basic stock of European names because of the popularity of St Martin of Tours (c. 316–97), the Roman soldier who cut his military cloak in half in order to share it with a beggar, became a pacifist and left the army, and eventually became a missionary and bishop of Tours. Feminine forms include **Martina** or **Martine**, and more rarely **Martitia**, **Martita** and even **Martinella**.

Marvin see MERVYN

Mary

A name of disputed meaning, Mary has long been one of the most popular and prolific of girls' names, used in honour of the Virgin Mary and the numerous other saints who bear the name. The Hebrew form of the name is **Miriam**, also found in the forms **Mariam**, **Maryam** and **Mariamne**. **Maria** is the Latin form of the name, now often used in the form **Mariah**, and **Marie** the French. These names have innumerable pet forms, including MAY, **Moll**, **Molly**, **Mally**, **Mamie**, **Minnie**, **Poll**, **Polly** and **Ria**. Diminutives from the Continent include **Mariel** and **Mariella**, **Mariette** and **Marietta**, **Marisa** or **Marissa** as well as MARIAN. **Marilyn** or **Marylyn** is a derivative. In Welsh the name appears as **Mair** or **Mari**, while in Ireland it is **Mhairi** or **Maire**, which has developed into the phonetic forms **Moira**, **Maura** or **Moyra** and **Maureen** or **Moreen**.

Mason

This surname from the occupation is a fashionable choice for boys in the United States. MACY seems to function as the feminine equivalent.

Mat, Mattie, Matty see MARTHA, MATILDA, MATTHEW

Matilda

This is a Germanic name, from *maht* ('might') and *hild* ('battle'), the same element as in the name HILDA. It is puzzling to be told that **Maud** or **Maude** is a variant form of the name, but the transformation comes through the French, where the Germanic *Mahthilda* became something like *Maheud*, anglicized as Maud. Matilda would then be the Latin form of the name, the form written down by the chroniclers, while Maud would be the way ordinary people pronounced the name. Just as Mary became Molly which changed to Polly, so the short form **Mat** or **Matty** had its first sound changed to **Patty**, a short form shared with Patricia (see PATRICK), PATIENCE and MARTHA. **Tilly** and **Tilda** are also used as short forms.

Matthew

This is the commonest form of the name of the first Evangelist; **Matthias**, the Greek form of the name, is the alternative. Both forms are found spelt with a single 't', and they are shortened to **Mat** or **Matt** and **Matty**. The name means 'gift of God'.

Maud, Maude see MATILDA, MADELINE

Maura, Maureen see MARY

Maurice
Maurice is the French form of the Latin *Maurus* ('a Moor'), which was used not only for those from North Africa, but for anyone with a dark complexion. The name gave us the surnames **Morris** and **Morse**, which have come in their turn to be used as first names. The Welsh form of the name, **Meurig**, gives us the surname **Merrick**, which is also found as a first name. (See also SEYMOUR.)

Mavis
An old dialect word for a song thrush, Mavis does not seem to have been used as a girl's name before the end of the nineteenth century. In the twentieth century a similar name, **Merle**, the French for 'a blackbird', came into use. It has been used in the American Bible Belt as a male name, but thanks to the actress Merle Oberon is now primarily a female name. **Merlene** is an elaboration of the name, probably influenced by MARLENE.

Maximilian
This is one of the best-known 'invented' names, having been made up by the Emperor Frederick III (1415–93) for his son. The name is a blend of the names of two admired Romans, Fabius Maximus and Scipio Aemilianus, whose qualities Frederick hoped his son would inherit. However, it is worth noting that *Maximilianus* already existed as a Roman name, based on the word for 'great'. The short form of the name, **Max**, is shared with the totally unrelated name **Maxwell**, which comes from a Scots place name meaning 'Mack's well', but the French name **Maxime**, used for either sex, does come from the word meaning 'great'. English speakers have used **Maxim** for the masculine, uncomfortable with the feminine feel of the final 'e' in the French form. **Maxine** seems to be a modern coinage, a female version of Max. There is also a feminine form of Maximilian, **Maximilienne**, or **Maxilmilianne**.

May
As well as being a pet form of MARGARET and MARY, May is used as an independent name, associated either with the other month names or the other flower names. **Mai** is the Welsh form of the name, while **Mae** is a common form in the United States. **Maia** and **Maya**, which have appeared in recent years, seem to be variants, rather than the name of the Central American people or a use of the obscure Roman earth-goddess or the legendary Greek mother of Hermes. They are also found as pet forms of Maria. A new name, **Myesha**, has been formed by blending Maya, currently popular in the USA, with AISHA.

Maybelle, Maybelline see MABEL

Mayra see MYRA

Meave, Meaveen see MAEVE

Meg, Meggie see MARGARET

Megan
Megan was originally a Welsh pet form of Margaret, but it has now become an

independent name, popular throughout the English-speaking world. It has become so separated from its origins that, in the United States at least, spellings such as **Maegan** or **Maygen** suggest that it is being analysed as an elaboration of May; while forms such as **Meghan** or **Meagan** suggest that some users regard it as Irish.

Mel see MELVIN

Melanie

This comes from the Greek word for 'black'. *Melaina* was one of the titles of the goddess Demeter (see DEMETRIUS) in her winter aspect, mourning for the loss of her ravished daughter **Persephone**. **Melany** is a variant, and **Melony** is said to be an old Cornish form. (See also CHLOE.)

Melchior see JASPER

Melicent, Melisande, Melisenda see MILLICENT

Melissa

The Greek for 'honey bee', Melissa was the name of a nymph who is said to have introduced the use of honey to mankind. She is probably the remnant of an earlier earth or fertility goddess, for there is evidence of an important goddess associated with bees in Minoan Crete and in even earlier cultures. Associated names which come from the word for 'honey' are **Melinda** (the pet form of which is **Mindy** or **Mindie**), **Melita** and **Melina**.

Melody

Melody is simply the word for a tune used as a first name. It was a twentieth-century innovation, along with a companion name, **Harmony**.

Melony see MELANIE

Melvin

With its variant **Melvyn**, this comes from a Scottish surname with various sources, the most important of which is a form of **Melville**, derived from a noble family taking its name from a place in Normandy, meaning 'poor settlement'. It has also been explained as a masculine form of MALVINA via the variant Melvina. **Mel** is the short form.

Mercy

Mercy is the Christian virtue used as a first name, and as such was popular with the Puritans. **Mercedes** (see DOLORES) is the Spanish equivalent. **Merry** is said to be a pet form of Mercy, but nowadays is probably more often used as an independent name or as a short form of MEREDITH. **Mercia**, the name of an Anglo-Saxon kingdom which came into use at the beginning of the twentieth century when Old English names were popular, can also be used as a Latinate version of Mercy.

Meredith

This is a Welsh masculine name, also found as **Meredydd** and **Maredudd**, which has been in use since the sixth century and means 'magnificent chief'. Its use as a girl's name, which probably started in the United States, was a twentieth-century development. **Merry** is used as a short form.

Merfin see MERVYN

Merial, Meriel, Merille see MURIEL

Merle, Merlene see MAVIS

Merlin, Merlyn see MERVYN

Merna see MYRNA

Merrick see MAURICE

Merry see MERCY, MEREDITH

Mervyn
The Welsh name **Myrddin** or **Merfin** has been anglicized as both Mervyn and **Merlin**, the wizard from Arthurian legend. Although the town of Carmarthen is traditionally said to take its name from Merlin, it seems probable that it was the other way round, and that the Welsh name for the wizard, Myrddin Emrys, means 'EMRYS from Carmarthen'. The town's name means 'fort by the sea'. There is a variant spelling, **Merlyn**, which is sometimes used for girls (and then perhaps thought of as an elaboration of MERLE). **Marvin** is an old variant of **Mervin**, an alternative spelling.

Meryl see MURIEL

Meta see MARGARET

Meurig see MAURICE

Mhairi see MARY

Mia
The source of this name is not clear. It is the Italian and Spanish word for 'my', and so may come from an endearment in one of these languages. On the other hand, this may be coincidental, and the name may be a pet form of some name such as Maria, as in the case of the actress Mia Farrow, whose fame has had a major influence in spreading the name.

Michael
This name comes from the Hebrew meaning 'who is like God?'. The name also appears in the Old Testament in the form of the name of the prophet **Micah** (now found used for both sexes). The popularity of the Archangel Michael, the defeater of Satan and weigher of souls, guaranteed the early spread of the name throughout Europe in various forms. **Miguel** is the Spanish form of the name. Michael also became a surname and, as **Mitchel**, is occasionally found re-used as a first name. Pet forms are **Mick**, **Micky** and **Mike**. **Misha** or **Mischa** is a Russian masculine pet form, which, because of its apparently feminine ending,

is sometimes used in the UK as a girl's name (see also Sasha under ALEXANDER). The French feminine forms **Michelle** or **Michèle** have recently popular and the German **Michaela** has also been fashionable. The name SHELLEY seems to have started life as a pet form of Michelle.

Mildred

Mildred is a form of the Anglo-Saxon name *Mildthryth* ('gentle strength'). St Mildred was a seventh-century abbess who seems to have been well named, for she had a reputation for kindness and as a great comforter of the afflicted. The short forms **Millie** or **Milly** are shared with MILLICENT and AMELIA.

Miles

Miles is an old name of disputed meaning, although it is generally agreed that the name being the same as the Latin word for 'soldier' is pure chance. In Ireland the name is used as an English version of **Maelmor** ('servant of the Virgin Mary'). **Myles** and **Milo** are variants.

Milla see CAMILLA

Millicent

Millicent is the English form of the French **Melisande**, itself from a German name meaning something like 'strong in battle'. **Melicent** and **Melisenda** are variants. The short form **Millie** or **Milly** is shared with AMELIA and MILDRED.

Millie, Milly see AMELIA, CAMILLA, MILDRED, MILLICENT

Milo see MILES

Milton

This English surname is made up of the elements 'mill' and the old word for 'an enclosure'. It is used as a first name in honour of the Puritan poet John Milton (1608–74), and is more common in the United States, where there is a stronger tradition of using surnames of the famous as first names.

Mima see JEMIMA

Mina, Minella see WILLIAM

Mindie, Mindy see MELISSA

Minerva see ATHENE

Minna, Minnie see MARY, WILLIAM

Minta, Minty see ARAMINTA

Mira see MYRA

Miranda

Miranda is the Latin for 'worthy to be admired, deserving admiration', and was coined by Shakespeare for the heroine of *The Tempest*. **Mirabel** or **Mirabelle** is an older name from the same root, meaning 'admirable, lovely'. The French name **Mireille** and its Provençal form **Mirèio** also come from the same root. One account of the introduction of Mireille says that the Provençal poet and champion of Provençal culture Frédérique Mistral (1830–1914) found the name in local legend and used it as the title for a verse epic. He wanted to use the name for his god-daughter, but the priest refused to use a non-liturgical name, upon which Mistral emphatically stated that the name was a Provençal form of Miriam. As he was an expert in such things, the priest could hardly demur, and so the name came to be officially accepted in France, despite the fact that the name actually comes from the Provençal *mirar* ('to admire'). There is a Welsh name **Mirain**, which means 'wonderful'.

Miriam see MARY

Mischa, Misha see MICHAEL

Misty
Misty has recently become fashionable as a girl's name in the USA, probably not so much in its sense of 'a light fog' as in 'misty eyed, sentimental'. **Mistie** and **Mistee** are also used.

Mitchel see MICHAEL

Moira see MARY

Moll, Molly see MARY

Mona
An Irish name, Mona comes from a word meaning 'noble'. However, in Wales it is sometimes used as the Welsh name for Anglesea, Môn, with a feminine ending. It can also be a short form of MONICA.

Monica
St Monica was the mother of St AUGUSTINE. We learn a lot about her in his autobiographical writings. She must have been a rather overwhelming as well as loving mother, combining ambition for her favourite son with a determination to save his soul. Because she was instrumental in his conversion to Christianity, her name was early on derived from the Latin *monire* ('to warn'), but the true source of her name is unknown, and may be Phoenician, as she was a native of Carthage. **Monique**, the French form of the name, is also used.

Montague, Montgomery
These two, which share the short form **Monty**, are both French baronial names brought over by the conquering Normans. Montague ('pointed hill') is a common place name in France, but the surname comes from the place in the district of La Manche in Normandy. Montgomery is a more complicated place name, being 'mount' plus the name of an earlier German invader made up of the elements *guma* ('man') and *ric* ('power'), and is a place in Calvados, a region of Normandy.

Montserrat see DOLORES

Morag

Morag is a Scots name, probably made up of the Gaelic element *mor* ('great') with a feminine ending indicating a pet form. However it has been suggested that it shares with MURIEL a derivation from the word for 'sea'.

Morcant see MORGAN

Mordecai

This is a biblical name, ultimately of Persian origin, meaning 'a follower of the god Marduk'. It is now very rare, but is kept before the public by the writer Mordecai Richler.

Moreen see MARY

Morfydd, Morfudd see MORWENNA

Morgan

This is a Welsh name of disputed meaning. It seems likely that it is actually a conflation of several names, made up of the Welsh *môr* ('sea') or *mawr* ('great'), coupled with *can* ('bright') or *gen* ('born'). The sense 'sea-born' is supported by the Latin name **Pelagius**, also meaning 'sea-born', which probably translates Morgan, and was the name of the only notable early British heretic (born c. 370). On the other hand, another early form of the name, **Morcant**, would support a sense 'great and bright'. It is primarily a masculine name, but the appearance of Morgan or **Morgana** Le Fey in Arthurian legend as Arthur's magic-working half-sister and implacable enemy has led to its use as a feminine, which is now popular in the USA.

Morna see MYRNA

Morris, Morse see MAURICE

Mortimer

Another Norman baronial name, Mortimer derives from a French place name which comes from *mort mer* ('dead sea or pond'). There are traditions associating the adoption of the name with Crusaders and the Dead Sea in the Holy Land. It came into fashion along with other aristocratic names in the nineteenth century, but to some extent its use as a first name is influenced by the Gaelic name **Murtagh** ('sea man') being translated as Mortimer.

Morwenna

This comes from the Welsh word *morwyn* ('a maiden'). **Morwena** is a variant spelling, and there are the names **Morwyn** and **Morwen** as variants. **Morfydd** or **Morfudd**, the name given to his beloved by the great medieval Welsh poet Davydd ap Gwilym, probably comes from the same root. It was the name of a sixth-century princess, daughter of Urien Rheged and sister to the heroic Owain (see EUAN). It was a popular Welsh name throughout the Middle Ages.

Moses

This is a biblical name of disputed meaning. It is possible that, since the original Moses was born and brought up in Egypt, the name may be of Egyptian origin (compare his brother, AARON). It was regularly used until the eighteenth century, but is now rare. **Moss**, both as a first name and surname, started as a diminutive of Moses.

Mostyn
This is a Welsh place name meaning 'field-fortress', which was adopted as a surname in the sixteenth century and then became a masculine first name.

Moyra see MARY

Muirne see MYRNA

Murdo, Murdoch
Murdo is the phonetic spelling of the Scottish masculine name Murdoch, which is in turn the English form of the Gaelic **Murchadh** ('seaman'). It is thus the equivalent of the Irish Murtagh (see MORTIMER), as well as being the source of the common surname. There is a rare feminine, **Murdina**.

Muriel
This is an ancient Celtic name meaning 'sea-bright' which came back into use in the nineteenth century. It was revived in two main forms, Muriel and **Meriel**, and has since developed a large number of variants including **Merial**, **Meryl**, **Merille**, **Merrill**, **Merril** and **Muryell**.

Murray
A surname, now used as a first name, Murray comes from Moray in north-east Scotland. This area got its name from the old Celtic meaning 'settlement by the sea'. **Murry** is the Irish spelling.

Murtagh see MORTIMER

Muryell see MURIEL

Myesha see MAY

Myfanwy
This is a medieval Welsh girl's name meaning 'my rare or fine one', which was revived in Wales in the nineteenth century. **Myf**, **Myfi** and **Myfina** are all used as short forms.

Myles see MILES

Myra
This is a poetic name invented in the seventeenth century by Fulke Greville, Lord Brooke (1554–1628), and remained a purely literary name until the nineteenth. Its intended meaning is not clear, but if it meant to include the sense of the Latin *mirare* ('to admire'), as seems likely, then the name would be similar to MIRANDA. In the United States it has been used as the female equivalent of MYRON. **Mira** is a variant, and **Mayra** is used in the United States.

Myrddin see MERVYN

Myrna, Morna

These two names are both forms of the Irish name **Muirne**, meaning 'beloved'. **Merna** is a rare, further variant.

Myron

Although this name is hardly used in the UK, it is not uncommon in the United States, where it belongs to the group of first names adopted from the names of the famous, in this case the fifth-century BC Athenian sculptor of the 'Discus Thrower'. In Greek, the name meant 'fragrant'.

Myrtle

This plant was probably adopted as a girl's first name because the plant has been used to symbolize love and fidelity. Until quite recently it was worn or carried by brides at weddings in the same way as orange blossom is today, and women would try to grow the plant from cuttings taken from their wreath or bouquet.

Mysie see MARGARET

Nn

Nadia
Nadia is the pet form of the Russian name **Nadezhda** ('HOPE'), although only the pet forms of the name seem to be much used outside Russia. **Nadine** is a French variant, and in the past the form **Nadège** was also used in France.

Nahum
A prophet in the Old Testament, Nahum wrote in the seventh century BC. As well as the usual oracles about the rewards of respecting God, and the vengeance that awaits those who do not, his book gives a vivid description of the fall of Nineveh. The name means 'full of comfort', and is probably a short form of a name describing God as comforter. It is rarely used, but an awareness of it is kept alive by the hymn writer Nahum Tate.

Nan, Nana, Nanette, Nanna, Nanny see ANN

Nance, Nancy, Nansi see ANN, AGNES

Nandy see FERDINAND

Nanty see ANTONY

Naomi
Naomi is the model mother-in-law of the Old Testament. When she and her daughter-in-law RUTH were left widows, Naomi wanted to travel back to her own land. Such was the love Ruth had for Naomi that she refused to be separated from her, even though it meant leaving her own people. Naomi means 'pleasant'.

Nat see NATHANIEL

Natalia, Natalie, Nataline, Natalya, Natasha, Natasja, Natassia, Nathalie see NOEL

Nathaniel
A Hebrew name meaning 'gift of God', Nathaniel was the name of one of the apostles, probably the same as BARTHOLOMEW. **Nathan** ('gift') was the name of a character in the Old Testament who was a prophet, and counsellor and

critic of kings David and Solomon. Nathan is sometimes used as a short form of Nathaniel, and they share the short form **Nat** and more rarely **Nath** and **Nate**. There has recently been an increase in the popularity of these names.

Neal, Neale see NEIL

Ned, Neddie, Neddy see EDGAR, EDWARD

Neil
The true Irish form of this name is **Niall**, correctly pronounced the same way as the English form, but often given a spelling pronunciation. **Neal** or **Neale** is a common alternative form. The name is also the source of **Nigel**, which comes from *Nigellus*, the form given to the name in written Latin. This was not at first a spoken form, but the Latin was later misunderstood, and the name Nigel born, and mistakenly linked with the Latin word *niger* ('black'). Admiral **Nelson** probably inherited his surname from a 'Neil son', and this is now used as a first name in memory of him. There have been attempts to form feminine forms of the name: **Nelda** from Neil and **Nigella** and **Nigelia** from Nigel, but none of them is very common. The name, the origin of which is obscure, came into use because of the fame of Niall of the Nine Hostages, a fifth-century Irish warrior-king around whom many legends have collected.

Neirin see ANEURIN

Nell, Nellie, Nelly see ELEANOR, HELEN

Nelson see NEIL

Nerissa
This is the name of the delightful and witty maid and companion to PORTIA in Shakespeare's *Merchant of Venice*. Not as common as some other Shakespearean girls' names, it is nevertheless steadily if quietly used. The name comes from the Greek sea nymphs, the Nereides, daughters of Nereus, the Old Man of the Sea, who also give us the rarer **Nerida** and **Nerina**.

Nerys
This Welsh girl's name is usually interpreted from the Welsh word *ner* ('lord'), plus a feminine ending, but a recent writer has suggested that it may be a shortening of **Generys**, a name popular in medieval Wales or derived from NERISSA. It is a recent name, given fame by the actress Nerys Hughes.

Nessa, Nessie, Nest, Nesta see AGNES, VANESSA

Net, Netta, Nettie, Netty see AGNES, ANTONY, JANE

Neville
Neville or **Nevil** is a noble surname used as a first name. The fifteenth-century earl of Warwick, known as 'Warwick the Kingmaker', was the first Neville earl of Warwick. Three of his five paternal uncles were earls, and all four of his aunts married dukes, so the family name spread through the aristocracy. The

name, which means 'new town', came into use as a first name in the seventeenth century, but only became popular in the nineteenth century.

Nia see NIAMH

Niall see NEIL

Niamh
Niamh or **Niav** in its anglicized spelling is an Irish name meaning 'bright', originally the name of a goddess. In Irish mythology, a woman of this name takes the poet OSSIAN to the otherworld Land of Promise where she is a princess. The name is pronounced 'neev'. A pet form, **Nia**, has become very popular in Wales. This popularity was inspired by a poem by T. Gwynn Jones in praise of *Nia Ben Aur* ('Nia of the golden head'). Black Americans also use Nia as a first name, in this case from the Swahili word meaning 'intention, purpose'.

Nic see DOMINIC

Nicholas
Nicholas comes from a Greek name meaning 'victory of the people'. **Nicolas** was the original form of the name, the insertion of the 'h' being a hypercorrect form, like the 'h' in Anthony. **Nicol** or **Nichol** is an old pet form, while **Nick**, **Nicky** and **Nico** are more common today. The old form was shortened to **Col**, the pet-form ending -in was added, and thus the now separate name COLIN developed. St Nicholas was a fourth-century bishop in Asia Minor, who, according to legend, secretly supplied three destitute girls with dowries by leaving the money at their windows. As his feast day is 6 December, this deed became associated with Christmas. The feast day of St Nicholas, or Santa Claus as he is known in Dutch, is still celebrated in many parts of Europe as the beginning of the Christmas season, or as a time for giving presents. Dutch settlers took the tradition to the United States, where it became more firmly associated with 25 December, and from there it spread to other parts of the world. **Nichola** is the commonest feminine form of the name along with the French **Nicole**; the latter has the diminutive **Nicolette**, which in turn leads to Colette (see COLIN). The short form of the name is spelt variously **Nicky**, **Nickie**, **Nikki** or **Nicci**. **Nikita** is strictly speaking a Russian masculine name, from a Greek name meaning 'unconquered', but is used, particularly in the United States, as a form of Nicola.

Nigel, Nigelia, Nigella see NEIL

Nikita see NICHOLAS

Nina, Ninette, Ninon see ANN

Ninian
St Ninian was a fifth-century Briton who became a missionary to the Picts in Scotland. This led to the name being a popular one in Scotland in earlier times. There has recently been something of a revival of interest in this as well as other local names, possibly helped by the name being kept alive by its appearance in Scott's *The Antiquary*. **Ringan** is a dialect form of the name.

Nita see ANN, JANE

Noah

Noah is a Hebrew name meaning 'repose'. The story of Noah and his ark must be one of the best-known Bible stories, but despite this the name has not been much used historically, although it is in fashion at the moment. One bearer of the name, Noah Webster (1758–1843), had a considerable impact on the cultural history of the United States, being not only the creator of Webster's *Dictionary*, but also introducing the spelling reforms that distinguish American English from that of Great Britain.

Noel

Noel or **Noël** is the French word for **Christmas** (itself occasionally used as a first name). It was originally given to children born on or about 25 December. **Noelle** or **Noëlle** is the French feminine form of the name, with **Noella** a variant. In English-speaking countries **Noele**, **Noleen**, **Noelena** and **Noeline** are also found. **Natalie** is a name with the same meaning, since it comes from the Latin *dies natalis* ('the birthday (of Christ)'), which is the root of the French *noël*. **Nathalie** is the French spelling. The Russian version of the name, **Natalia** (occasionally found as **Natalya** and shortened to **Talia**) has a pet form **Natasha** (sometimes spelled **Natasja** or **Natassia**). These have been used steadily since the 1960s, and Natalie has developed a variant, **Nataline**.

Nola see FENELLA

Nolan

Nolan is an Irish surname, ultimately going back to the word *nuall* ('famous'), now used as a boy's name in the USA.

Noll, Nolly see OLIVER

Nora

Nora or **Norah** started life as a pet form of such names as HONORIA, LEONORA and ELEANOR, but has long been used as an independent name. Honoria was a particularly popular name in Ireland, and was frequently reduced to Nora. It then acquired a diminutive suffix, and **Noreen** was formed. This name has been further elaborated to **Norlene** and **Noreena**. **Nonie** is a pet form of Nora.

Norman

Norman means 'man from the north', and was in use in England for Scandinavian settlers even before the country was invaded by the Normans, who were themselves Scandinavian settlers in France. In Scotland, the name was used to anglicize another Viking name, **Tormod**, adopted by Gaelic speakers from their Norse conquerors. This is formed from the name of the pagan god Thor, and *mod* ('mind, courage'). (For other Thor names see THORA). **Norma**, which is used as the feminine form of the name, seems to have been invented by Felice Romani, the librettist of Bellini's opera of that name, which was first performed in 1832. Some would derive it from the Latin *norma* meaning 'rule, standard, measure'.

Normandy, Normandie see BRITTANY

Nuala see FENELLA

Nye see ANEURIN

Oo

Oberon see AUBREY

Octavia
This is the Latin feminine for 'eighth', originally a Roman name given to an eighth child, but later it was associated with the imperial family – the first emperor, AUGUSTUS, being called **Octavius** or **Octavian** before he took his title. Octavia is shortened to **Tavy**, **Tave** or **Tavia**.

Odette, Odile, Odo see OTTO

Odysseus see ULYSSES

Oighrig see AFRIC, EUPHEMIA

Olaf see OLIVER

Olga
Olga is the Russian version of the Scandinavian name **Helga**, meaning 'holy, blessed'. Although Helga was found in pre-Conquest England, its use today is a modern re-introduction. The predominance of Olga over Helga probably reflects the popularity of Russian literature.

Oliver
ROLAND and Oliver were inseparable companions and the two greatest of Charlemagne's peers in the old French stories. Their friendship was so great that it became proverbial. The followers of Charlemagne in both fact and fiction were Franks, a Germanic people, and their names reflect this. Thus, although Oliver looks as if it is based on the olive, symbol of peace, and the French form of the name, **Olivier**, is identical with the French for 'an olive tree', the name most probably is a form of the Scandinavian name **Olaf**, formed from elements meaning 'ancestor' and 'heir, descendant', which in its old form *Olafr* (*Olvir* in many early texts) would have a very similar pronunciation. Oliver was long out of fashion after the fall of Oliver Cromwell (whose nicknames illustrate the old pet forms **Noll** and **Nolly**), but time has reduced the close association of the Protector and the name, and Oliver is now firmly back in fashion in the UK. **Ol** and **Ollie** are now the more common short forms. The name **Havelock** is said to be the Welsh form of the name.

Feminine forms of the name are even more closely associated with the plant, being **Olive** and **Olivia**. Olivia is another Shakespearean introduction, used for the noble lady beloved by the duke in *Twelfth Night*. The name is sometimes shortened to **Livia** or **Livy**, although Livia is a name in its own right, being a Roman family name made famous by the wife of the emperor AUGUSTUS.

Olwen

Olwen is a character from the medieval Welsh story of *Culhwch and Olwen* in which her wise advice enables her lover to win her from her ogre father. She possessed outstanding beauty, and four white trefoils sprang up in her footprints wherever she trod, hence her name, which means 'white footprint'. **Olwyn** is a frequent variant of the name, and it is not surprising that this charming legend has made the name popular with Welsh parents.

Olympia

Mount Olympus was the home of the gods in Greek mythology. From this mountain the Greek name **Olympias** was coined. It was the name of the ruthless but admired mother of ALEXANDER the Great, and from there spread through the lands he conquered. It was given to a fourth-century AD Byzantine woman of equally strong but rather more attractive character who was later canonized, and as St Olympia the name spread through Europe. Both forms of the name occur early on in England, but now the name is rare, except among those of Greek descent. **Olympe**, the French form, and **Olympie** are also used.

Omar

As a boy's name, this can have three different sources. It is a well-known Arabic name meaning 'flourishing'. It can be a biblical name mentioned in the book of Genesis. Finally, some uses may be inspired by the fame of US general Omar Bradley (1893–1981), who distinguished himself as a commander in World War II.

Onyx see JEWELL

Oona, Oonagh see UNA

Opal see JEWELL

Ophelia

Another Shakespearean introduction, Ophelia is the tragic and rather ineffective heroine of *Hamlet*. Although this is not one of the commonest Shakespearean names, parents do not seem to have been put off by the story of her madness and suicide, and the name has a steady use. It was probably coined from a Greek root meaning 'help'.

Oran see ORRIN

Oriel, Oriole see AURELIUS

Orin see ORRIN

Orla

An Irish name meaning 'golden lady', Orla thus has the same meaning as the AURELIAN group of names. In Irish it is spelt **Orfhlaith**, and it can also be found in the form **Orlagh**. **Aurnia** is a variant. There is also a masculine Orla who occurs in the poems of OSSIAN, but while this was used at the height of the European Ossianic craze in the nineteenth century, it is probably now obsolete.

Orlanda, Orlando see ROLAND

Orrin

Orrin or **Orin**, a name largely confined to the southern United States and in use since at least the eighteenth century, is probably a form of the Irish name **Oran** ('grey-brown, dark') and the name of a number of Irish saints. **Orna** is the female equivalent.

Orson

Orson means 'bear cub'. In medieval legend Valentine (see VALERY) and Orson were twins born to an exiled Byzantine Princess. The new-born Orson is stolen by a bear, who brings him up. Despite his rough behaviour and ursine appearance, his noble nature shows through in his fighting skills, and after many adventures he is finally reunited with his family and regains his rightful place in society. By no means a common name, it became well known in the twentieth century through the fame of Orson Welles (1915–85). URSULA is the feminine equivalent of the name.

Orville see WILBUR

Osbert

This is one of a group of Old English names containing the first element *os*, meaning 'god', combined with other common name elements. Thus we have **Osric** ('god' + 'rule') **Oswald** ('god' + 'power') and **Oswin** ('god' + 'friend'). They all share **Os**, **Oz**, **Ozzie** and **Ossy** as short forms. There was a revival of these names in the nineteenth century, but they are not popular at the moment.

Oscar

Although some authorities give this name a German source meaning 'divine spear', it is much more likely to be an Irish name meaning 'champion warrior'. It has strong associations with Scandinavia, but despite its being a Swedish royal name, this is not evidence for a Germanic inheritance, for it comes from Napoleon Bonaparte's passion for the poems of OSSIAN. In 1799 Napoleon was godfather to the first son of his Marshal, Jean-Baptiste Bernadotte, who became king of Sweden as Karl XIV Johan. Napoleon chose to name his godson Oscar after the hero of Macpherson's poems, and this child became Oscar I of Sweden in 1844. From him the name spread to the general population, along with a number of other Ossianic names. King Oscar had as his court physician a certain Sir William Wilde, and it is probably this connection, rather than the Irish one, that led to his son being christened with two Ossianic names, Oscar FINGAL O'Flahertie Wilde. Oscar had been a popular name in the nineteenth century, but the scandalous trial of Oscar Wilde in 1895 led to a distinct fall in its popularity and it became rare in the UK, although there are now signs of its returning to use, but Scandinavian immigration made sure that it never suffered the same fate in the USA.

Osric see OSBERT

Ossian
Ossian means 'fawn' and is the name of the legendary son of Finn (see FINLAY). The name is also found as **Ossin**, **Oisin** and in a phonetic spelling of the Irish form **Osheen**. According to legend, Ossian was the leader of the Irish Fenians who were defeated at the battle of Fabhra by King Carbery in 283. Ossian was left as the last survivor of the Fenians and after spending some years in fairyland (see NIAMH) he was converted to Christianity by St Patrick. In the eighteenth century James Macpherson created a great stir by publishing a series of poems associated with Ossian, supposedly ancient but in fact mainly his own work, and this led to a number of names which occurred in these poems, such as OSCAR, FINGAL, SELMA and MALVINA, coming into use. A feminine form, **Ossia**, is also found.

Ossy, Oswald, Oswin see OSBERT

Otis see OTTO

Otto
The Germanic name element *ot* or *od*, meaning 'riches, prosperity', has developed into a number of names. Otto is the German form which has not been used that long in this country, but the name came over with the Normans in the form of **Odo**, William the Conqueror's avaricious half-brother. The French feminine forms of the name, **Odile** and **Odette**, reflect this form in 'd', but the 't' forms are also to be found in **Ottilie**, **Ottoline** and **Ottilia**. The name Otis comes from a surname which developed from the same root. It came into use in America as a first name out of respect for James Otis (1725–83), a campaigner for American rights in the lead up to the Revolution.

Owain, Owen see EUAN

Oz, Ozzie see OSBERT

P**p**

Pablo see PAUL

Paddy, Padraic, Pàdraig, Padrig see PATRICK

Paige
This surname, originally given to someone who was a page, has been one of the most successful new names in recent years. It was well established in the USA in the late 1980s, but did not enter the British top 50 until the second half of the 1990s.

Paloma
This is the Spanish for 'dove'. It was used by Picasso for his daughter's name, and is occasionally found in this country, probably as a direct result of Paloma Picasso's fame. For masculine names meaning 'dove', see under MALCOLM.

Pamela
Pamela was invented by Sir Philip Sydney (1554–86) as a name in his pastoral *Arcadia*. From the way his verse scans, he seems to have intended the word to be pronounced with the stress on the second syllable, and may have intended it to be understood as from the Greek meaning 'all honey'. It became a famous name with the success in 1740 of Samuel Richardson's long novel *Pamela: or Virtue Rewarded*. **Pamella** is a variant and **Pam** or **Pammie** the pet form.

Pandora
In Greek mythology Pandora plays the same role as EVE in the Bible, bringing misfortune upon mankind. She was created by the gods on the orders of Zeus, to take vengeance for the stealing of fire for mankind's use. Each god gave her a gift of some desirable quality (the name means 'all gifts'), but she was also made inquisitive. Her husband had a sealed box which she had been forbidden to open, but she did so, and out flew all the ills which afflict mankind. Hope had also been sealed in the box, which alone made the afflictions bearable. Despite this story, Pandora is now quite regularly used, and can be shortened to **Panda**.

Pansy
One of the less common flower names, Pansy has been in use since the end of the nineteenth century. The name of the flower comes from the French word *pensée* ('a thought'), from the way in which the markings on the flowers and the way they grow can look like a face bent in thought.

Paola, Paolo see PAUL

Paris
Although Paris was originally a man's name (see ALEXANDER, HELEN), it is now more common as a first name for girls. The occasional male uses probably hark back to the original Trojan hero (the name is also used in passing by Shakespeare), but for girls, parents are probably thinking of the French city of Paris (which got its name from the ancient Gaulish tribe who lived there, the Parisi) and all the associations of culture and the good things in life that are associated with it.

Parker
Parker, or its shortened form **Park**, has come into fashion in the USA as a boy's name. It comes from a surname which would have been given in the Middle Ages to a gamekeeper.

Parnel see PETER

Parthalon, Partholon see BARTHOLOMEW

Pascal
Pascal means 'Easter' and was originally given to those born at that time of year, just as NOEL was given to those born at Christmas. The surname **Pascoe** comes from the Cornish form of the name. **Pascale, Pascalle** or rarely **Pascaline** are its feminines.

Pat see PATRICK

Patience
Patience is one of the Christian virtues, and as such was brought into use in the seventeenth century by the Puritans. It has recently been rather out of favour, but now shows slight signs of coming back into fashion.

Patrick
Patrick comes from the Latin *patricius* ('a nobleman'). The Irish form of their patron saint's name is **Pádraig**, with **Padraic** and **Phadrig** as variants, but the name was not used in Ireland in early times, possibly out of reverence for the great saint. St Patrick was not a native Irishman, but a Briton, and his name has survived in Welsh as **Padrig**. **Pat** and **Paddy** are the commonest short forms of Patrick, with **Patsy**, once common, now more generally female. **Patricia**, the feminine, comes from the Latin form of the name, and has a number of short forms such as **Pat, Patty, Patsy, Tricia** and **Tisha**. **Patrice**, used in France for both sexes, is usually feminine in English-speaking countries.

Pattie, Patty see MARTHA, MATILDA, PATRICK

Paul
This name comes from the Latin *paulus* ('small'), and was therefore a suitably humble name for SAUL of Tarsus to adopt after his conversion from persecutor of Christians to Apostle. **Pablo**, the Spanish form, and **Paolo**, the Italian, are found in the USA. **Paula** is the direct Latin feminine of the name, with **Pauline** a

diminutive derived from the Latin alternative **Paulina**. **Paola** is the Italian form and **Paulette** a French pet form. **Polly** is occasionally a pet form of Pauline.

Pearce see PETER

Pearl
Although it is one of the jewel names, Pearl has the same meaning as MARGARET, so is also found as a pet form of that name.

Pedran, Pedr see PETER

Peg, Peggie, Peggy see MARGARET

Pelagius see MORGAN

Penelope
In Homer's *Odyssey*, Penelope is the faithful wife of Odysseus (see ULYSSES), who successfully resists the wooing of the 50 suitors who wish to win the kingdom by marrying her, for the 10 years it takes for her husband to reach home after the fall of Troy. Her main ploy is to say that she will not choose a new husband until she has woven a shroud for her father-in-law. Although she diligently weaves all day, at night she unpicks her work. The meaning of the name is something of a problem. It appears to come from the word for 'a duck', but it is very difficult to see why the ancient Penelope should have been named after this bird. The name may be so early, possibly pre-Greek, that its meaning has been lost. **Pen** and **Penny** are its short forms.

Pepita see JOSEPH

Percy
The first of the Percys came over with the Conqueror and founded the great Northumbrian family of that name. The surname comes from the common French place name Percé, in his case probably from the village near St Lô. The village name, in its turn, comes from the Gallo-Roman name *Persius*. The surname came into use as a first name in the eighteenth century. Percy is also used as a short form of the name **Percival**, which comes from Arthurian romance. It was invented in the twelfth century by the French writer Chrétien de Troyes for his perfect knight. It seems to be made up of the elements *perce-val* ('pierce-valley'), although the reason for this is not clear, and it may be that the name is a corruption of the Welsh name for a hero who shares some of the same adventures, **Peredur**, whose name means 'hard spears'. Percival is sometimes shortened to **Val**.

Perdita
This name means 'the lost one' and was created by Shakespeare for the heroine of *The Winter's Tale*, who is abandoned as an infant. Despite the charming personality of the original, and the happy outcome of the play, this is not one of the commoner Shakespearean names, although it was certainly in use among the ruling classes by the early part of the twentieth century, for the name was given to the granddaughter of the prime minister H.H. Asquith in 1910.

Peredur see PERCY

Peregrine
Peregrine comes from the Latin for 'a pilgrim, traveller', and was a common early Christian name, emphasizing the transitory nature of life on earth against the eternity of heaven. Its only connection with the peregrine falcon is that they share a common root. Most birds used for falconry were taken from the nest, but the peregrine was captured while travelling to its breeding ground; hence its name. **Perry** can be used as a short form of Peregrine, but is also used as an independent name in the United States in honour of two Admiral Perrys, one of whom, Oliver Hazard Perry, defeated the British fleet on Lake Erie in 1812, while Matthew Galbraith Perry opened up Japan to foreign interests. However, the best-known Perry, the singer Perry Como, was originally Nick Perido, so got his stage name from his surname.

Perkin, Pernel see PETER

Pernilla see PETER

Perry see PEREGRINE

Persephone see CORINNA, MELANIE

Perseus see DANÄE

Persis
Persis means 'Persian woman'. It is now a rare name, but was not uncommon in the seventeenth century, when obscure names from the Bible were in fashion. The biblical Persis is mentioned in the Epistle of St Paul to the Romans (16. 12), when he writes 'Salute the beloved Persis, which laboured much in the Lord'. Nothing else is known of her.

Peter
Peter means 'stone', and started life as a nickname, given to the Apostle SIMON by Jesus, who, punning on the word, says 'thou art Peter, and upon this rock I will build my church' (Matthew 16. 18). Peter is formed directly from the Latin *petrus*; but **Piers**, the alternative form of the name, comes via the French **Pierre**. Piers was the common vernacular form of the name in the Middle Ages, and gives us the surnames **Pearce** and **Pierce**, sometimes used as first names. **Pete** is now the common pet form, but in the past **Peterkin** and **Perkin** were used. In Welsh the name became **Pedr**, with the pet forms **Pedran** and **Petran**.

There are a large number of feminine versions of the name. According to legend, St **Petronilla** or **Petronella** was the daughter of St Peter (the name is actually a form of the Roman family name of the Petronii), and this was used as a feminine equivalent. It was very common in medieval England, when it was shortened to **Petronel**, **Pernel** or **Parnel**. In Scandinavia it became **Pernilla**. **Peta**, **Petra** and **Petrina** are based more closely on the masculine.

Phebe see PHOEBE

Phelim see FELICITY

Phemia, Phemie see EUPHEMIA

Phia see SOPHY

Philip
A traditional name in the Macedonian royal family, Philip means 'loving horses'. It was spread by the conquests of Philip the Great of Madeconia's son Alexander (see further under ALEXANDER), became common throughout the Middle East, and was the name of one of the Apostles and a number of saints, which guaranteed the spread of the name through Europe. It is sometimes spelt **Phillip**, as in the surname, and shortened to **Phil** and **Pip**. **Flip** is a contracted form of the name. **Philippa** (sometimes **Phillipa**, **Phillippa** or **Philipa**) is the usual feminine and this is shortened to **Pippa**, which was originally an Italian form. The French feminine **Philippine** is occasionally found.

Phillida, Phillis see PHYLLIS

Philomena
Philomena means 'beloved'. In 1802 an inscription and some bones were discovered in the Catacombs at Rome, and a dedication to the bereaved's 'beloved' was interpreted as indicating that these were the bones of a St Philomena. In 1863 Charlotte M. Yonge could write, 'So many wonders are said to have been worked by this phantom saint, the mere produce of a blundered inscription, that . . . she is by far the most fashionable patroness in the Romish Church.' The name was particularly popular in Ireland, but has lost favour there since the saint was declared spurious. However, the name is still regularly used, with the French form **Philomène** occasionally found.

Phineas
This is the name of two minor characters in the Old Testament, where the name appears as **Phinehas**. Its meaning is obscure, but it may mean 'oracle'. Little used now, the name is kept alive by the stories about the showman Phineas T. Barnum (1810–91), and in literature by Trollope's novel *Phineas Finn* (1869).

Phoebe
Phoebe means 'the shining one' and was an epithet of the goddess Artemis, sister of Phoebus Apollo, in her aspect of moon goddess (see also DIANA, CYNTHIA). It is found in the Bible in the same chapter of Romans as PERSIS, in the form **Phebe**, and this justified it being adopted as a Christian name. It has been rather out of favour since the early part of the twentieth century, but is now showing distinct signs of coming back into fashion. Phoebe is also used as a short form of EUPHEMIA.

Phyllis
This is a Greek name meaning 'leafy'. In mythology, Phyllis is a Thracian maiden who hangs herself when her lover does not return from his own country, where he has gone to settle his affairs, within the promised time, and is transmogrified into an almond tree. When her delayed lover finally returns he embraces the almond tree, and the plant, hitherto barren, puts forth green leaves. **Phyllida** is a literary elaboration of the name. Other forms are **Phillis**, **Phylis** and **Phillida**.

Pia

The Latin feminine for 'pious', Pia is an Italian name which has only recently come into use in this country, although the masculine, Pius, has long been familiar as the name of numerous popes.

Pierce, Pierre, Piers see PETER

Pip, Pippa see PHILIP

Pollux see COSMO

Polly see MARY, PAUL

Poppy

This is another flower name which became particularly popular at the end of the nineteenth century and the beginning of the twentieth. Out of favour for a number of years, it is once more coming back into use.

Portia

A Roman family name, coming from the word for 'pig', Portia has become dissociated from its roots thanks to Shakespeare. He has two Portias in his plays. One, Cato's daughter and Brutus' faithful and stoical wife in *Julius Caesar*, is a Roman matron who really existed. The other, the heroine of *The Merchant of Venice*, combines charm with wit and wisdom, and it is after her that most Portias are named. The name has been fashionable in recent years, and in the United States many phonetic forms have developed, the most common of which is **Porsha**. Since the pronunciation of the name and that of the German Porsche car is all but identical, one name blends imperceptibly into the other, and as well as **Porsche**, spellings such as **Porchia**, **Porscha** and **Porshia** are found.

Precious

This name, generally a term of affection, is now being used as a girl's given name, and is also occasionally used for boys.

Preston

This surname, now a common choice for a boy's first name in the USA, comes from a place name that can either be interpreted as 'village with a priest', or 'village on land owned by the church'.

Primrose

Primrose, like POPPY, was a very popular name at the turn of the nineteenth and twentieth centuries but there does not seem to have been the same return of interest in it. **Primula**, the Latin name for the plant, has also been used.

Priscilla

This is a biblical name. Priscilla was very active in the early Church, being both a supporter and follower of St Paul. She is mentioned in various books in the New Testament, including the chapter of Romans that gives us PHOEBE and PERSIS. Priscilla is an old Roman family name meaning 'ancient'. **Prissy** and **Cilla** are the short forms.

Prudence

Like other virtue names, Prudence was much loved by the Puritans. An earlier form of the name is **Prudentia**, a saint's name, probably in its turn modelled on **Prudentius**, a much admired early Christian poet of the fourth century. **Prue** is the short form.

Prunella

Prunella may be a diminutive of the Latin *prunus*, both the word for 'a plum tree' and for the group of winter-flowering trees that do so much to lighten winter gardens. Prunella is also the name for a kind of silk and the Latin name for both the wild flower self-heal and the hedge sparrow, but this is probably coincidental. An alternative suggestion is that it is a variant of **Brunella**, a feminine form of BRUNO, which is also used to indicate a brunette.

Qq

Queenie see REX

Quentin

Quentin comes from the Latin name *Quintus* ('fifth'), traditionally given to a fifth son. St Quentin was a third-century missionary and martyr who met his death at the French city now named after him. **Quintin** is a common variant, while **Quinton** is the commonest form in the USA. This reflects the spelling of the surname, which can either be from Quentin, or from a place name meaning 'the queen's settlement'.

Quincy

An aristocratic surname, Quincy comes from the French place name of Cuinchy (north of Arras). This, in its turn, comes from a Roman personal name *Quintus*, so the name has the same root as QUENTIN. Quincy (sometimes **Quincey**) is used more frequently in the United States, where it came into use in honour of John Quincy Adams (1767–1848), the 6th president of that country.

Quinn

This boy's name comes from an Irish surname meaning 'descendant of Conn', CONN meaning 'chief, leader'.

R**r**

Rab, Rabbie see ROBERT

Rachel

A Hebrew name meaning 'ewe', Rachel was a suitable name for a girl who kept her father's sheep (Genesis 29. 6.) The biblical Rachel was 'beautiful and well favoured' and dearly loved by her husband JACOB, although she did not get on with her sister and co-wife LEAH. The name is often spelt **Rachael** and has developed in a number of different directions. The variant **Rachelle**, with a 'sh' sound in the middle, has in turn developed the form **Rochelle**. This is a more likely source of the name than the Breton port meaning 'little rock', although it is worth noting that it is an American name, and Rochelle is also a transatlantic place name, for example Rochelle Park in New Jersey. Rachelle and Rochelle use SHELLEY as a short form. Rachel can be shortened to **Rae** or **Ray**, and this has been elaborated into **Raelene**. **Raquel**, the Spanish form of the name, has come into use since it was made famous by the actress Raquel Welch. Rachel has been a popular name since the 1970s.

Rae see RACHEL, RAYMOND

Raeven see RAVEN

Rafael, Rafaela see RAPHAEL

Rafe see RALPH

Raina, Raine see REX

Ralph

This comes from an old Germanic name *Rad(w)ulf* made up of the elements meaning 'counsel' and 'wolf'. The spelling **Ralf** is closer to the original, the -ph form being an eighteenth-century 'improvement'. The variant **Rafe**, found since the Middle Ages, reflects the pronunciation which was the norm until the twentieth century. **Raoul** is the French form of the word. **Rolf**, from *Hrodulf* ('fame' + 'wolf'), is a closely allied name, which was absorbed by Ralph in the Middle Ages, and obsolete until revived as a separate name in the nineteenth century. **Rollo** was the medieval Latin form of Rolf, while in Germany the name became **Rudolph** or **Rudolf**, with a short form **Rudy** or **Rudi**. This was introduced into the English-speaking world in the nineteenth century, but despite the enormous popularity of Rudolph Valentino in the 1920s, the name has never been very common. Its more recent association with red-nosed reindeer cannot have helped.

Ramon, Ramona see RAYMOND

Ranald see REGINALD

Randolph, Randall
Randolph or **Randolf** is an Old English name meaning 'shield wolf'. It has two major variants, **Ranulf** (very occasionally **Renouf**), and **Randal** or **Randall**, which at the moment is probably more frequently given than the original form. The short form **Randy** is now treated as an independent name (and **Randi** is sometimes found as a feminine form), especially in the United States, but the alternative **Dolph** is rarely heard now.

Raoul see RALPH

Raphael
The archangel Raphael's name means 'God heals', reflecting his role in the Apocryphal *Book of Tobit*, where he restores Tobit's sight. The name has been less popular than the other archangels MICHAEL and GABRIEL, despite his being the patron of doctors and travellers, and for a long time it was regarded as a particularly Jewish name. Nowadays it is probably most closely associated with the Renaissance painter. **Rafael** is a variant, and the Italian feminine **Raphaela** or **Rafaela** is sometimes found.

Raquel see RACHEL

Rasmus, Rastus see ERASMUS

Raven
Recorded from as early as 1869, Raven (sometimes **Raeven** or **Ravyn**) has been fashionable as a girl's name in the USA for the last decade, presumably because of its associations with glossy darkness shared with EBONY and Sable.

Ray see RACHEL, RAYMOND

Raymond
The old Germanic name *Raginmund*, formed from words meaning 'counsel' and 'protection', became *Raimund* in Old French and was brought over to England by the Normans, where it became Raymond or **Raymund**, with the short form **Ray** or **Rae**. When the Normans later conquered Ireland, they took the name with them, and there it became **Redmond** or **Redmund**, an increasingly popular name. In Spanish it became **Ramon**, well used in the United States, with a feminine **Ramona**, made famous as the title of a popular song. The French feminine **Raymonde** is also occasionally found.

Rayna see REX

Reanna see RHIANNON

Rebecca
The meaning of the name Rebecca is not clear, although it may mean either 'cow' or 'noose'. She appears as **Rebekah**, a form that is occasionally used, in the Old Testament, Rebecca being the spelling used in the New. She was the mother of Esau and JACOB, the founder of the house of Israel. Jacob was her favourite son, and it was Rebecca who planned the scheme by which Jacob deprived his brother of his birthright (Genesis 27). Rebecca comes across as a strong-minded woman, used to giving orders and with no patience if contradicted; but also as a woman capable of great love. **Becky** is the usual short form but **Becca** is also used.

Redmond, Redmund see RAYMOND

Redvers
General Sir Redvers Buller (1836–1908) played a prominent part in the Boer War. He was greatly criticized for his conduct of the war, and was later dismissed from his post after coming into conflict with the government of the day, but his actions were often prompted by a care for his troops, and he was popular with the men under his command, which is no doubt the reason for the brief popularity of this name at the turn of the nineteenth and twentieth centuries. It comes from an aristocratic surname which derives from the French place name Reviers. The name is very rarely used today.

Reece, Rees see RHYS

Regina, Regine see REX

Reginald
Reginald, with its short forms **Reg**, **Reggie** and occasionally REX, comes from *Reginaldus*, the Latin form of the name **Reynold**, the Norman form of an old Germanic name *Reginwald*, formed from elements meaning 'might' and 'rule'. **Ronald** (often **Ronnald** in the USA), with its short forms **Ron** and **Ronnie**, is from the Old Norse form of the same name. In Scotland, **Ranald** is found as an occasional variant.

Reina, Reine see REX

Rena see ANDREW

Renée
Also found without the accent as **Renee**, this is the French form of the Latin name **Renata** ('reborn'), referring to Christian baptism. It can also be spelt **Rennie** or **Renie** (see also IRENE), **Rene** and **Renny**. The masculine form **René** from **Renatus** is very common in France, but little used here.

Renouf see RANDOLPH

Reuben
The name given to the eldest son of JACOB, Reuben was interpreted in the Bible (Genesis 29. 32) as meaning 'behold a son'. It is also spelt **Ruben**.

Rex

Rex, the Latin word for 'king', came into use as a first name in the nineteenth century (see also REGINALD). The French equivalent of Rex is **Regis**, the inflected form of the Latin, although this was adopted as a first name in honour of St Jean François Regis, the apostle of the Vivarais region. There is a wide range of feminine equivalents. **Regina** (sometimes shortened to **Gina**) is the Latin for 'queen' and **Queenie** started life as a pet form of this name (although it was also used for VICTORIA, a name which only became popular during Queen Victoria's long reign). In French, the name becomes **Regine**. **Raine** and **Reine** are based on the French word for 'queen', while the Spanish form is **Reyna** (sometimes found as **Rayna**, **Raina** or **Reina**). The Irish name **Riona** has the same meaning, and ultimately the same root.

Reynold see REGINALD

Rhiannon

An important figure in early Welsh literature, Rhiannon's antecedents go back even before the earliest surviving legends, for she seems to be a survival of an ancient Celtic goddess, possibly having some connection with horses. Her name means 'nymph, goddess'. It is also spelt **Rhianon**, and use has spread to non-Welsh parents, perhaps as a result of the Fleetwood Mac hit single *Rhiannon* (1978). As a result, variants such as **Rhianna** and spellings without the 'h' have developed. There are a number of other Welsh girls' names which come from the same root. Another popular Welsh name **Rhian** (now also **Rhianne**, **Rhianna**) could be a short form of Rhiannon or from *rhiain* ('maiden'), an interpretation backed by names such as **Rhianedd** and **Rhianydd**, which are based on the plural form of the word, and **Rhianwen** or **Rhiainwen**, which combines the word for 'maiden' with that meaning 'white' or 'fair'. **Reanna**, used in the USA, is either from Rhiannon or is a pet form of Adriana.

Rhoda

Rhoda is from the Greek meaning 'rose' and is another example of an apparently pagan name being made 'respectable' by being that of a minor New Testament character. It was very popular at the turn of the last century, but is not much used now.

Rhodri see RODERICK

Rhona, Rona

This is a difficult name. It may be from a Scottish island, in which case it means 'rough island'; it may be a short form of ROWENA, or it may be a feminized form of **Ronan**, the name of a fifth-century Irish saint which probably comes from the word for 'seal'. It seems to have been in use only since about 1870, and became fashionable in the 1930s when it was given glamour by the successful 'Rhona Roy' fashion clothes.

Rhonda

This is probably a respelling of the Welsh Rhondda valley, which takes its name from its river. The word means 'noisy'.

Rhonwen see ROWENA

Rhys

A Welsh masculine name, Rhys means 'ardour' and so implies 'fiery warrior'. It was the name of two twelfth-century warriors who fought successfully against the English invaders of Wales. It is frequently found in the forms **Rees(e)** and **Reece**, more common as surnames.

Ria see MARY

Riana see ADRIAN

Richard

Richard comes from a Germanic root meaning 'strong ruler'. It was in use among the Anglo-Saxons in the form *Ricehard*, but the modern form was introduced by the Normans. It has long been a popular name, as can be seen from the number of pet forms it has developed, which include: **Dick, Dickie, Dicky, Diccon** or **Dickon; Rick** and **Ricky** (see also ERIC, FREDERICK), **Rich** and **Richie**. In the USA, the Spanish form **Ricardo,** and its shortening **Rico,** are well used. Attempts at forming feminines have been less successful, but **Ricarda, Richenda** and **Richelle** are all used.

Rick, Ricky see CEDRIC, ERIC, FREDERICK, RICHARD

Riley

This Irish surname, of obscure origin, is now also used as a first name, most often for boys, but increasingly for girls.

Ringan see NINIAN

Riona see REX

Rita see MARGARET

Robert

A Germanic name, Robert is formed from elements meaning 'fame' and 'bright'. Like Richard, it has long been part of the basic stock of English names and has consequentially developed a large number of pet forms. Dod, Dobbin, Hob and Hobbie were all used in the past but are now obsolete, but that still leaves **Bert** and **Bertie; Bob** and **Bobbie** or **Bobby; Rob, Robbie, Robby, Robo,** and in Scotland **Rab** and **Rabbie. Robin** (sometimes **Robyn** in Wales) is now often used as a separate name, but started life as a French pet form of Rob. **Roberta** and **Robina** are the older feminine forms, and more recently **Robyn** (or **Robin**) and **Bobbie** have been well used for girls. In Germany, the 'o' of Robert became a 'u', the 'b' changed to 'p' and the name became **Rupert.** This name was introduced into England by Prince Rupert of the Rhine (1618–92), a romantic figure who combined a keen interest in science with great bravery displayed while fighting on the side of his uncle King Charles I during the English civil war. Although used steadily in the UK, Rupert is an unusual name in the USA.

Rochelle see RACHEL

Roderick

Roderick comes from two Germanic name elements meaning 'fame' and 'power' and has short forms **Rod** and **Roddy**. It is also used as the English equivalent of two ancient Welsh names, **Rhodri**, formed from 'circle' (possibly implying a coronet) combined with 'ruler' and **Rhydderch** ('exalted ruler'). The Welsh patronymic 'ap (son of) Roderick' developed into the surname **Broderick**, which is sometimes used as a first name. In Scotland, Roderick has also been used as the equivalent of the Gaelic **Ruairi** (see RORY).

Rodge see ROGER

Rodney

This is a surname which came to be used as a first name in honour of Admiral George Rodney (1718–92), an outstanding commander who was instrumental in bringing much of the West Indies under British rule. It has the same short forms as RODERICK.

Roger

Roger comes from the Germanic elements 'fame' and 'spear' and is the French form of the name that appears in the great Anglo-Saxon epic *Beowulf* as *Hrothgar*. **Hodge** and Hodgekin were used as diminutives in the past and became the typical names of rustic labourers. **Rodge** is now sometimes used as a short form.

Roisin see ROSE

Roland

Roland or **Rowland** (the commoner form for the surname) is a Germanic name combining 'fame' with 'land'. It is sometimes shortened to **Roly**. The *Song of Roland* is the great epic of medieval France in which Roland, brave and honourable above all, but lacking the wisdom of his close friend OLIVER, is betrayed by his step-father Ganelon and killed by the Saracens, but is afterwards avenged by his uncle, Charlemagne. This character became the hero of later stories in Italy, where his name became **Orlando**, a form that has been growing in popularity in recent years. A feminine form, **Orlanda**, has been recorded.

Rolf, Rollo see RALPH

Roma

This is one of a group of names connected with the city of Rome, although none of them is particularly common. Roma is simply the Italian form of the city's name. **Romaine**, more common on the Continent, is the feminine of **Roman** ('a citizen of Rome'), and the same name as the Italian **Romeo**. **Romola**, the heroine of George Eliot's novel (1863), is a feminine form of the name **Romulus**, the legendary founder of Rome. **Romilly**, a surname occasionally used as a name (now more often for girls than boys), comes from a French place name, but this in its turn would have come from a founder whose name derived from Romulus.

Romy see ROSEMARY

Ron, Ronnie see AARON, REGINALD

Rona see RHONA

Ronald, Ronnie see REGINALD

Ronan see RHONA

Ronee, Roni see VERONICA

Rory
Rory or **Rorie** is the anglicized form of the Gaelic **Ruairi** or **Ruairdhri** ('the red-haired one'), originally a nickname. In Scotland it is still very much a Highlander's name, and its spread to England is probably from Ireland rather than Scotland (see also RODERICK). **Roy** is from the same root, the Gaelic *ruadh* ('red').

Rosaleen see ROSE

Rosalind, Rosamund
Rosalind is originally a Germanic name made up of elements long interpreted as meaning 'horse' and 'serpent'; but now the philologists seem to prefer the meaning 'fame' and 'shield'. However, like BELINDA, the name has long been thought of as if it comes from a Romance language, and analysed as 'rose' + 'beautiful'. Variants are **Rosalyn, Rosaline, Roslyn** and **Rosalinda**. In the same way Rosamund ('horse (or fame)' + 'protection') has been thought of in terms of the Latin *rosa munda* ('pure rose') or *rosa mundi* ('rose of the world'), both of which are images that have been used to describe the Virgin Mary. It has **Rosamond** as a variant and the two groups of names share **Roz** as a short form.

Rose
Historically, Rose may not be the simple plant name that it appears, but a Germanic name from the same root as ROSALIND and Rosamund. However, there can be little doubt that since the Middle Ages it has been thought of as a flower name, despite the fact that such names were unusual at that time. Because the rose is symbolic of so many things – the Virgin Mary, love, England and much else – it is hardly surprising that the name has enjoyed such long use. Although in recent decades the name has been out of favour, in the last few years it has enjoyed a sudden burst of popularity with parents. It has developed a large number of pet forms, compounds and elaborations, many of them based on the Latin form of the name, **Rosa**. Thus we find: **Rosabel, Rosabella, Rosalia** and **Rosalie** along with **Rosetta, Rosie, Roseanna, Roseanne, Rosina** and **Rosita**. In Ireland the name became **Roisin** or **Rosheen** (a phonetic spelling), which is anglicized to **Rosaleen**.

Rosemary
One of the nineteenth-century flower names, Rosemary is an obvious elaboration of ROSE. The plant's symbolism – rosemary for remembrance – is well known thanks to the mad Ophelia's speech in *Hamlet*. In the past this strongly scented herb was used to make crowns and garlands as well as to scent clothes and protect them from moths. The true meaning of the name has nothing to do

with the rose, but comes from its Latin name *ros marinus* ('sea-dew'), so-called from the plant's liking to grow near the sea, and the misty bluish colour of its leaves. **Rosemarie** is a variant, and Rose is used as a short form. The name **Romy**, made popular in recent years by the actress Romy Schneider, is a Germanic pet form of the name.

Rosetta, Rosheen, Rosie, Rosina, Rosita see ROSE

Ross

Ross is a surname used as a first name. The surname has a number of different origins, but is particularly common in Scotland and Ulster, where it has been used as a first name since at least the sixteenth century, and in these cases it comes from the Gaelic meaning 'a promontory'. Nowadays it is also used occasionally for girls.

Rowan

As a masculine name, this comes from the Irish *Ruadhán* ('little red one') and thus like RORY and RUFUS would have started life as a nickname for someone with red hair. As a feminine name it could be a transferred use of the masculine, but just as probably refers to the plant name, which is the alternative name for the slender and graceful mountain ash. As a boy's name its use is old, but for girls it is recent, and no doubt its similarity to the already well-established ROWENA has helped its spread. **Rowann** or **Rowanne** are also found.

Rowena

According to the traditional history of Britain, Rowena was the beautiful daughter of the Saxon invader Hengist, who used her beauty (and some say witchcraft) to persuade the ruler of Britain, Vortigern, to give large areas of the country to the Saxons in return for marriage to Rowena. It is possible to construe the name as Anglo-Saxon, composed of such elements as *hrod* and *wynn* ('fame' and 'joy'); but the name appears in very early sources as *Renwein* or *Ronnwen*, and since most of the early accounts come from the British side, the name is most probably a form of the Welsh **Rhonwen**, made up of the elements *rhon* ('a pike or lance', thus figuratively 'tall, slender'), and *gwen* ('fair, blessed'). Rowena came into general use after Sir Walter Scott used it as the name of his heroine in the novel *Ivanhoe* (1819).

Rowland see ROLAND

Roxana

Also found as **Roxanne** or **Roxane**, this was the name of an Asian princess who was married to ALEXANDER the Great after he defeated her father in 327 BC. According to the Greek biographer Plutarch (c. 46–120), the marriage took place not for political ends but because Alexander had seen Roxana and fallen in love with her. Her son by him, Alexander IV, was at one time joint ruler of his father's empire, but both he and his mother were murdered in the power struggles that followed Alexander's death. Her romantic story was turned into a play in the late eighteenth century, which dealt with the rivalry between her and Statira, her co-wife, and stories circulated about how various actresses playing the two women carried the stage rivalry over into their own lives, so that the conflict between the two women became proverbial. The name was given a further boost by the publication of a novel called *Roxana* by Daniel Defoe in 1724, and more recently by Edmond Rostand's *Cyrano de Bergerac* (1897), in which the heroine is called **Roxane**. It is not clear where the name comes from. It is traditionally said to be from the Persian for 'dawn', but it may be connected with the name of the central Asian district of Roshan. **Roxy** is used as a short form.

Roy see RORY

Roz see ROSALIND

Ruairdhri, Ruairi see RODERICK, RORY

Ruben see REUBEN

Ruby
Ruby is another of the gem names so popular in the nineteenth and first part of the twentieth centuries. This popularity dated bearers, and it was for a long time out of fashion, but is now being used once again.

Rudi, Rudolf, Rudolph, Rudy see RALPH

Rufus
Rufus comes from a Latin word used as a nickname for someone with red hair, and thus has the same meaning as the names under ROY and ROWAN. It is particularly associated with the assassinated Norman king William Rufus (William II), but his unsavoury reputation did not stop nineteenth-century parents adopting it as a first name. The Old French equivalent of Rufus was **Russell**, which became a surname, and later a first name. **Russ** is a short form also used as an independent name.

Rupert see ROBERT

Russ, Russell see RUFUS

Ruth
Ruth is a Hebrew name of uncertain meaning. The Old Testament Book of Ruth tells the charming story of Ruth's devotion to NAOMI, and of how Boaz, whom she later married, saw the poor widow gleaning in his field and ordered his men to drop grain on purpose, so that she could have more to collect.

Ryan
Ryan is an Irish surname of unknown meaning which has come into use as a first name, particularly since the 1970s when the actor Ryan O'Neal made it well known. It has remained among the most popular first names on both sides of the Atlantic since then.

Ss

Sabina
Sabina and its German form **Sabine** (pronounced in the same way) mean 'Sabine woman'. In the legendary history of Rome told by the historian Livy, the neighbouring Sabine people refused to intermarry with the newly founded Rome, where there was a desperate shortage of women. To avoid their city dying after one generation, the Romans invited the Sabines to a festival, ambushed them, and then carried off all the young women and married them by force. This became known as 'The Rape of the Sabine women'. It took a long time before the Sabines could organize their revenge. When battle was finally joined, the Sabine women found themselves faced with the prospect of losing either their parents or their husbands, now the fathers of their children. To escape from this situation they forced their way between the two armies and imposed peace. For this they were greatly honoured. The name is used in Ireland to anglicize the Irish name **Sive** ('goodness'), which is also anglicized as **Sabia**.

Sable see EBONY

Sabrina
According to the mythological history of Britain, Sabrina was the daughter of Locrine, the second king of Britain. Her stepmother Guendolen (see GWEN) rebelled, killed her father, took over the government and ordered her to be thrown into the nearby river, ever since called the Severn after Sabrina. She is probably best known as the nymph of the Severn in Milton's masque *Comus*, where she is addressed with the words: 'Sabrina fair,/ Listen where thou art sitting/Under the glassy, cool, translucent wave,/In twisted braids of lilies knitting/The loose train of thy amber-dropping hair.' However, in the 1960s the name was most closely associated with a certain voluptuous actress, Britain's answer to the Hollywood starlet of the time. In the USA, where these associations are not so prominent, Sabrina has been quite fashionable, sometimes in the form **Zabrina**, and is now closely associated with the television series *Sabrina the Teenage Witch*.

Sacha see ALEXANDER

Sade
This is the name of the British-Nigerian singer. It is actually a shortening of her full name, Folashade, which means, in the Nigerian Yoruba language, 'honour

confers a crown'. She pronounces her name **Sharday** and parents often spell it this way or give it a similar phonetic twist.

Sadie see SARAH

Saffron
This is the name of the autumn-flowering crocus, as well as of the flavouring and and colouring agent obtained from it. The plant was at one time extensively cultivated in Cornwall, but its use as a first name is modern, and it was probably not used before the 1960s.

Safire see SAPPHIRE

Sage
The herb sage got its name from the reputation tea made from its leaves has for improving the memory, making the drinker more sage. Thus this name is both a plant and a virtue name. It has been fashionable for both sexes for a number or years, but is not a new name, having been well used in Wales in the fifteenth to seventeenth centuries.

Sahara
This place name, with all its romantic associations, has been quietly but steadily used as a girl's first name for a number of years. One of the attractions is probably the form of the name. It not only ends in -a, like so many girl's names, but shares the sounds and form of a number of other new names, such as SAVANNAH, found on these pages. The Sahara desert gets its name from the Arabic word for 'deserts'.

Sal, Sally see SARAH

Salome see SOLOMON

Sam, Sammy see SAMANTHA, SAMUEL

Samantha
The origin of Samantha is not known. It appears in the eighteenth century and it has been conjectured that it is meant to be a feminine form of SAMUEL. It really took off as a name after the 1950s when the song 'I love you, Samantha' and the character of Tracy Samantha Lord in the film *High Society* (1956) gave the name a great deal of exposure. Use of TRACY seems to have increased at the same time. **Sam** and **Sammy** are used as short forms as they are for all Sam- names.

Samson
Although the Bible claims Samson as one of the judges of Israel, he appears in the stories about him as a violent, vengeful and unrestrained folk-hero, notable chiefly for his strength, sarcastic sense of humour and weakness for Philistine women. The name can be interpreted as a diminutive of the Hebrew for 'sun' or as meaning 'son of the sun god Shamash'; and this latter, with the similarities between his adventures and those of demigods of other cultures such as Hercules and the Babylonian Gilgamesh, has led to suggestions that he

represents a reworking of the myths of a sun god. The name is not much used at the moment, but has been very popular at various times in the past. **Sampson** is an alternative form.

Samuel
One of the great judges and prophets of the Israelites, Samuel was instrumental in making kings of both SAUL and DAVID. The name means 'name of God', and he was destined for a holy life from birth. His mother Hannah (see ANN), desperate to have children, had vowed to God that if she had a son he should be dedicated to His service. The infant Samuel was therefore taken to the Temple and given to ELI to bring up. **Sam** and **Sammy** are short forms. The name is popular at the moment on both sides of the Atlantic.

Sanchia
This is a Spanish name meaning 'holy'. **Sancha** and the German form **Sancia** can also be found. The masculine is not used in this country, but is famous thanks to the resourceful servant **Sancho** Panza in Cervantes' *Don Quixote* (1605–15).

Sander, Sandor, Sandra, Sandy see ALEXANDER

Sapphire
One of the rarer gem names, Sapphire was no doubt kept from popularity when other gem names were current by its associations with the biblical **Sapphira**, wife of the Ananias who in the Acts of the Apostles sells some of his goods to give to the Church, but keeps back a part of the proceeds for his own use. They are both struck dead for this deception. As a first name, the spelling is sometimes simplified to **Safire**.

Sarah
This is the Hebrew for 'princess' and the name of the wife of the patriarch ABRAHAM in the Old Testament. The name takes the form **Sara** in the Greek New Testament. **Sadie, Sal, Sally** and even **Sallie** are short forms. In Ireland the name has been used to anglicize the native **Saraid** ('excellent'), probably influenced by the similarity of the names and by the fact that Sarah was originally called by the even more similar-looking Sarai ('contentious'), before her name was changed as a sign of God's blessing.

Sasha see ALEXANDER

Saskia
This was the name of Rembrandt's wife, who was painted by him in some memorable portraits. It was also used by John Buchan as the heroine of his adventure story *Huntingtower*, which would have made the name more widely known. Its origin is not clear, but it may mean 'Saxon woman'. There has been a marked increase in use of the name in recent years, perhaps as a result of the fame of the actress Saskia Reeves.

Saul
Saul is the Hebrew for 'asked for (child)'. The Old Testament Saul is elected the first king of Israel, but his sins lead to God's favour being taken from him and

given to DAVID, at one time Saul's favourite, but whom he now persecutes. Saul was also the name of St PAUL before his conversion to Christianity (see further under STEPHEN).

Savannah
As a term for 'a grassy plain', savannah comes from the Caribbean Taino Indian language word *zabana* ('meadow'). However, as a first name use is probably most influenced by the Georgian city of Savannah and the associations that go with it.

Sawnie see ALEXANDER

Scarlett
This name, which has been fashionable for a number of years, is one of the many names brought to the attention of the public by the book (1936), and particularly the film (1939), of Margaret Mitchell's *Gone with the Wind*. In this Scarlett O'Hara is actually named from her grandmother's maiden name, and it is her middle name, although (like many other characters in the book) she is generally known by her middle name. The surname would have originated with someone who dealt with the costly cloth called scarlet in the Middle Ages: a cloth that was worthy of the expense of being dyed bright red, then a rare shade, and so transferred its name to the colour.

Schuyler see SKYLER

Scott
This popular name is simply a surname which would have been given to someone from Scotland, particularly a Gaelic speaker, transformed into a first name. The admired American novelist Francis Scott Fitzgerald (1896–1940), like Scarlett O'Hara above generally referred to by his middle name, may have been influential in the rise of the name, which has been steadily popular since the 1960s. The pet forms **Scottie** or **Scotty** are also used as independent names, perhaps influenced by *Star Trek*'s 'Beam me up, Scottie'.

Seamus, Seumus see JAMES

Sean see JOHN

Searlait see CAROL

Sebastian
This means 'man from Sebastia', a town (now Sivas) in central Asia Minor that got its name from the Greek translation of the name AUGUSTUS. St Sebastian was a martyr of unknown date. According to his highly dubious legend he was a Roman officer who was sentenced to be shot to death with arrows for his faith, a subject very popular with Renaissance artists. Left for dead, he was healed of his wounds by a pious widow, but on confronting his persecutors he was beaten to death. **Seb** is a short form, and **Bastian** is also used.

Sedrick see CEDRIC

Seisyllt see CECIL

Selina
This is probably originally a variant of CELIA and CELESTE, names meaning 'heavenly', a derivation which seems to be confirmed by the form **Celina** and the French **Céline**. However, the name looks very like a Latinate form of **Selene**, the Greek moon goddess, and is often understood in this way.

Selma
Selma is another of the names that came into use from the popularity of the poems attributed to OSSIAN. It is not a personal name in these poems, but the name of Fingal's castle (see FINN). However, when these poems were translated into Swedish it was not clear what 'Selma' was, and it was taken to be a feminine personal name. It then became popular in Sweden from the fame of the Selma poems of the Finno-Swedish poet Frans Mikael Franzén (1772–1849). More recently the name became well known through another Swedish writer, Selma Lagerlöf (1858–1940). The name spread from Scandinavia to the English-speaking world through Scandinavian immigration in the USA. It is also an American place name, the town from which Martin Luther King led a 50-mile civil rights march in 1965. **Zelma** is an occasional variant.

Senga see AGNES

Seonaid see JANE

Septimus
A Latin name meaning 'seventh', Septimus was originally given to a seventh child (compare OCTAVIA and QUINTUS). The feminine is **Septima**.

Serena
Serena is the feminine form of an old Roman name meaning 'serene'. It was the name of a minor saint, but until the twentieth century its use in Britain was mainly literary. In Edmund Spenser's *The Faerie Queen* (1590–96), Serena is a character who is gathering flowers for a garland when she is attacked by the Blatant Beast, who seizes her in his mouth and carries her off, until her cries attract the attention of a wandering knight who comes to her rescue. **Serina** is a variant, used by the seventeenth-century playwright Thomas Otway in *The Orphan* (1680).

Serge
The old Roman name **Sergius** became **Sergei** in Russian, but it is often found in its French form Serge, in part because at one time French was the dominant language in polite society in Russia. The enormous popularity of the name in that country is due to St Sergius of Radonezh, a fourteenth-century hermit who became the founding father of Russian monasticism. He lived in the woods and had a close relationship with nature not dissimilar to that of St FRANCIS. This and his reputation as a saint that embodied all the virtues associated with the Russian peasant – humble simplicity, gentleness, gravity and good-neighbour-liness – has led to his being regarded as the embodiment of all that a Russian saint should be. The Spanish and Italian form **Sergio** is well used in the USA.

Seth

In chapter four of the Book of Genesis we are told 'And Adam knew his wife again; and she bare a son, and called his name Seth: For God, said she, hath appointed me another seed instead of Abel, whom Cain slew'. This has led to the name traditionally being interpreted as 'appointed', but it actually means 'a setting, a cutting', the pun being on the word translated as 'seed'. It was a popular name among the Puritans and remained in use in the USA, and has now come back into fashion.

Seumas, Seumus see JAMES

Sextus see CECIL

Seymour

A masculine name, Seymour is taken from the surname of a noble family. This in its turn came from the French village (now a southeastern suburb of Paris) of St-Maur-des-Fossés, where the saint's name is the local form of MAURICE.

Shaina

This is a Yiddish girl's name meaning 'beautiful', used increasingly in the USA. However, many parents may use it because it fits in with names derived from Shane (see JOHN), a view reinforced by spellings such as **Shaine**, **Shana** and **Shayna**. The country singer **Shania** Twain's name is not a variant, but an Ojibwa Indian name meaning 'I'm on my way'.

Shakila

A new girl's name, coined from the Arabic man's name **Shakil** ('well-formed, handsome').

Shakira

The spread of this Arabic name meaning 'thankful, grateful' is probably inspired by the beauty of the actress Shakira Baksh, now married to the actor Michael Caine.

Shameka

This is a Black American girl's name, apparently a blend of TAMIKA and the fashionable Sha- found in names on these pages (see particularly under SHANAE).

Shamus see JAMES

Shana see SHAINA

Shanae, Shanice, Shanika, Shaniqua

Sha- (also found as Cha-, pronounced with a soft 'ch' sound, as in CHANEL) has become a very active element in the creation of new names for some time. The sound first became popular in the name SHARON, which although recorded as a male name in the eighteenth century, as a popular name began life in the 1930s, reaching the 20s in the most-used names statistics in the 1940s in America, and being the tenth most popular name in the UK in 1965. The sound was then found in another new name, SHANNON, which first enters the charts in the USA in the late 1960s but does not make significant inroads in the UK until the late 1990s. Evidence for the popularity of Sha- names, particularly for girls but also for boys, will be found in the surrounding entries. The ones grouped here are, like many of the new names, typically African-American, although many of these names are adopted by the more general population; and, like all new names, they come in a variety of spellings. They can be analysed as blends, but are best viewed as creations combining attractive, fashionable sounds. Thus while Shanae can be analysed as Sha- plus the ending of Renee, the -ee or -ae ending is a common one in names, as is the -ice of Shanice. Shaniqua and Shanika use a newly fashionable ending, perhaps inspired by TAMIKA.

Shane see JOHN

Shanel, Shanelle see CHANEL

Shani see JANE

Shania see SHAINA

Shannon
Shannon comes from the name of the longest river in Ireland and means 'the old one'. It is used for both sexes, but predominantly for girls. Like other recent names with strong Irish associations, such as ERIN, the name is little used in Ireland itself, but seems to have arisen from the sentiment of those of Irish emigrant stock. More recently **Shanna** has appeared, either as a short form of Shannon, or from **Shannagh**, an Irish name coming from a word meaning 'old, wise'.

Shantal see CHANTAL

Shante see ASHANTI

Shara, Shari see SHARON

Sharday see SADE

Sharice see CHARIS

Sharlene, Sharley, Sharlotte see CAROL

Sharmaine see CHARMAINE

Sharon
Sharon means 'the plain' and in the Bible refers to the rich and fertile coastal plain of Palestine. In the Song of Solomon the 'rose of Sharon' is an image of beauty (although 'rose' is a mistranslation; the flower referred to may be the narcissus). At one time the name was pronounced with its first syllable lengthened as in 'share' (still the pronunciation preferred by the actress Sharon Stone), but a pronunciation as in 'shan't' is now otherwise almost universal, and is reflected in the spelling **Sharron**. **Sharyn** is also found, while **Shara** and **Shari** are pet forms and **Sharona** is an elaboration.

Shaun, Shauna, Shawn, Shawndelle see JOHN

Shavon see JANE

Shayla, Shaylee, Shaylyn see SHEA

Shayna see SHAINA

Shea
This is an Irish surname meaning 'descendant of the fortunate one', used more or less equally for boys and girls in the USA. It is also found as **Shaye** or **Shay**, which has been the base of a number of new blends (used for girls) such as **Shaylee**, **Shaylyn** and **Shayla** (although some users may regard the latter as a form of SHIELA).

Sheba see BATHSHEBA

Sheelagh, Sheila see CECILIA

Sheena see JANE

Shelby
This is a surname now used as a first name. The surname, like the first name, is more common in the USA than in the UK, and can come from a number of sources, one of which is a place meaning 'hut-farm'. The similar-sounding **Sheldon**, mainly used for boys, probably contains the place-name element meaning 'shelf, ledge' combined with *don* ('settlement').

Shelley
This, with its variant **Shelly**, is a girl's name with a number of sources. The actress Shelley Winters, who made the name more widely known, is really a SHIRLEY, which is probably the most important source; but other names ending in the -shell sound such as Michelle (see MICHAEL) and Rachelle or Rochelle (see RACHEL) have also contributed. In addition the surname, reinforced by the fame of the poet, has contributed to the name, and the occasional masculine use of the name comes from this source.

Sheralyn, Sherel, Sherell see CHERYL

Sherise see CHARIS

Sherrel, Sherrell, Sherri, Sherry, Sheryl see CHERYL

Sheyenne, Shianne see CHEYENNE

Shiela see CECILIA

Shirley
This is a place name made up of elements meaning 'shire' and 'meadow', which became a surname. Originally a man's name (and still occasionally found as one – the wrestler known as Big Daddy (1937–97) was christened Shirley

Crabtree), it came into fashion as a girl's name in 1849 after Charlotte Brontë gave it to the heroine of her highly successful novel *Shirley*, a work which urged the public to accept a wider choice in life for women.

Shivaun see JANE

Sholom see SOLOMON

Sholto
This is a Scottish name, restricted at one time to the Douglas family, and still particularly used by that family. It has been derived from the Gaelic for 'sower', probably indicating fertility.

Shona see JANE

Shura see ALEXANDER

Shyann, Shyanne see CHEYENNE

Sian see JANE

Sib, Sibyl, Sibylla see SYBIL

Sidney
Sidney and its alternative spelling **Sydney** is an aristocratic surname, traditionally derived from the French name Saint-Denis, used as a first name for both sexes. The 'i' spelling is now primarily male, the 'y' female. It has been suggested this feminine use comes from the name **Sidonia** or **Sidony, Sidonie** ('woman of Sidon'), but Sidney has a long history of use as a woman's name, and there is no reason why it should not be from the surname. An early female bearer was Sydney Owenson, Lady Morgan, whose novel *The Wild Irish Girl* (1806), which passionately supports Irish nationalism, was considered by the authorities so dangerously subversive that she was put under surveillance at Dublin Castle. **Sid** is a short form of Sidney, **Siddy** of Sidonia. Not much used in the UK at the moment, as a male name Sidney is now undergoing something of a revival in the USA, and Sydney is also well used for girls.

Siegfried
This is a Germanic name, from the elements meaning 'victory' and 'peace', introduced into this country in the last century by admirers of Wagner's *Ring Cycle*. Other Germanic names which have the element meaning victory are **Sigurd** ('victory' + 'word'), the earlier name for the hero Wagner calls Siegfried, **Sigmund** ('victory' + 'protection'), the name of Sigurd's father; and its variants **Siegmund** (the German rather than Scandinavian spelling), and **Sigismund**, a name much used by the Polish royal family. **Sigrid** ('victory' + 'beautiful') is the only well-known feminine name with this element.

Sierra
This Spanish word for a mountain range, with its associations with the Wild West and the natural world, has become a well-used name for girls in the USA.

Sigourney

The actress Sigourney Weaver chose to change her first name when still a child, feeling that her given name of Susan did not match the striking nature of the names borne by the rest of her family, such as her brother Trajan. She chose Sigourney because it was the name of a favourite character, Sigourney Howard, in Scott Fitzgerald's novel *The Great Gatsby* (1925). A number of parents have since chosen to follow her lead.

Silas see SILVIA

Sile see CECILIA

Silvia

Silvia and its alternative spelling **Sylvia** mean 'of the wood', and would therefore be a suitable epithet for numerous goddesses and nymphs, such as DIANA. **Silvie** or **Sylvie** is the French form, also used as a diminutive of Silvia. An early use of the name is found in Rhea Silvia, the mythical mother of Romulus (see ROMA) and Remus. However, as a Vestal Virgin her associations are with the worship of the hearth and state, and in her case the name may have been changed from some earlier form that sounded as if it came from the Latin *silva* ('a wood'). The name was given Christian respectability by being the name of a saint, the mother of GREGORY the Great. There is a large group of less frequently used names which come from the same root. **Silvius**, the masculine of Silvia, does not seem to be used, and **Silvanus** is most often found in the New Testament short form of the name, **Silas**, although the feminine **Silvana** or **Silvania** is sometimes found. **Silvester** or **Sylvester**, the name of an outstanding early pope, is more common, and has the feminine **Sylvestra**.

Simon

Simon is a name that occurs frequently in the New Testament, the best-known holder being the apostle Simon Peter. It is the Greek form of the Hebrew **Simeon**, the name of one of the tribes of Judah, and of the 'righteous and devout' old man who took the infant Jesus in his arms when He was presented at the temple and blessed Him. It probably comes from the Hebrew word for 'to listen'. **Sim**, **Simmy** and **Simkin** are old pet forms of Simon, but **Si** is used now. **Simone** is a French feminine that has been gaining ground in recent years.

Sindy see CYNTHIA, LUCY

Sine, Sinead see JANE

Siobhan see JANE

Sion see JOHN

Siriol

Siriol or **Sirol** is a Welsh feminine name meaning 'cheerful'. It is a fairly recent name, but currently popular with Welsh parents.

Sis, Sisley, Sissie, Sissy see CECILIA

Sive see SABINA

Siwan see JANE

Skye
The name of this Hebridean island is one of the names currently making its mark as a new name. It is used for both sexes, but most often for girls. The island has a reputation for beauty and is a favourite holiday place, as well as having a reputation as a good place to seek an alternative life style. To these associations is probably added those that come from it having the same sound as 'sky'. Use may also have some overlap with SKYLER, below.

Skyler
This is a phonetic spelling of the old Dutch surname **Schuyler**, meaning 'scholar'. Schuyler Colfax (1823–85) was the 17th vice president of the USA, serving under Ulysses S. Grant, and other nineteenth-century bearers of the name are found. Skyler is currently used for boys and girls, both in the original and modern spellings, but is more frequent for boys.

Solomon
The name of the Old Testament king famous for his wisdom, Solomon comes from the Hebrew **Shalom** ('peace'), which, with the variant **Sholom**, has been used as a girl's name. **Sol** and **Solly** are short forms of Solomon. The better-known feminine equivalent of Solomon is **Salome**, a name which was much used by the ruling family of the kingdom of Judea, but best known as the name of the girl who danced before Herod, and when asked to name her reward asked for John the Baptist's head. However, it was also the name of one of the women who stood at the foot of the cross during the crucifixion, and occasional uses of the name are probably inspired by her.

Somerled, Somhairle see SORLEY

Sondra see ALEXANDER

Sophy
This is the traditional English form of **Sophia**, which comes from the Greek word for 'wisdom', used to denote the holy wisdom of God, as in the great sixth-century church of Santa Sophia built in Constantinople (now Istanbul). Sophia is sometimes shortened to **Phia**. **Sophie** is the French form of the name, and **Sonia** (**Sonya, Sonja**) a Slavic pet form.

Sorcha
This is an increasingly popular early Irish name meaning 'bright, radiant'. The actress Socha Cusack has made the name more widely known outside Ireland.

Sorel, Sorell see SORREL

Sorley
Sorley, in Irish **Somhairle** and in the Scottish islands **Somerled**, despite being a Gaelic name, comes not from the Celtic language but from Old Norse, for it represents a form of the words *sumar* ('summer') and *lithr* ('warrior'), a term

used for the Vikings who made regular raids on these areas during the sailing season. They later settled, founded new communities such as Dublin, and passed on some of their names, while at the same time Celtic names passed into the stock of Norse names.

Sorrel
This girl's name can be derived either from the plant name, or from the rich reddish brown colour found in the coat of some horses and of dogs such as red setters; the latter seems the more likely, as the plant is notorious for its sourness. It is also spelt **Sorrell** or **Sorell**, and Noel Coward used the name **Sorel** Bliss in his play *Hay Fever* (1925). This form is probably a direct allusion to the notorious Agnes Sorel (c. 1422–50), mistress of and procuress for King Charles VII, known as 'Dame de Beauté' from the estate at Beauté-sur-Marne, which he gave her. Her undoubted beauty has been preserved in a portrait where she is shown in the role of the Virgin Mary breast-feeding her child, but which has rather more to do with pornography than with religion.

Spencer
This surname, originally given to the steward of a medieval household, has come into fashion as a boy's name in the USA, sometimes in the form **Spenser**.

Spring see AUTUMN

St John see JOHN

Stacey, Stacy see ANASTASIA, EUSTACE

Stanislaus
This is the Latin form of the Slavic **Stanislav**, a name made up of the verb 'to be' combined with a word meaning 'glory'. **Stanislas** is the French form of the word. It is occasionally used by English speakers – for instance it was the name of James Joyce's brother – but usually by those of Slavic descent, in honour of St Stanislaus of Cracow, an eleventh-century Polish bishop and martyr, probably murdered by his king, whom he had frequently rebuked for his irregular private life.

Stanley
As a surname, Stanley belongs to one of the oldest and most distinguished aristocratic families in England, with an ancestry going back to the Norman Conquest. It is the family name of the earls of Derby who were at one time kings of the Isle of Man, and who over the centuries have provided many famous politicians. The word means 'stoney field', and refers to property owned by the family. It had been used quietly from the eighteenth century as a first name, but became popular in the next century in honour of the journalist and explorer Henry Morton Stanley (1841–1904) of Dr Livingstone fame. His background was anything but aristocratic, as he was born illegitimate, spent part of his childhood in a workhouse and ran away to America, where he was adopted by a family named Stanley. Despite these beginnings, he did in fact join the nobility when he became a knight of the Order of the Bath in 1899.

Steenie, Stefan, Steffan see STEPHEN

Steffi, Steffie see STEPHEN

Stella
The Latin for 'star', Stella seems to owe its use as a first name to Sir Philip Sidney (1554–86), who wrote a sonnet sequence called *Astrophel and Stella*, using the name to show how far above her lover Stella was. However, he was not the first to use the idea, for **Estelle**, which comes from the same root, was an Old French name. Along with the Latinate **Estella**, Estelle became popular in the nineteenth century.

Stephen, Steven
St Stephen was the first person to be martyred for his Christian faith, stoned to death as a blasphemer after accusing the Jewish Elders of rejecting the Messiah. Among those who supported his execution was SAUL of Tarsus, the young man who was later to see the light on the road to Damascus, and on his conversion take the name PAUL. Stephen's name reflects the martyr's crown he won, for it comes from the Greek for 'crown'. St Stephen's feast day is 26 December, the day on which the Bohemian King **Wenceslas** (nowadays more usually found in central Europe in the forms **Vaclav** or **Wenzel**, a name that shares Stephen's meaning, being made up of Slavic elements meaning 'crown' and 'glory') looked out and saw the poor man gathering winter fuel. Continental forms such as **Stefan, Steffan** or **Stephan** are sometimes found. The form Steven is simply a modern respelling of the Greek 'ph'. There is an old Scots form **Steenie** but **Steve** or **Stevie** are the usual pet forms. **Stephanie** is the French feminine of the name which has been popular in recent years, and which has short forms **Steffi(e)** and **Stevie**, while there is an older, rarer form **Stephana**.

Sterling see STIRLING

Steuart, Stewart see STUART

Stirling
This is the name of the Scottish city, of unknown meaning, used first as a surname and then as a first name. In America it is more frequently spelt **Sterling**.

Storm, Stormy
These have been used as girls' names since about the 1960s. The associations are presumably not of cold and wet, but of romantic adventures and the sort of personality that could also be described as 'tempestuous'; indeed **Tempest** is, itself, occasionally used.

Stuart
Stuart, **Stewart** and **Steuart** are all forms of the Scottish surname and royal name. The name means 'steward' and was adopted from the title of hereditary Steward of Scotland conferred by King David I on Walter Stewart (d. 1177). His great-grandson and great-great-grandson were both regents of Scotland, and the marriage of the son of the next generation into the royal family led to *his* son becoming King Robert II (1316–90). Short forms are **Stu** or **Stew**.

Sukie, Suky see SUSAN

Suleika see ZULEIKA

Summer see AUTUMN

Susan

In the Apocryphal story of Susanna and the Elders, **Susanna**, whose name means 'lily', is a very beautiful woman who two old men try to blackmail into going to bed with them by threatening to say that they have seen her sleeping with a young man in a garden. Susanna defies them, and when they accuse her the judge DANIEL takes a hand in the case. He questions the old men individually, and when they differ in their accounts of what species of tree the couple were making love under, Susanna's innocence is proved, thus giving the tale a claim to be the earliest recorded detective story. **Susannah** and **Suzanna** are variants of the name; **Susan** is the English form and **Suzette** (Susette) the French pet form of **Suzanne**. **Sue**, **Sukie** or **Suky**, **Susie**, **Susy** and **Suzy** are the short forms.

Sybil

This is now the more common spelling of **Sibyl**, the title given to the women who spoke the oracles in various religious centres in the ancient world. Collections were made of these prophecies, and in the Middle Ages some of these were interpreted as foretelling Christ, so that sibyls became associated with the biblical prophets, and it became possible for Christians to use the word for a pagan priestess as a first name (this also explains the presence of sibyls in such otherwise incongruous places as Michelangelo's ceiling in the Sistine Chapel). **Sib** is a short form and variants include **Sibylla**, **Sybilla** and **Sybella**, while the actress **Cybill** Shepherd has recently given publicity to another spelling of the name.

Sydney see SIDNEY

Sylvester, Sylvestra, Sylvia, Sylvie, Sylvius see SILVIA

Syril see CYRIL

Tt

Tabitha

This comes from an Aramaic word meaning 'gazelle', **Dorcas** is the Greek translation of the name. In the Bible we are told 'there was at Joppa a certain disciple named Tabitha, which by interpretation is called Dorcas' (Acts 9. 36). She died, and the Apostle Peter was summoned. He went to the body and said 'Tabitha, arise. And she opened her eyes: and when she saw Peter, she sat up'. The trouble taken in this account to give the Aramaic as well as the Greek form of the name probably arises from a desire to echo Jesus' words in Mark 5. 41, when He performs a similar miracle: 'And he took the damsel by the hand, and said unto her, Talitha cumi: which is, being interpreted, Damsel, I say unto thee, arise.' **Talitha** ('damsel') is sometimes used as a first name. Although Tabitha is now the more frequent form of the name, Dorcas was popular in the past and Dorcas Societies were formed where women would meet to make clothes for the poor, inspired by the biblical Dorcas, who was 'full of good works and almsdeeds.'

Tacey

Tace or Tacey was a name coined by the Puritans from the Latin meaning 'be silent', as a reminder to women that the New Testament says that they should be silent in church (and no doubt hoping for silence elsewhere). It was sometimes used in its English translation – for instance, Conwy parish church has a seventeenth-century plaque commemorating a Silence Jones. Despite a meaning that might be expected to be too sexist for modern use, the name is still regularly encountered.

Tad see THADDEUS

Tadhg see TIMOTHY

Taffy see DAVID

Talia see NOEL

Taliesin

An ancient Welsh bard, supposedly from the sixth century, Taliesin's name means 'radiant brow'. Much of the tradition about him is mythical, but the very earliest manuscripts of Welsh poetry have works that are said to be by him. (See also EUGENE, CERIDWEN.)

Talitha see TABITHA

Tallulah
This name was introduced to the general public by the American actress Tallulah Bankhead (1903–68), who was named after her grandmother, who had in turn been named after Tallulah Falls in Georgia. The place name is said, on rather shaky evidence, to come from a Native American word meaning 'terrible'. The name got a further boost after the success of the film of the musical *Bugsy Malone* (1976), where the female lead, called Tallulah, was played by the young Jodie Foster.

Tam see THOMAS

Tamara
This is the Russian form of the biblical name **Tamar**, which means 'date palm'. **Thamar** or Tamara was a highly successful, twelfth-century queen of Georgia in Russia and her fame helped to spread the name throughout the country. Tamara, along with **Tamsin**, is one of the sources of the name **Tammy** (see THOMAS).

Tamika
In 1962, a film called *A Girl Called Tamiko* was shown in the USA. Tamiko is a Japanese name formed from *tami* ('people') and the feminine ending *-ko*. The name obviously struck a chord, but the Japanese name endings -o for women and -a for men are counterintuitive to Western ears; the name was changed to Tamika, and widely adopted by Black Americans. Not only did this introduce a new name and new variants such as **Tamisha**, but it is probably also the source of -ika as a fashionable ending for names.

Tammie, Tammy, Tamsin, Tamzen, Tamzin see TAMARA, THOMAS

Tania
Tania or **Tanya** is the Russian pet form of the name **Tatiana**. This popular Russian name comes from ancient Rome; it means 'belonging to the house of Tatius', a Roman family name which seems to go back to the Roman baby word for 'daddy'. Tatiana spread to Russia as the name of a martyr venerated by the Eastern Church who died c. AD 228. **Tonya** can be viewed as a variant of this, or as from Antonia.

Tanisha
This widely used Black American name may be a modern blend of a name like Tanya and the fashionable -isha, but it can also be linked to the name *Tani*, used by the Hausa of Nigeria, meaning 'born on Monday'.

Tanith
The Phoenician goddess of love and fertility, Tanith was worshipped in Carthage as the Great Goddess under the name **Tanit**. The name has come into limited use in recent years, mainly in a literary context.

Tanner
This is a surname which would originally have been given to someone who had that job, now used as a boy's name.

Tansy see ANASTASIA

Tara
This is the hill in County Meath in Ireland where the ancient high kings of Ireland were crowned. The remains of prehistoric earthworks can still be seen there today. Although the name was certainly in use by the end of the nineteenth century, it was widely used only in the last half of the twentieth century, due largely to its use for the name of the house in *Gone With the Wind* (see further SCARLETT). It has been used for both sexes, but is predominantly female.

Tarquin
Tarquin was the name of two semi-legendary kings of Rome in the sixth century BC. The second of these, Tarquin the Proud, was a murderous tyrant who tried to reverse many of the reforms that had recently been made. His conduct, together with his son's rape of LUCRETIA, led to revolt and the institution of the Republic. Despite the name's reputation, it is in limited use (for example Sir Laurence Olivier gave it to his first child), although it is more frequent as a literary name.

Taryn see TYRONE

Tatiana see TANIA

Tavia, Tave, Tavy see OCTAVIA

Taylor
For some reason this surname, from the occupation, has become enormously popular in the USA as a first name, and is beginning to be used in the UK. It is particularly popular for girls, but is well used for both sexes.

Teah, Teia see TIANA

Tearra, Teaira see TIARA

Tecla see THEKLA

Ted, Teddie, Teddy see EDGAR, EDMOND, EDWARD, EDWIN, THEODORE

Teesha see LAETICIA

Tegwen
A Welsh woman's name, Tegwen means 'fair and white (or blonde)'. Another name based on the word *teg* ('beautiful') is the Cornish **Tegan**, now beginning to be used, particularly in Australia, in the form **Teigan**. For some reason this has become a popular name for dogs in the UK. The masculine equivalents are **Tegwyn** and **Tegyd** or **Tegid**.

Tempest see STORM

Terence
This is the anglicized form of the name of a Roman comic playwright of the

second century BC. He is said to have been a Carthaginian who was brought as a slave to Rome, where his owner freed him. There is an obscure saint of the same name, which may have helped make the name more popular, but it seems likely that the short form of the name holds the key to its spread. **Terry** is also a form of the group of names that give us DEREK, and it may well be that many a Terry was interpreted as a pet form and 'corrected' to Terence. Terence occurs in variants such as **Terrance** (the most popular form in the USA), **Terrence** and **Terance**. **Tel** is a recent short form of Terence. **Terrel** or **Terrell** is a variant. It seems to have arisen in the United States was in use by the beginning of the twentieth century, and may owe something to the city of Terrell in Texas. **Tyrrel**, a surname of uncertain origins now used as a boy's name, could have evolved in turn from Terrel, as some forms blur the distinction. **Terron** seems to be a blend of Terrance and DARREN. (See also under THORA.)

Teresa see THERESA

Terrel, Terrell, Terrance, Terrence see TERENCE

Terri, Terrie, Terry see DEREK, TERENCE, THERESA

Terron see TERENCE

Tess, Tessa see THERESA

Tevin
Well used as a first name for boys in the USA, this is of obscure origin. It may be from a French surname which was in turn based on a medieval French form of STEPHEN, but it may well simply have been made up, attractive because of its echo of the popular name KEVIN.

Tewdwr see THEODORE

Thaddeus
Thaddeus or **Thaddæus** was the name of one of the Apostles. He may be the man identified elsewhere as 'Judas, not Iscariot', and so identical with St JUDE. Thaddeus would therefore be a surname to distinguish him from the treacherous man of the same name. Its meaning is disputed. It may be from the Aramaic meaning 'praise' or 'desired', or it may be a local variant of THEODORE. In the past it was used in Ireland to render the native Tadhg (see TIMOTHY), but was not much used elsewhere until a revival of the name in the United States in the 1970s. **Thaddy** or **Thady** is sometimes found as a short form, but **Tad**, sometimes used independently, is the most common form.

Thea see DOROTHY, THEODORE

Thekla
This means 'god's glory' and is the name of the first female martyr. Unfortunately, unlike St STEPHEN whose story is well authenticated, little is known for sure about Thekla, as most of her legend is highly romantic and thus dubious, and even her existence has been doubted. However, in the fourth century St Thecla's church in Milan was one of the largest buildings in the Western World.

There was a later St Thekla, an Anglo-Saxon Abbess who worked as a missionary in Germany in the eighth century, so it is surprising that this name has not been more widely used in this country. **Thecla** and **Tecla** are variants.

Thelma
This is a name invented by the writer Marie Corelli for the heroine of her novel of that name, published in 1887.

Theobald
Theobald is a Germanic name made up of elements meaning 'people' and 'bold'. It is one of a number of Germanic names starting with the element *theo-* ('people'), which have at times been confused with those names from the Greek *theo-* ('God') (see THEODORE below). Shakespeare's **Tybalt** shows an early form of the name, reflecting the old pronunciation, and it was also found as **Tibald**, a name which was once traditional for cats, but which is now best known as a surname.

Theodore, Theodora
Of the many names that contain the Greek element *theos* ('God'), the most common are Theodore and Theodora ('gift of God'), although the latter is more likely to appear in its reversed form of DOROTHY or Dorothea, both forms using **Thea** and **Dora** for short. **Theo** and **Teddy** are the commonest male short forms. Although the associations of Theodora are nowadays Christian, it is a very ancient name, a form of it having been found on a Minoan Linear B clay tablet from Knossos in Crete. The Russian form of the name is **Feodor, Fedor**, and the feminine **Fedora** is occasionally found. The Welsh **Tudor** (**Tudyr, Tewdwr**), an ancient name which eventually became the surname of the ruling family of Britain, is traditionally supposed to be a form of Theodore, but may owe something to the Welsh word *tud* ('country, tribe'). **Theodosius** and **Theodosia** are related names, meaning 'given by God'. **Theophilus** ('beloved by God' or 'loving God') and its even rarer feminine **Theophila** are little used by English speakers, but in France **Théophile** is not uncommon. Although *theos* names were in use in the pagan world, they were particularly popular with early Christians, and most of the names were used by a number of saints. Since the meaning of the names is quite transparent, this group of names is found translated literally into other languages. Thus the sense of Theodore is found in Latin as **Deodatus**, and in French as **Dieudonné**, while Theophilus is the Greek form of Mozart's middle name, **Amadeus**, or in German, **Gotlieb**. The feminine **Amadea** has also been recorded, perhaps used by admirers of Mozart for their daughter.

Theodoric see DEREK

Theophania see TIFFANY

Theresa
This is a name of unknown meaning. The name has been derived from the Greek for 'to reap' and from the Greek island of Thera (Santorini), but since it seems to have arisen in Spain, neither of these seems very likely. The spread of the name owes much to the popularity of St Theresa of Avila, the sixteenth-century nun. Her complex and engaging personality, said to be a combination

of 'the eagle and the dove', has led to many being devoted to her. She was a gifted writer and combined great practicality with being a mystic. She has the distinction of being one of the first two women ever to be officially declared doctors of the Church, in 1970. **Teresa** is an alternative spelling; the German form is **Theresia**, and the name is shortened to **Terry** or **Terri(e)**, **Tess**, **Tessie** and **Tessa**. **Tracy** or **Tracey**, now an independent name, started out as another pet form of Theresa, helped by the use of the surname as a masculine first name. The surname comes from a village in the Calvados region of France, which would have come from a Gallo-Roman personal name meaning 'an inhabitant of Thrace'.

Thierry see DEREK

Thomas

This is the name of one of the 12 Apostles. The word is Aramaic for 'twin', and sometimes appears in the Bible in its Greek equivalent, *Didymus*. It was probably a nickname, and although no other name for him is mentioned in the Bible, there is a tradition that his name was really Judas, in which case Thomas would have been used to distinguish him from the other Judases – Judas Iscariot and the Judas also known as THADDEUS. The popularity of the name throughout Christendom may owe something to the Apostle's character, as he is shown in the Bible as one of the more fallible and human of the 12. When Jesus appears after His Resurrection to the assembled Apostles, Thomas is not there, being too depressed to join them. When he is told what has happened, he declares that until he has touched Christ's wounds he will not believe; whence the expression 'doubting Thomas'. When this happened and his doubts were removed, he immediately declared Jesus to be God. Thomas became a particularly favoured name in medieval England, in honour of the immensely popular St Thomas à Becket (1118–70). The name is shortened to **Tom** or **Tommy** and, in the north, **Tam** and **Tammie**. 'Tommy' for a soldier comes from the use of the name Thomas Atkins on sample forms for recruitment by the War Office in the nineteenth century.

There are a good number of feminine forms of the name. Formerly **Thomasina** or **Tomasina** was the most common, but this has now been easily outstripped in popularity by the Cornish **Tamsin**, with its variants **Tamzin** and **Tamzen**. This is the main source of the name **Tammy**, although it can also be a pet form of any name beginning Tam-. **Thomasa** and **Tomina** have also been used.

Thora

When the Viking raiders came to stay and settle in northern England, Scotland and Ireland, they brought with them a set of names based on their favourite god Thor, the god of thunder and fighting. Thora ('dedicated to Thor') is the only feminine name to have survived, and of the many masculine names based on the god only the rare names **Thurstan** or **Thurston** ('Thor's stone (?altar)'), **Torquil**, a contracted form of *Thorketill* ('Thor's cauldron') and **Turlough** (in Irish **Toirdhealbhach**), meaning 'like Thor' and often anglicized by TERENCE, are still found. More recently **Torrin** or **Torin** and **Tory** (**Torey**, **Torry**, not to be confused with the pet form of VICTORIA), both forms of the name Thor, have become quite fashionable.

Tiana

This American name can be a Cherokee variant of the name DIANA, or else a German form of Christiana. The more popular name **Tia** may be a short form of this, or of other names beginning or ending in the letters -tia; but it is also the Spanish word for 'aunt', often used as a term of affection. That it is regarded as an independent name is shown by spellings such as **Teah** and **Teia**.

Tiara

This word for a jewelled headpiece was adopted unchanged from Latin into English, the Romans having borrowed the word from the Greek, where it meant 'turban'. The sound, however, may be more important than the meaning, for at the same time as girls began to be called Tiara, they were also being called **Tierra**, the Spanish for 'earth, land', and spellings such as **Tearra** and **Teaira** blur the distinction between the two. **Tia** is used as a pet form of these names.

Tib, Tibbie, Tibby see ISABEL

Ticia, Tiesha see LAETITIA

Tierra see TIARA

Tiffany

Theophania is a Greek name meaning 'divine appearance', which was given to girls born around the time of the Epiphany, a word that comes from the same root. This became *Tiphaine* in French, and **Tiffania** or **Tiphany** in English. In medieval romance Tiphany appears as the name of the mother of the Three Kings whose gifts mark Epiphany. The name more or less disappeared in English-speaking countries, but was known as a French surname, which belonged to a jeweller who set up in New York. Tiffany's famous shop featured in the title of the very successful film *Breakfast at Tiffany's* (based on Truman Capote's novel, 1958), where, out of context, it could be understood as a proper name; and it is this that seems to have led to a revival of this name in recent decades.

Tilda, Tilly see MATILDA

Timothy

This really belongs with the THEODORE group of names, for it comes from *Timotheos*, a Greek name meaning 'honouring God'. In the Acts of the Apostles, Timothy is a young man of Asia Minor, carefully brought up in religion by his mother EUNICE and grandmother LOIS, who is chosen as an able companion and assistant by the Apostle PAUL. **Tim** and **Timmie** or **Timmy** are the usual short forms. In Ireland the name has been used to replace the native **Tadhg**, which means 'poet'.

Tina see CHRISTINE

Tisha see LAETITIA, PATRICK

Titus

A Roman family name, Titus is probably of Etruscan origin and thus of unknown meaning. There was an Emperor Titus, chiefly remembered for his destruction of the Temple at Jerusalem, who was very popular with the people of Rome on account of his generosity to them, but luckily for them died young and thus avoided bankrupting the state as he looked set to do. Like so many other Roman names, its use is largely due to its appearance in the Bible. It was the name of a follower of St Paul who, with TIMOTHY, was the most trusted of his followers. The notoriety of Titus Oates, fabricator of the Popish Plot in the seventeenth century, probably helped a long-lasting decline in the name, but there are slight signs of a revival at the moment, possibly helped by the publicity given to the name by Titus Groan, hero of Mervyn Peake's *Gormenghast* books.

Toby

Toby is the English, **Tobias** the Greek form of a Hebrew name meaning 'Jehovah is good'. The name comes from the Apocryphal Book of Tobit, a highly romanticized account of how Tobias, with the help of the Archangel RAPHAEL, set out with his dog, won himself a wife and cured his father Tobit's blindness. It was a popular subject for painting, and since Tobias's dog is a notable feature of such works, Toby was transferred to the animal, and became the name of Mr Punch's dog.

Tod, Todd

A surname used as a first name, Tod is a dialect word for 'fox', and would originally have been given as a nickname to someone who either had red hair or else was known for his cunning. As a first name it has been in use from at least the latter part of the nineteenth century, for the expression 'on your tod', Cockney rhyming slang for 'on your own', refers to the American jockey Tod Sloan (1874–1933).

Toirdhealbhach see THORA

Tom, Tomina, Tommy see THOMAS

Toni, Tonia, Tonie, Tonio, Tony, see ANTONY

Tonya see ANTONY

Topaz see JEWELL

Torey see THORA

Tori, Toria, Torie see VICTORIA

Torin, Torrin see THORA

Tormod see NORMAN

Torquil see THORA

Torry, Tory see THORA, VICTORIA

Toya see LAETITIA

Tracey, Tracy see THERESA

Travis

This is a form of the surname **Travers**, which comes from the Old French word for 'a crossing', and would have been given to someone who lived at a ford or crossroads, or possibly someone who gathered tolls at such a place. It has been a popular boy's name in the USA since the later 1970s. **Travon** or **Trevon** seems to be a development of this.

Trent, Trenton

Both these boys' names go back to the English river Trent, whose name dates back to prehistoric times and has tentatively been identified as meaning 'the flooder'. The river name became a surname, which was taken to America, where these names are most used. In the eighteenth century William Trent founded a settlement, now a city in New Jersey, which was known as Trenton ('Trent's town'), which in turn has become a first name.

Trevor

This is the English form of the Welsh name **Trefor**. It means 'large homestead' and is the name of a number of places in Wales. It has been in use in Wales since the tenth century, but only came to England in the middle of the nineteenth, and was particularly popular in the middle years of the twentieth century. **Trev** is the short form.

Trey

It has been suggested that Trey is a form of the Latin *tres* ('three') and was originally a nickname given to a boy who was the third generation to bear the same name and had the Roman numeral III after his name. It may, however, simply be a made-up name, influenced by the older TROY. Trey Parker, the creator of the cartoon series *South Park*, has recently made the name more widely known.

Tricia see PATRICK

Trina see CATHERINE

Triss see BEATRICE

Tristan

Tristan, **Tristram** or **Tristam** is the hero of the tragic love-story of Tristan and ISOLDA. Sir Tristan of Lyonesse was famous for his skill as a huntsman, one of the best fighters in Arthurian legend, the bravest knight in Cornwall and a faithful follower of his uncle, King Mark, until he fell in love with Mark's wife. The meaning of the name is not known, but it has a complex history. In the romances his name is linked with the French word *triste* ('sorrowful'), and a story was told that after his father had been captured by an enchantress his mother went searching for her husband, even though her baby was due to be born. She fell into labour in the forest, and died from a combination of complications and exposure. Before she died, she held her son and said to her waiting woman (in Malory's words): 'Because I shall die of the birth . . . I charge thee, gentlewoman, that thou pray my lord, King Melodias, that when he is christened let call him Tristram, that is as much to say as a sorrowful birth.' However, this is an example of folk etymology, with the name being altered to fit a recognizable word, and a story made up to go with it. The early form of the name seems to have been Drustan, derived from the Pictish name Drust, and the form **Drystan** is occasionally used in the United States. The Scottish connection is not surprising, for scholars interpret Tristan's homeland of Lyonesse as a form of the Scottish place name Lothian. There are, however, very early associations of the name with Cornwall. Near Castle Dore in Cornwall, in romance the capital of King Mark, a sixth-century tombstone was found inscribed in Latin 'Here lies Drustan son of Cynvawr', and it may be no coincidence that Cynvawr is recorded as the name, along with the later GERAINT, of one of the sixth-century Cornish kings. The name has been quietly fashionable in the UK for a number of years, and has recently become well used in the USA. (See also BRONWEN.)

Trix, Trixie SEE BEATRICE

Troilus SEE CRESSIDA

Troy
As a surname Troy can be either from someone who originally lived in the French town of Troyes, or an Irish surname from the Gaelic for 'a foot soldier'. Modern use of the name as a first name also comes from the story of the great city of Troy in Asia Minor, whose siege and destruction by the Greeks is told in Homer's *Iliad* and by many later classical writers.

Trudie, Trudy SEE GERTRUDE

Tudor, Tudyr SEE THEODORE

Turlough SEE THORA

Ty SEE TYLER, TYRONE

Tybalt SEE THEOBALD

Tyler
This is a name that has been popular in the USA in recent years. It is simply a surname, a respelling of the occupation of tiler, used as a first name. Predominantly a boy's name, which can be shortened to **Ty**, it is now also used for girls.

Tyrone
Tyrone is the name of an Irish county which, in its turn, gets its name from a person, for it means 'Owen's land'. Two American actors, father and son, called Tyrone Power who appeared in films in the first part of the twentieth century did much to spread the name there, while in the UK the director Tyrone

Guthrie (1900–71) gave it fame. Guthrie was called Tony as a pet form of his name, but **Ty** is the more usual short form. The girl's name **Taryn** was invented by the younger Tyrone Power and his wife Linda Christian by combining letters from their names, and given to their daughter. Its use has spread, and it is now not uncommon both in the USA and UK. The same Gaelic element *ty*, meaning 'land, territory', is also found in **Tyree**, the name of an island off the coast of Scotland, now used for boys.

Tyrrel see TERENCE

Uu

Ulick see HUGH, ULYSSES, WILLIAM

Ulric

This name appears in Old English as **Wulfric** ('wolf' combined with 'power'), which was the name of an English saint of the twelfth century who had been a self-indulgent parson in his younger days, devoted to hunting, but who reformed in later years, to end his days a recluse in the delightfully named Haselbury Plucknett in Somerset. It is also the name of a number of German saints, and modern use of Ulric is probably due to its introduction from Germany. This is certainly the case for **Ulrice**, the German feminine form, also found as **Ulrica** or **Ulrika**, all forms being pronounced the same way. Ulrica seems to have been a popular literary name in the nineteenth century, appearing, among others, as characters in two of Sir Walter Scott's books, *Ivanhoe* (1819) and *Count Robert of Paris* (1831).

Ulysses

This is the Latin form of **Odysseus**, Homer's great Greek hero, famous for his wisdom, cunning and eloquence and the faithfulness of his wife PENELOPE. It is little used in modern times, but when it occurs it is probably through an association with General Ulysses S. Grant (1822–85), commander of the Union armies in the American Civil War and 18th president of the United States. In Ireland **Ulick** is sometimes anglicized as Ulysses.

Uma

Made famous by the actress Uma Thurman, whose father is a noted Buddhist scholar, Uma is the name of an Indian goddess whose name comes from the Sanskrit word for 'flax' or 'turmeric'. English speakers had been exposed to the name earlier, for it is used by R.L. Stevenson for a character in his spooky novella *The Beach of Falesa* (1893).

Una

Una is an early Irish name, often found as **Oona** or **Oonagh**. In the past it has sometimes been anglicized as JUNO. Its meaning is not clear, but it has been argued that it is from the Irish word *uan* meaning 'lamb'. Another source of the name Una is Spenser's poem *The Faerie Queene* (1590–96), in which she is the heroine of Book I. Here the name is based on the Latin for 'one', for Una is truth personified and is so-called because Truth is one, while Error is multiform.

However, it is probably no coincidence that Spenser was a resident of Ireland, and he was very possibly influenced by the Irish name. The sense of 'one' is found in another name, **Unity**, introduced as an abstract name by the Puritans but often regarded as a variant of Una.

Unice see EUNICE

Unity see UNA

Urban

This Latin name, meaning 'townsman', was chosen by eight medieval popes, probably because it was the opposite of 'pagan', which originally meant 'country dweller'. It is rarely found in modern times. There is a Welsh name Urien, which is thought to come from the same root, being a form of the Latin *urbigenus* ('town-born'). It was the name of a leader of the Northern Britons in the sixth century, who also appears as one of King Arthur's knights in the medieval romances.

Uriah see BATHSHEBA

Urien see URBAN

Ursula

Ursula means 'little bear'. St Ursula was a very popular saint in the Middle Ages who had a church dedicated to her by the late fourth or early fifth century. According to legend, she and 11,000 virgin companions were martyred at Cologne by the Huns on their way back from a pilgrimage to Rome. She is said to have been a British princess fleeing from an unwanted marriage. Other than that she probably existed and that her companions were originally recorded as 10 in number, little can be confidently asserted about Ursula, for the stories about her are no less fictitious than those told about her masculine equivalent ORSON.

Vv

Vaclav see STEPHEN

Val see PERCY, VALERY

Valda, Valdemar see WALDO

Valery
Valery with its alternative spelling **Valerie** is the English form of the Roman family name **Valeria** (masculine **Valerian**), a name coming from the Latin verb *valere* ('to be strong, healthy, flourish'). From the same root comes **Valentine**, the name of a third-century martyr. Nothing is known about him for sure, for all the stories revolve around customs associated with St Valentine's Day, and these evolved from pagan Roman fertility customs associated with mid-February. Valentine's only connection is that his feast day falls on 14 February. In the Middle Ages the name is found in the romance of *Valentine and ORSON*, in which Valentine is a brave and doughty prince. The name is especially given to children born on or about the saint's day and can be given to both sexes, although it is more commonly masculine, with **Valentina** being used as an alternative feminine. **Val** is used as a short form of these names for both sexes, and for women it has been elaborated into a new name, **Valene**.

Vanda see WANDA

Vanessa
This is a name invented by Jonathan Swift (1667–1745) for a poem called *Cadenus and Vanessa* (1726), in which he declines the offer of marriage made to him by a young woman called Esther Vanhomrigh, Cadenus being an anagram of *decanus*, the Latin for his rank of Dean, and Vanessa a play on elements of her name. **Ness**, **Nessa** and **Nessie** are common short forms.

Vanora see JENNIFER

Vashti
Vashti is the name of the Old Testament queen whose refusal to display herself at her husband's feast leads to her replacement by ESTHER. The name probably comes from the Persian for 'beautiful'. It is still in occasional use, but mainly in literary contexts, often with rather voluptuous connotations.

Vasilie see BASIL

Vaughan

A Welsh first name and surname, Vaughan is the English form of the adjective *fychan*, a form of the Welsh word meaning 'little', and would originally have been given to someone small as a nickname.

Velda see WALDO

Velma

This name is something of a mystery. It seems to have come into use in the United States in the 1880s, at a time when names such as THELMA were also popular. It may well be that the -elma sound was felt to be particularly attractive by parents, in the way that certain sounds seem to become strangely fashionable for a while, and that Velma was a name invented to fit this fashion. However, it has been linked with Wilhelmina (see WILLIAM), and there may be a progression of Wilhelmina moving to the pet form Wilma, then becoming **Vilma** (the German pronunciation), with Velma as a variant.

Venetia

This is the Latin name for the city of Venice, although in the past the name was associated with the name of **Venus**, the Roman goddess of fertility and love, and some uses may have been in this sense. A famous early bearer of the name was Venetia Stanley (1600–33). She was a lady of noble family and outstanding intellect, who set up house on her own in London, thereby earning the description by one contemporary of 'that celebrated beautie and courtezane'. In 1625 she secretly married her childhood playmate Sir KENELM Digby against his family's wishes. It was a love match and a happy marriage, and after Venetia's early death Digby erected an elaborate monument to her and was so overcome with grief that he went into complete seclusion for two years. Her death was lamented in verse by numerous poets, including Ben Jonson.

Venus see JULIA, VENETIA

Vera

Vera looks as if it is from the Latin for 'truth', which would give it the same sense as the English name **Verity**; in fact, it comes from Russian and means 'FAITH'. It is sometimes used as a short form of VERONICA. The rare spelling **Viera** is closer to the Russian original. **Vere** is sometimes regarded as a masculine form of Vera, but is actually a French place name which became an aristocratic surname and then a first name.

Verena

Verena is the name of an obscure third-century saint. The name is probably a form of the Latin word for 'truth' (see VERA). Modern use probably owes much to Henry James having given this name to the central character of his novel *The Bostonians* (1886).

Vergil see VIRGIL

Verity see VERA

Vernon

Vernon is a French place name which comes from a Gaulish word meaning 'where alders grow'. A Richard de Vernon was one of the Norman conquerors of England, and he founded a noble family. In the nineteenth century, when such practices were popular, the surname was adopted as a first name. **Verna** has been used as a feminine form of the name, but is usually traced back to the Latin word *vernus* ('spring').

Veronica

The story told of St Veronica says that she was a witness of Christ's suffering as he carried His cross through Jerusalem to the site of the crucifixion. Moved with pity at his suffering, she used her veil to wipe the sweat from His face, and an image of His face, like that of the Turin shroud, was left on her veil and became a sacred relic. In fact, the name of the relic seems to have been transferred to the (possibly fictional) woman, for Veronica means 'true image or icon'. **Véronique**, the French form, is occasionally found. An alternative interpretation of the name links it with the Macedonian Greek name **Berenice** ('bringer of victory'). Berenice was a popular name with the third-century BC rulers of Egypt, descendants of ALEXANDER'S Macedonian conquerors, and a story is told of how one Berenice dedicated a lock of her hair at a temple as an offering for the safe return of her husband from war. The lock disappeared and a new constellation was seen in the sky, ever after known as the Lock of Berenice. The Greeks would have pronounced the name with the 'c' hard and the final 'e' pronounced; it was formerly given a soft 'c' and a final 'e' in England, but its modern pronunciation is reflected in the form **Bernice**. **Bunnie** or **Bunny** and **Bernie** are short forms of Bernice, with **Roni** or **Ronee** for Veronica.

Vesta

This is the name of the Roman goddess of the hearth and home. The name was the stage name of the music-hall stars Vesta Tilley (1864–1952) and Vesta Victoria, but was never widely used.

Victoria

The Latin for 'victory', both Victoria and **Victor** (the masculine form) are found at an early date on the Continent, but are very rare in Britain until the nineteenth century, when Queen Victoria was christened after her German mother. **Vic** is used as a short form for both sexes and **Vicky**, **Tory** or **Tori(e)**, **Toria** and **Vita** for Victoria. Vita has been associated with the Latin word for 'life', but its most famous bearer, the writer Vita Sackville-West (1892–1962), was a Victoria. The pre-Roman British already had a name with the same meaning, used by the chieftainess and rebel leader the Romans called **Boadicea** or **Boudicca**. This name has come down to us as the Welsh name **Buddug** or **Buddic**. The masculine name **Gwythyr**, found in some of the earliest surviving Welsh literature, is said to be a form of Victor.

Vida see DAVID

Viera see VERA

Vilma see VELMA, WILLIAM

Vina see DAVID, LAVINIA

Vincent

Vincent is a name allied to VICTORIA, for it comes from the Latin verb for 'to conquer'. The name was popular in the Middle Ages, particularly among the French, who introduced it into this country. At a later date, St Vincent de Paul (1580–1660), one of many saints called Vincent, brought the name fame. He organized societies of laymen to care for the poor and neglected, as well as founding the Vincentian Fathers and the Sisters of Charity.

Violet

One of the best known of the flower names, Violet is also found in the French form **Violette**, in the Italian **Violetta** – famous as the name of the heroine of Verdi's opera *La Traviata* (1853) – and in the Latin form **Viola**, possibly influenced by Shakespeare's heroine of *Twelfth Night*. The flower and its colour seem to go back to a Greek word *ion*, which has the same meaning and which lies behind a group of less common girls' names. **Ione** means 'violet', and is the feminine of Ion, the name of the king of Athens who gave his name to the Ionian people. Edward Bulwer-Lytton seems to have invented it for the heroine of his highly successful novel *The Last Days of Pompeii* (1834). **Ianthe** ('violet flower') is an ancient name which has a long literary history. It was taken from ancient mythology by Ovid (43 BC–AD 18), picked up by a number of sixteenth- and seventeenth-century poets and playwrights, used by Byron for a pseudonym for the dedicatee of the poem which brought him fame, *Childe Harold's Pilgrimage*, and used by Shelley for his first daughter and for a character in *Queen Mab* (1813). **Iolanthe,** used by Gilbert and Sullivan for their opera, is a form of the name **Yoland** (**Yolande** or **Yolanda**), a name of disputed origin which may belong to this group.

Virgil

This is the usual form, as a first name, of the Latin poet, more correctly spelt **Vergil**. It is primarily an American name, as in the composer Virgil Thomson (1896–1989), although it can also be found in Ireland as an anglicization of FERGUS. To the Romans, Virgil became almost the national poet, his epic *The Aeneid* becoming the accepted account of how Rome came to be. In the Middle Ages he was thought to have prophesied the coming of Christ in a poem which actually celebrated the birth of a grandchild of the Emperor AUGUSTUS; and from this he developed into a powerful magician in popular literature, with a magic looking-glass in which he could see whatever was happening in the world.

Virginia

Virginia is a Roman symbolic name. The Romans told a story of a corrupt ruler who lusted after a beautiful young girl called Virginia, who virtuously rejected his advances. He got a dependant of his to claim that the girl was actually his slave, and the ruler gave judgement in his favour, having agreed in advance that the girl would then be handed over into his power. Virginia's father realized what was happening and the fate which awaited his daughter and killed her on the spot, preferring her death to dishonour. Despite this ancient precedent, the real source of Virginia as a modern name is the American state named in honour of Elizabeth I, the Virgin Queen, by Sir Walter Raleigh when he founded a colony there. The first child born to the settlers was christened Virginia, and for a long time the name remained primarily an American one, although this is no longer the case. It is shortened to **Ginny** or **Jinny**.

Vita see VICTORIA

Vivian
Derived from the Latin meaning 'lively', Vivian was originally a masculine name, with the elaborations **Vyvyan** and **Vyvian**. **Vivien** and **Vivienne** were the feminines. However, this distinction has now become blurred, and while you are unlikely to find the feminine forms used for men, women now use all the forms along with **Viviana** (an obscure early martyr) and **Vivianne**. **Viv** is a short form of all these.

Vonda see WANDA

Vyvian, Vyvyan see VIVIAN

Ww

Wade

Wade was the name of an obscure character in Anglo-Saxon pagan legend, but modern use of this as a boy's name comes from the surname. Some bearers of the surname may in fact get it from the Anglo-Saxon name, but other Wades get their surname either from an ancestor who lived by a ford ('wade' in Middle English), or because they originally came from the Suffolk town called Wade.

Waldo

This comes from a Germanic word meaning 'power' and is also a pet form of **Waldemar** or **Valdemar**, meaning 'great ruler'. **Valda**, which has a variant **Velda**, is the feminine equivalent. The word 'Waldo', as used to mean a mechanical device for handling things by remote control, comes from a science-fiction novella by Robert Heinlein, where the hero is a physically handicapped man of that name who invents devices to compensate for his inabilities. When, soon afterwards, the nuclear industry developed means of extensive remote manipulation, the name of Heinlein's fictional devices was transferred to the real ones.

Wallace

The use of this as a surname probably arose from admiration of Sir William Wallace (c. 1274–1305), the great Scottish patriot who fought against the English under Edward I and temporarily drove them out of his country, until he was captured and executed by them. In contemporary accounts his name is spelt *Walays*, or in Latin *Wallensis*, which means 'the Welshman'. It comes from the word *waleis*, which originally meant 'foreign' but came to be given to all the Celtic minorities in the British Isles, including those living in the Scottish border area from whom Wallace is thought to have been descended.

Walter

Walter is another of the Germanic names brought to England by the Norman Conquest. It is made up of elements meaning 'rule' and 'army'. In the past, the pet forms were **Wat** and **Watty**, reflecting the old pronunciation which swallowed the 'l'; but now **Wally** and **Walt** are used.

Wanda

It has been said that Wanda is a form of 'Vandal', the wandering tribe that so devastated Europe in the Dark Ages that their name has become a part of the language; but this is not well supported. It is a Slavic name, found in Poland from the nineteenth century, but seems to have reached English speakers only when Ouida published a novel called *Wanda* in 1883. The variant **Vanda** reflects the German pronunciation of the name, and has the variant **Vonda**.

Warren

Warren is a surname used as a first name. Unlike the majority of such names, which only came into use in the nineteenth century, it has been a first name since the seventeenth century. The name has a number of different sources. There was a Germanic name *Varin*, meaning 'to watch, guard', which the Normans brought over as *Guerin* and which became Warren in English; it can be from the French place name La Varenne (near Nantes), meaning 'warren'; or it can be a name given to someone who lived near a warren or was a warren-keeper.

Warwick

This is a surname and place name used as a first name. The town of Warwick, to judge by its meaning, was originally a suburb which grew up by a weir. Guy, Earl of Warwick, was a popular hero of medieval romance. There were also two real-life earls of Warwick in the fifteenth century whose lives could have come from the story-books – one a model of knightly courtesy and prowess, the other so influential in the Wars of the Roses that he has come down to us as Warwick the Kingmaker. The pub sign of the Bear and Ragged Staff is taken from the Warwick coat of arms. **Warrie** is used as a short form.

Wat, Watty see WALTER

Wayne

This is most emphatically a twentieth-century name, since it owes its use to the popularity of the film star John Wayne. As a surname, it is the old word for 'a cart', and would have been given to a carter or cart-maker.

Wenceslas see STEPHEN

Wendy

Wendy has one of the best-recorded histories of any first name. It was introduced by J.M. Barrie in 1904 for the girl in *Peter Pan*. He said that he took it from the nickname that a child called Margaret Henley used for him: she regarded him as her friend, so called him 'Fwendy-Wendy'. *Peter Pan* was enormously successful and the name Wendy spread rapidly. Its spread must have been helped by its similarity to the Welsh names starting with GWEN which had been popular shortly before. With variants such as **Wenda** it is difficult to draw a line between Wendy and the Welsh Gwenda.

Wenonah see WINONA

Wenzel see STEPHEN

Wesley

Another name with a clear history, Wesley was introduced as a first name in honour of John Wesley (1703–91), the founder of Methodism, and his brother

Charles (1707–88), evangelist and hymn writer. **Wes** is the short form. The surname means 'west meadow'. **Weston**, another surname which has recently come into use as a first name, has a similar origin, meaning 'west farm'.

Whitney
This is an English place name meaning 'white island'. In the United States the Californian Mount Whitney is the highest peak in the country outside Alaska; it was named after Josiah Dwight Whitney (1819–96), the geologist who surveyed the Rockies and established the height of many of the mountains' highest peaks; he is probably the main American source of the name. Whitney has been used as a first name for both sexes, but is mostly feminine. **Whitley** ('white meadow' in Old English) is also used for girls, probably because of its similarity to Whitney.

Wilbert
An Old English name combining 'will' with 'bright', Wilbert is little used now, but it is known to generations of *Thomas the Tank Engine* fans as the first name of the Rev. Awdrey who created him.

Wilbur
This is a surname, probably from the Old English words meaning 'will' and 'fortress', used as a first name. It is mainly an American name, its use inspired by Wilbur Wright (1867–1912) who, together with his brother **Orville** (which appears to have been a surname invented by Fanny Burney for her novel *Evelina* (1778), was a pioneer of aviation.

Wilfred
Wilfred, with its variant **Wilfrid**, is an Old English name made up of the elements 'will' and 'peace'. It was the name of an outstanding Northumbrian bishop in the seventh century, but it died out after the Norman Conquest until revived in the saint's honour by High Church Anglicans in the nineteenth century. **Wilf** and **Fred** are the short forms.

William
A Germanic name, William is compounded from elements meaning 'will' and 'helmet' (signifying 'protection'), and literally came over with the Conqueror, who was better known in his own time as William the Bastard. It rapidly became popular, and has remained among the favourite boys' names from the Norman Conquest to this day. It is shortened to **Will**, **Willie** or **Willy** and its variants **Bill**, **Billie** or **Billy**. In Welsh the name became **Gwilym** or **Gwillym**, with a short form **Gwil**; in Ireland **Ulick** (see HUGH) may be a form of the name, while **Liam**, the Irish short form of William, has become popular as a name in its own right and spread to other countries. **Wilhelmina** is the basic feminine form, taken from the German. This has evolved a large number of short forms such as **Elma**, **Willa**, **Wilma** or **Vilma**, **Mina**, **Minna**, **Minnie** and **Minella** which, along with the masculine pet forms, are used as independent female names (see also VELMA).

Winifred
This is the English form of the Welsh name **Gwenfrewi** ('blessed reconciliation': see further under GWEN). St Winifred was a seventh-century princess who,

according to legend, rejected the advances of a prince who then decapitated her in fury. When her head was restored to her body she miraculously came back to life, and was allowed to end her days as a nun. Her relics were moved to Shrewsbury in 1138, which accounts for the name developing an English form. Short forms are **Win**, **Winnie** and **Freda**. The name was very popular at the end of the nineteenth century and beginning of the twentieth.

Winona

This is the name of a number of places in the United States, including a city and county in Minnesota, used as a first name. It is the Sioux word for 'first-born daughter', so is particularly suited to be a first name. The name occurs as **Wenonah**, the mother of Hiawatha in Henry Longfellow's poem (1855). It is often found in the form **Wyn(n)ona**.

Winston

Winston owes its modern popularity as a boy's name to Sir Winston Churchill (1874–1965). It was a traditional name in his family. The first Sir Winston Churchill, father of the first Duke of Marlborough, was born in 1620. He was named Winston in honour of his mother, who was born Sarah Winston. The surname came from a place name made up of Old English elements meaning 'joy' and 'stone'.

Wulfric see ULRIC

Wyatt

The modern use of Wyatt as a boy's name is probably linked to the fame of the Western lawman Wyatt Earp. As a surname, it is a contracted form of the Old English name *Wigheard*, formed from elements meaning 'battle' and 'brave'.

Wyn, Wynford, Wynn see GWEN

Wynona, Wynnona see WINONA

Wyvonne see YVONNE

X

Xandra, Xandrine see ALEXANDER

Xanthe

The Greek for 'yellow', Xanthe is thus the equivalent of the Latin names FLAVIA and Fulvia. Although Dunkling suggests that the name is obsolete, or at least obsolescent, it is still being used by parents, even if it is not the most common of names.

Xavier

St Francis Xavier (1506–52), the patron saint of missionaries, got his name from the Spanish-Basque village where he was born. He was one of the founding members of the Jesuits and devoted his life to spreading Christianity in the Far East, particularly in India, China and Japan. He is buried in Goa (India), where his tomb is still a popular place of pilgrimage. Xavier is most often found as a second name, often following Francis. It is occasionally spelt Zavier, and there are feminine forms **Xaviera, Xavia** or **Zavia, Xaverine** and **Xavière**.

Xenia

This is the full form of the name more often found as **Xena, Zena** or **Zina**. It comes from the Greek word for 'hospitable', which in turn comes from *xenos* ('stranger, foreigner'). It is too soon to see if the success of the television series *Xena, Warrior Princess* will affect use of this name.

Yy

Yasmin, Yasmine see JASMIN

Yehudi see JUDE

Yesenia
The origin of this name is unknown, but it became popular, particularly with Spanish speakers in the USA, after it was used for the titular gypsy heroine of a 1971 melodramatic Mexican film set in the nineteenth century. This was later developed into a television series.

Ynyr see HONORIA

Yoland, Yolande, Yolanda see VIOLET

Ysabel see ISABEL

Yseult, Yseut, Ysold, Ysolda, Ysolde see ISOLDA

Yvonne
This is the most common form of a group of names which come from a Germanic root meaning 'yew', the tree used for making longbows. **Yves**, the French form of Ivo (see IVOR), a popular name in France but rare elsewhere, developed two feminine diminutives, Yvonne and **Yvette**. There are a number of spelling variants, of which **Yvone** and **Evonne** are the most common. In the United States in the 1930s and 1940s it was considered a rather exotic name, and some users were not sure how to pronounce it, others how to spell it. This led to a number of extraordinary variations in both spelling and pronunciation, of which the most extreme were **Javonne**, as if the name were Slavic (perhaps an influence on the development of **Javon** as a Black American masculine name), and **Wyvonne**.

Zz

Zabrina see SABRINA

Zac see ISAAC, ZACHARY

Zachary
The English form of the Hebrew name **Zachariah** (**Zacharias** is the Greek), Zachary means 'God has remembered'. It is probably the most used of the masculine 'Z' names, particularly in its short form **Zac** (see also ISAAC). **Zach, Zack, Zacky** and **Zaz** have also been recorded as short forms. The name is attached to eight different people in the Bible, the most prominent of whom was the father of John the Baptist, who was punished with dumbness when he did not believe what the Angel Gabriel told him of his future son, and on the restoration of his voice was inspired to compose the hymn of praise known as the 'Benedictus'.

Zandra see ALEXANDER

Zane
The use of this surname of unknown meaning for boys comes from the author Zane Grey (1872–1939), who was largely responsible for creating the western as a literary genre. He was christened Pearl Grey, but not surprisingly chose to change this, and took his pen name from his home town of Zanesville, Ohio. This in turn was named from its founder, Ebenezer Zane.

Zara
An Arabic name meaning 'brightness, splendour of the dawn', Zara was introduced by William Congreve as the name of an African queen in his play *The Mourning Bride* (1697). It was then used by Aaron Hill in 1735 as the title and name of the heroine of his translation of a melodramatic tragedy by Voltaire, in the original French called *Zaïre* (1733). However, it was rarely found in real life until the 1960s. Surprisingly, although its use by The Princess Royal for her daughter in 1981 brought the name to the attention of the general public, it does not seem to have led to any marked increase in the name's use.

Zavia, Zavier see XAVIER

Zebedee

The father of the Apostles James the Great and John 'the disciple whom Jesus loved', Zebedee was a successful fisherman, working on the Sea of Galilee. His name means 'my gift'. However, the modern associations of this name are not biblical, for generations of children grew up linking the name with the spring-based puppet of television's *The Magic Roundabout* and the catch-phrase 'Time for bed, said Zebedee'.

Zeke see EZEKIEL

Zelda see GRISELDA

Zelma see SELMA

Zena see XENIA

Zenaida see ZINAIDA

Zenobia

Zenobia was a queen of Palmyra in Syria, famous for her intellect and beauty. When her husband Odenathus died in AD 267 (some say by her hand), she took over the throne. At first the Roman emperors supported her, but she became over-ambitious, and when she invaded the Roman territories of Asia Minor and Egypt she was captured and deposed, and her city-state and its unique culture were obliterated. The name is interpreted as the Greek for 'force of Zeus', but it is probably an adaptation (which at that time could go a long way from the original) of her native name found in local inscriptions, which was Septimia Bathzabbai, meaning something like 'dowry of God'.

Zillah

This is a Hebrew name meaning 'shadow'. In Genesis she is the mother of Jabal and Jubal, co-wife of Lamech with ADAH. The name was used by the poet laureate Robert Southey (1774–1843) in a tale he took from a medieval source about the origin of the rose, in which a fair maiden of Bethlehem called Zillah rejects the advances of a sottish brute, is accused by him of having dealings with the devil, and is condemned to be burned at the stake. The flames destroy her false accuser, but she is unharmed and from the stake white roses blossom, 'the first ever seen on earth since paradise was lost'.

Zilpha

Zilpha, more correctly spelt **Zilpa**, is a biblical name from the Arabic meaning 'with the little nose'. She was a slave girl given to LEAH by her father Laban, and by her to her husband JACOB as a concubine to be a sort of surrogate mother for Leah. Zilpa became the mother of Gad and Acher, from whom two of the 12 tribes of Israel descended.

Zina see XENIA

Zinaida

This is the Russian form of a Greek name meaning 'daughter of Zeus'. It is the name of two early martyrs, but its introduction to the English-speaking world is probably due to its use for the heroine of Turgenev's novella *First Love* (1860). **Zenaida** is an alternative form.

Zinnia

This is a modern flower-name, the flower being named after J.G. Zinn, a German botanist.

Zita

Zita seems to be from an Italian dialect word for 'child'. It was the name of a Tuscan saint of the thirteenth century, who at the age of 12 started work as a domestic servant. Her care over her work and her habit of giving food to the poor brought her into conflict with both her fellow servants and her employer, but her devotion and meek patience won her respect in the end, and she spent most of her later life in good works. She became the patron saint of domestic servants, with a bunch of keys as her emblem. Despite these lowly associations, Zita was the name of the last empress of Austria, who lost the throne after the dissolution of the Austro-Hungarian empire at the end of World War I, but who lived on in retirement until 1989.

Zoe

Zoe or **Zoë** is the Greek word for 'life', and as such was used by Greek speakers for the Hebrew EVE. It was introduced to this country in the nineteenth century and has been popular since the 1970s, with a phonetic spelling, **Zowie**, an occasional variant.

Zola

Although the name Zola is most closely associated with the South African runner Zola Budd, she is by no means the first user of the name, for it has been in use, particularly in the United States, for many years. For example, the lead singer of the Black American pop group The Platters, who had a hit single in 1956, was called Zola Taylor. It must be assumed that the name is a use of the surname of the French writer Emile Zola (1840–1902). His father was Italian and the name comes from a dialect word meaning 'bank, mound of earth'.

Zowie see ZOË

Zuleika

This is a Persian name meaning 'brilliant beauty'. It is traditionally the name of both Joseph's and Potiphar's wives but it first gained fame in the English-speaking world when Byron used it for the tragic heroine of his poem *The Bride of Abydos* (1813). Its greatest fame, however, comes from Max Beerbohm's comic novel *Zuleika Dobson* (1911). When this was broadcast on the radio and his heroine's name was, in his view, mispronounced, Beerbohm sent an angry telegram to the producer, which ran 'ZULEIKA SPEAKER NOT HIKER BEERBOHM'; but although the pronunciation rhyming with speaker is the traditional one, that rhyming with hiker is now the more common. **Suleika** is a variant.